Lecture Notes of the Institute for Computer Sciences, Social Informatics and Telecommunications Engineering 527

The LNICST series publishes ICST's conferences, symposia and workshops.

LNICST reports state-of-the-art results in areas related to the scope of the Institute. The type of material published includes

- Proceedings (published in time for the respective event)
- Other edited monographs (such as project reports or invited volumes)

LNICST topics span the following areas:

- General Computer Science
- E-Economy
- E-Medicine
- Knowledge Management
- Multimedia
- Operations, Management and Policy
- Social Informatics
- Systems

Leandros A. Maglaras · Christos Douligeris
Editors

Wireless Internet

16th EAI International Conference, WiCON 2023
Athens, Greece, December 15–16, 2023
Proceedings

 Springer

Editors
Leandros A. Maglaras
Edinburgh Napier University
Edinburgh, UK

Christos Douligeris
University of Piraeus
Piraeus, Greece

ISSN 1867-8211   ISSN 1867-822X (electronic)
Lecture Notes of the Institute for Computer Sciences, Social Informatics
and Telecommunications Engineering
ISBN 978-3-031-58052-9   ISBN 978-3-031-58053-6 (eBook)
https://doi.org/10.1007/978-3-031-58053-6

This Springer imprint is published by the registered company Springer Nature Switzerland AG
The registered company address is: Gewerbestrasse 11, 6330 Cham, Switzerland

If disposing of this product, please recycle the paper.

Preface

We are delighted to introduce the proceedings of the 16th EAI International Conference on Wireless Internet (WiCON 2023). This conference brought together researchers, developers and practitioners around the world who are leveraging and developing wireless technologies, AI algorithms and novel applications for a smarter and more digital life. The focus of WiCON 2023 was on the challenges of wireless Internet communications.

The technical program of WiCON 2023 consisted of 14 full papers, including 2 invited papers, in oral presentation sessions at the main conference tracks. The conference tracks were: Track 1 – Wireless Networks; Track 2 – AI/ML Systems; Track 3 – 5G/6G Networks; and Track 4 – Digital Services. Aside from the high-quality technical paper presentations, the technical program also featured two keynote speeches and one tutorial. The two keynote speeches were from Andreas Mitrakas from ENISA on "Cybersecurity certification: delivering measurable trust in the EU" and Massimo Villari from University of Messina, Italy on "Foresee Possible Evolutions of Distributed Intelligence in Cross Domains". The tutorial was delivered by Dimitrios Zorbas from Nazarbayev University, Kazakhstan. The tutorial was entitled "LoRa and LoRaWAN: Advantages, Pitfalls, and Countermeasures" and explored their advantages, such as their extensive range, cost-effectiveness and low power consumption along with their disadvantages such as security vulnerabilities and potential network congestion issues.

Coordination with the steering chair, Prof. Imrich Chlamtac, was essential for the success of the conference. We sincerely appreciate his constant support and guidance. It was also a great pleasure to work with such an excellent organizing committee team for their hard work in organizing and supporting the conference. In particular, the Technical Program Committee, led by our TPC Chairs and Co-Chairs, Bill Buchanan, Mohamed A. Ferrag, Helge Janicke and Charalampos Konstantopoulos, completed the peer-review process of technical papers and made a high-quality technical program. We are also grateful to the Conference Manager, Veronika Kissova, for her support and to all the authors who submitted their papers to the WiCON 2023 conference.

We strongly believe that WiCON provides a good forum for all researchers, developers and practitioners to discuss all science and technology aspects that are relevant to wireless communications. We also expect that future WiCON conferences will be as successful and stimulating, as indicated by the contributions presented in this volume.

December 2023

Leandros A. Maglaras
Christos Douligeris

Organization

Steering Committee

Chair

Imrich Chlamtac   University of Trento, Italy

Organizing Committee

General Chairs

Leandros Maglaras   Edinburgh Napier University, UK
Christos Douligeris   University of Piraeus, Greece

TPC Chairs and Co-chairs

Bill Buchanan   Edinburgh Napier University, UK
Mohamed A. Ferrag   TII, UAE
Helge Janicke   Edith Cowan University, Australia
Ioanna Kantzavelou   University of West Attica, Greece
Charalampos Konstantopoulos   University of Piraeus, Greece

Sponsorship and Exhibit Chairs

Naghmeh Moradpoor   Edinburgh Napier University, UK
Tiago J. Cruz   University of Coimbra, Portugal

Local Chair

Rosa Mavropodi   University of Piraeus, Greece

Workshops Chairs

Ying He   University of Nottingham, UK
George Xylomenos   Athens University of Economics and Business, Greece
Nineta Polemi   University of Piraeus, Greece

Publicity and Social Media Chairs

Theodoros Karvounidis	University of Piraeus, Greece
Xenofon Vasilakos	University of Bristol, UK

Publications Chairs

Naghmeh Moradpoor	Edinburgh Napier University, UK
Dimitrios Kallergis	University of West Attica, Greece

Web Chair

Yagmur Yigit	Istanbul Technical University, Turkey

Posters and PhD Track Chairs

Dimitrios Zorbas	Nazarbayev University, Kazakhstan
Aris Leivadeas	ÉTS Montréal, Canada
Konstantinos Kantelis	Aristotle University of Thessaloniki, Greece

Panels/Demos/Tutorials Chairs

Rania Garofalaki	University of West Attica, Greece
Naghmeh Moradpoor	Edinburgh Napier University, UK
Tiago J. Cruz	University of Coimbra, Portugal
Anna Maria Vegni	Roma Tre University, Italy
Eirini Eleni Tsiropoulou	University of New Mexico, USA

Technical Program Committee

Angelos Rouskas	University of Piraeus, Greece
Christos Tselikis	University of Piraeus, Greece
Dimitrios Kosmanos	University of Thessaly, Greece
Iryna Yevseyeva	De Montfort University, UK
Nestoras Chouliaras	University of West Attica, Greece
Nineta Polemi	University of Piraeus, Greece
Vasileios Germanos	De Montfort University, UK
Vasilis Papaspirou	University of West Attica, Greece
Xenofon Vasilakos	University of Bristol, UK

Contents

5G/6G Networks

Digital Services

Wireless Networks

Cellular-V2X and VANET(DSRC) Based End-to-End Guidance for Smart Parking

Mohamed Darqaoui$^{(\boxtimes)}$, Moussa Coulibaly, and Ahmed Errami

NEST Research Group, LRI Laboratory, ENSEM,
Hassan II University of Casablanca, BP 8118 Oasis, Casablanca, Morocco
{mohamed.darqaoui.doc21,m.coulibaly,a.errami}@ensem.ac.ma

Abstract. Nowadays, Vehicle-to-everything (V2X) is one of the main emerging technologies attracting significant interest of researchers and industries who aim to improve traffic efficiency. C-V2X which stands for Cellular Vehicle-to-everything is a technology that enables communication between vehicles (V2V), vehicles and infrastructure (V2I), vehicles and pedestrians (V2P), and vehicles and other devices (V2D) using cellular networks (LTE or 5G). DSRC which stands for Dedicated Short-Range Communication Standard, specifically IEEE 802.11p, is a communication standard enabling vehicles to exchange real-time information with each other and roadside infrastructure within short distances. VANET DSRC's main purpose is to enhance road safety and improve traffic efficiency. Another essential system which in turn contributes to improved traffic efficiency and reduced congestion in urban areas is the Smart Parking System (SPS). SPS is a technology-driven approach to managing parking spaces more efficiently. In This paper, integration of a Smart Parking System with C-V2X and VANET(DSRC) is proposed, we suggest a new C-V2X and VANET (DSRC) based End-to-End guidance scheme for smart parking. The C-V2X network provides external guidance in this system, while the VANET (DSRC) infrastructure handles internal guidance. By integrating both external and internal guidance, we offer parking users a comprehensive End-to-End guidance experience. This paper introduces the fundamental aspects of the proposal, which will be further developed and validated through simulation in our future works.

Keywords: Smart Parking · Parking Guidance · VANET · DSRC · Cellular-V2X · Internal Guidance · External Guidance

1 Introduction

VANET and C-V2X are two related but distinct technologies for enabling communication between vehicles and between vehicles and their surrounding environment such as network, infrastructure, and pedestrians. VANET [1] is an emerging technology, the term Vehicular Ad Hoc Network associated is developed and standardized under the umbrella work of intelligent transport systems (ITS) [2]. VANETs are a subset of Mobile Ad Hoc Networks (MANETs), which

© ICST Institute for Computer Sciences, Social Informatics and Telecommunications Engineering 2024
Published by Springer Nature Switzerland AG 2024. All Rights Reserved
L. A. Maglaras and C. Douligeris (Eds.): WiCON 2023, LNICST 527, pp. 3–13, 2024.
https://doi.org/10.1007/978-3-031-58053-6_1

are known for their dynamic topology, self-organization, and absence of a fixed infrastructure, it allows different deployment architectures in highways, urban and rural environments. VANET uses vehicles as nodes equipped with Onboard Unit (OBU) creating a wireless network for communication and information sharing among vehicles and with roadside infrastructure (RSU). Communication in VANET is enabled through the use of IEEE 802.11p recognized as "Wireless Access in Vehicular Environments" (WAVE), developed specifically for VANET communications and it allows different deployment architectures in highways, urban and rural environments (Fig. 1). The main motivations behind VANETs include enhancing road safety and optimizing traffic efficiency [1].

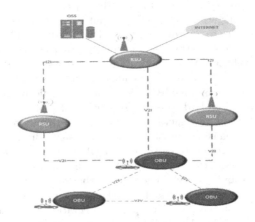

Fig. 1. VANET DSRC/WAVE architecture.

C-V2X (Fig. 2) is the technology developed within the 3 Generation Partnership Project (3GPP) and designed to provide wider coverage and higher data rates compared to VANETs. It encompasses both direct vehicle-to-vehicle (V2V) and vehicle-to-everything (V2X) communications [3]. C-V2X stands for cellular Vehicle-to-Everything operates in tow modes, direct mode (PC5) and network mode (Uu interface) [4]. In direct mode, often referred to as PC5, communication takes place directly between vehicles and infrastructure without relying on a cellular network. Network mode, also known as Uu, involves communication between vehicles and infrastructure using the cellular network infrastructure.

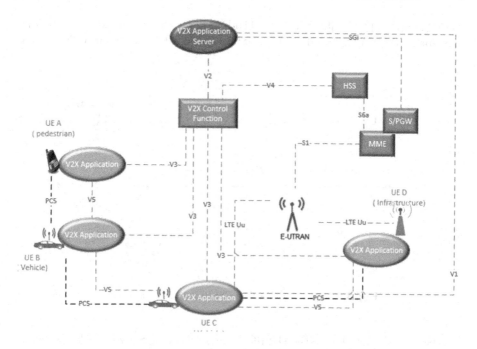

Fig. 2. 3GPP LTE C-V2X architecture.

Network Communication V2N (Uu Mode): C-V2X can connect vehicles to cellular networks, enabling them to access cloud-based services, traffic updates, and other relevant information.

Direct Communication V2V and V2I (PC5 mode): The direct mode, referred to as the PC5 interface, enables vehicles to communicate directly with each other (V2V) and with roadside units (V2I) without the need for cellular networks.

The 3GPP LTE standard's Release 14 introduced several new network architecture entities to fulfill the requirements for supporting V2X communications. These entities include:

- V2X Control Function: Supplies configuration parameters for the vehicular UEs(cars) for both in-coverage and out-of-coverage UEs.
- V2X Application Server: Handles a majority of the network functions associated with V2X. This encompasses receiving uplink V2N messages, disseminating unicast or multicast data to vehicular User Equipments (UEs)...
- V2X Application located on board of each vehicular UE or RSU that communicates with the V2X Application Server.

have the common goal of enhancing road safety, optimizing traffic efficiency, and delivering infotainment services. From the performance perspective, C-V2X was explored as an alternative or complementary technology due to the limitations of VANET (DSRC) and was expected to improve performance of vehicular

communications (V2X) [5]. IEEE 802.11bd and 5G-NR are the next generations
for respectively VANET-DSRC (IEEE 802.11p) and LTE Cellular-V2X [6] (see
Fig. 3).

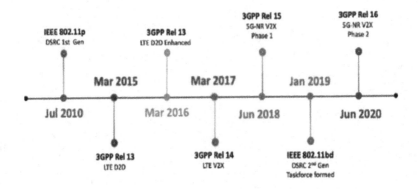

Fig. 3. C-V2X and VANET DSRC standardization.

Beside C-V2X and VANET (DSRC), Smart Parking System (SPS) is also a
key element in smart city context. Smart parking system is an essential component witch is expected to play a considerable role in traffic efficiency especially in urban area. The smart parking concept combines traditional parking
methods with recent technologies, including the Internet of Things (IoT), Radio
Frequency Identification (RFID), Wireless Sensor Networks (WSN), Ultra-
WideBand (UWB), Artificial Intelligence (AI), Cloud Computing (CC), and
others. Smart parking strategies encompass various technologies and approaches
designed to optimize parking management and improve parking experience [7].

Guidance plays a crucial role in smart parking system by enabling drivers to
easily locate parking spaces. There are two distinct methods, outdoor and indoor
guidance, employed to assist individuals in reaching their destinations [8]. In the
realm of smart parking, external guidance systems are created to aid navigra-
tion through outdoor spaces like city streets, parks, or campuses. Meanwhile,
indoor guidance systems are specifically designed to assist people in navigat-
ing through enclosed spaces such as airports, hospitals or shopping malls. For
external localization in open spaces Global Navigation Satellite Systems (GNSS)
such as Global Positioning System (GPS), GLObalnaya NAvigatsionnaya Sput-
nikovaya Sistema (GLONASS) as well as GALILEO have demonstrated high
efficiency. Indoor systems typically utilize technologies such as Bluetooth beacons, Bluetooth Low Energy (BLE), WiFi, Zigbee, UWB, RFID tags to provide
location information. Additionally, visual cues such as signs or arrows, maps can
be utilized to provide directions and facilitate individuals in finding the route to
the parking spot.

The remainder of the article is structured as outlined below: Section 2 delves
into discussions on guidance within the context of smart parking. In Section 3,

an analysis and critique are presented concerning existing works that address guidance in smart parking. Section 4 introduces our proposed End-to-End parking guidance scheme. Finally, Sect. 5 is dedicated to concluding remarks and considerations for future work.

2 Related Works

One widely adopted application in smart cities involves the deployment of intelligent parking solutions. These solutions enable individuals to optimize their time, decrease fuel consumption, and reduce carbon dioxide emissions, ultimately contributing to the enhancement of traffic efficiency within the smart city. Guidance for drivers in parking is a pivotal component of smart parking systems. It employs computer technology, communication mechanics, control techniques, and more to offer driving route suggestions, berth order, traffic state forecasts, and additional services based on a traveler's driving destination and current traffic conditions. The primary objective is to guide drivers in anticipating available parking spaces.

The state of the art define two parking guidance solutions, outdoor parking guidance and indoor parking guidance [9]. For the parking external guidance, the widely used technology is Global Positioning System (GPS), GPS give real time location and guidance toward outdoor destination. GPS signals experience signal weakening and exhibit restricted penetration capability when used indoors. In indoor areas such as shopping malls, airports, etc., rather than the classical methods used for guiding drivers inside, which are based generally on panels, screens and directions, different technologies could be used to provide positioning and route drivers to the free parking slot.

WIFI, Bluetooth Low Energy, Zigbee, RFID and UWB are the technologies widely used in indoor positioning solutions [8,9]. A WiFi-based positioning parking guidance system is proposed in this work [10], a system framework composed of ultrasonic, databases, location server, web server, and mobile app is developed, with the use of fingerprint technique for positioning.

In [11], a straightforward parking system utilizing Bluetooth Low Energy (BLE) is created and implemented. The system assigns a unique BLE beacon to each parking spot, offering users guidance to available parking spaces and incorporating a secure, automated payment system based on real-time usage.

In this study [12], a parking management system is designed using RFID technology along with wireless RF ZigBee to control and manage parking spaces. An Indoor Parking Guidance System has been successfully developed and designed accordingly.

In [13] an indoor parking guidance system for multi-level building based on wireless networks sensors and ultrasonic sensors prototype is developed and tested for only one floor. The solution can be extended to a building with multi floors.

In [14], authors explore an intelligent parking guidance system utilizing computer vision. The study delves into the essential technologies of a real-time parking recognition system founded on image recognition. Additionally, the paper discusses a vehicle guidance system based on the Dijkstra algorithm.

In [15], a novel smart parking system (SPS) scheme known as SPARK is presented, leveraging Vehicle Ad Hoc Networks (VANETs). SPARK introduces three crucial use cases, including real-time navigation for users. The system involves Roadside Units (RSUs) actively monitoring parking areas to ensure users receive current information on available parking spaces, facilitating efficient navigation to the nearest open spots. A comprehensive review of VANET localization techniques is conducted in [16].

In [17], R. Raghu et al. introduce an Effective Dead Reckoning Approach for forecasting a vehicle's future position. The algorithm uses the current position of the vehicle to anticipate its future location. This is accomplished by taking into account a forthcoming time-space window, allowing for a precise estimation of the vehicle's future position.

3   Analysis and Critical

Indeed, Global Navigation Satellite Systems (GNSS) demonstrate exceptional efficiency in external localization within open areas. Nevertheless, their effectiveness diminishes in indoor environments such as malls, tunnels, and enclosed spaces. In such situations, GNSS signals may encounter obstruction or weakening, leading to decreased accuracy or even signal loss. In a smart parking system, GNSS is employed to offer external guidance, assisting drivers in reaching their intended destinations.

The predominant strategies for smart parking systems primarily emphasize external guidance, typically relying on GPS and maps to provide drivers with instructions on reaching the parking facility. There are only a limited number of studies that delve into providing guidance specifically for parking inside smart parking environments. Moreover, with respect to the literature, the concept of End-to-End guidance in smart parking has not been previously addressed. The End-to-End guidance system is a navigation system, combination of external guidance and internal guidance, which provide route and instructions for drivers to reach directly their booked parking free slot inside parking facility.

Each of the previously mentioned technologies has the capability to offer either outdoor localization only or indoor localization only or a combination of both [Table 1].

Table 1. Positioning technologies

Technology	Positioning Type	
	Outdoor	Indoor
GNSS	*	
WIFI		*
Bluetooth		*
BLE		*
RFID		*
UWB		*
Zigbee		*
Hybrid (VANET + C-V2X)	*	*

4 Proposal

To the best of our knowledge, this work is the initial endeavor to introduce smart parking services into the domain of cellular vehicular networks (see Fig. 4). C-V2X and VANET (DSRC) technologies exhibit a key advantage by providing both external and internal guidance in smart parking, enabling an End-to-End (E2E) parking guidance experience.

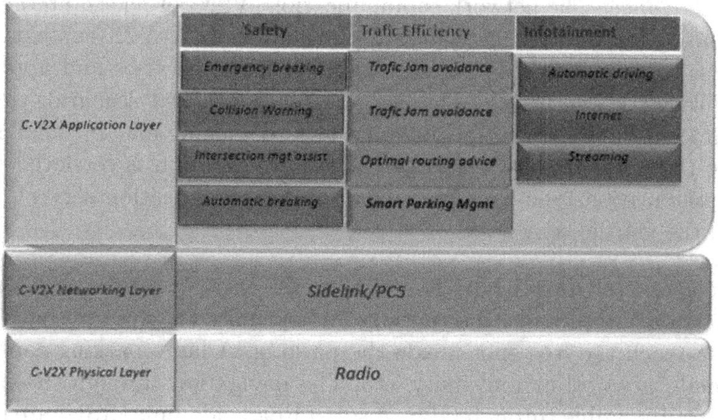

Fig. 4. C-V2X: Smart parking use case.

We leverage these two emergent and extensible technologies, C-V2X and VANET (DSRC), to propose an End-to-End parking guidance scheme (see Fig. 5).

Our smart parking management approach is based on C-V2X and VANET dual mode RSUs (C-V2X mode and DSRC mode support). the C-V2X provides

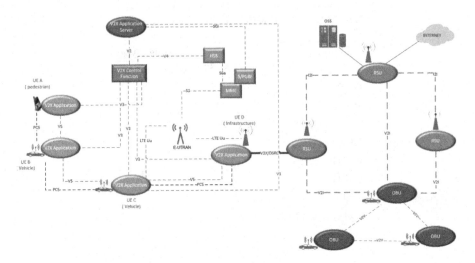

Fig. 5. C-V2X and VANET (DSRC) interoperability architecture for smart parking use case.

online reservation, payment, parking location and route to reach the parking. While the parking status (free/busy spot), entrance, exit is controlled by the RSUs installed in the parkin space. A smart parking application server is used to host all the parking related information.

External Guidance: The network communication (V2N) provides internet access and optimised route to reach a parking destination. In C-V2X context, devices have access to the internet as well as to cloud based services and applications servers through Uu interface. Therefore, in our proposed scenario, the smart parking information such as availability lots, payment, and optimal route is hosted by the V2X application server. These information is retrieved through V2N communication (vehicle communication with application server) and displayed on the vehicle screen.

Internal Guidance: Once the driver arrives to the entry of the parking, the direct communication V2I provides instructions and optimised routes to vehicle's driver in order to reach the free spot inside the parking. A large parking could be an airport, mall, hospital or university, etc. The navigation through these kind of building is not possible through GPS. A set of Road-side-unit (RSU) are installed around the parking space. The vehicle and RSU specifications are as follow:

- V2I communication at the entrance, inside and exit of the parking.
- The parking space spot status (free/busy) is recorded in The RSUs database. Updates are regularly sent to the smart parking application server.
- Dual mode RSU: The RSUs are equipped with two different modes of communication: DSRC for Vehicle-to-Infrastructure (V2I) communication and Cellular-V2X mode for Infrastructure-to-Network (I2N) communication (to share parking status with smart parking application server).

- The RSU hosts the online map: the online map is used for indoor navigation, typically designed to help drivers navigate and locate specific spot within the parking.
- The vehicle is equipped with an dual mode OnBoard Unit (OBU) for V2V, V2I and V2N communication.

At the entrance of the parking, the vehicle and RSU initiate V2I communication. This exchange between the RSU and the vehicle aims to authenticate, authorize and then guide the vehicle to its reserved parking spot:

- Authentication phase: RSU triggers the authentication phase by challenging the vehicle to authenticate itself. Various authentication criteria could be used during this phase (keys, plat number, RFID tags...).
- Authorization phase: The RSU determines whether the vehicle is granted access to the parking facility or not. Typically, this decision relies on the payment status, indicating whether the driver has paid for parking or not.
- Positioning technique: fingerprinting, Trilateration or Multilateration are the widely used techniques in the field of wireless positioning and location-based services. While fingerprinting involves creating a database of signal strength patterns (fingerprints) at various locations within a given area, and then when a device wants to determine its location, it measures the signal strengths of nearby Wi-Fi access points, Bluetooth beacons, or other wireless signals and compares these measurements to the stored fingerprints in the database. The technique relies on signal strength data, called RSS (Received Signal Strength), which represents the distance of each beacon or sensor from a user's device. Trilateration/Multilateration is used to determine the position of a device based on its distance measurements from at least three reference points with known coordinates. Vehicle localization is achieved using V2I communication, in which the RSUs installed in the parking facility calculate the vehicle position using the positioning technique.
- Guidance phase: Subsequently, based on the previous phase result, the route towards the free spot is displayed on the vehicle screen or driver's phone.

End-to-End Guidance: End-to-end guidance is the combination of external guidance and internal guidance. The external guidance provides assistance to vehicles and individuals by giving them precise location information and directions. The parking location stored in the smart parking application server database is requested by the driver through V2N communication, and subsequently, the GPS is involved in route calculation.

On the other hand, the internal guidance assists the driver in the process of parking their vehicle. Once the driver arrives at the parking entrance, and after successful authentication and authorization procedures, the drivers use the online map downloaded by RSU on the vehicle OBU and displayed on the screen, or alternatively, the driver may have previously downloaded this map onto their vehicle or smartphone. Subsequently, after entering the parking zone, the wireless communication (V2I) between the vehicle and the RSUs in place started in order to calculate the vehicle localization utilizing fingerprinting approaches as it can provide high accuracy in indoor environments. then the driver follows the route displayed on the online map to the free spot.

5   Conclusion

This paper presents a novel smart parking guidance system that utilizes the promising capabilities of Cellular-V2X (C-V2X) and VANET (DSRC), an evolving and adaptable technologies. The objective of this scheme is to enhance the management of parking lots and offer a comprehensive End-to-End guidance service for vehicles, covering both external and internal aspects. Our subsequent efforts will delve deeper into the architecture and procedures of the proposed scheme. Moreover, we aim to develop a model for our solution and then perform a simulation to validate its functioning. The modeling step consists of developing a model where we define the components and the data flow of the system; the system involves "parking facility position" and "parking spot ID " as inputs, and provides "external guidance" and "internal guidance" as results. To validate our model, we will choose the most appropriate simulation tools namely traffic and network simulators. By performing these simulations, we will be able to extensively evaluate and validate the effectiveness and performance of the proposed scheme.

References

1. Raut, C.M., Devane, S.R.: Intelligent transportation system for smartcity using VANET. In: 2017 International Conference on Communication and Signal Processing (ICCSP), pp. 1602–1605 (2017). https://doi.org/10.1109/ICCSP.2017.8286659
2. Maimaris, A., Papageorgiou, G.: A review of intelligent transportation systems from a communications technology perspective. In: 2016 IEEE 19th International Conference on Intelligent Transportation Systems (ITSC), pp. 54–59 (2016). https://doi.org/10.1109/ITSC.2016.7795531
3. Papathanassiou, A., Khoryaev, A.: Cellular V2X as the essential enabler of superior global connected transportation services. IEEE 5G Tech Focus 1(2), 1–2 (2017)
4. Kiela, K.: Review of V2X-IoT standards and frameworks for ITS applications. Appl. Sci. 10, 4314 (2020). https://doi.org/10.3390/app10124314
5. Bey, T., Tewolde, G.: Evaluation of DSRC and LTE for V2X. In: 2019 IEEE 9th Annual Computing and Communication Workshop and Conference (CCWC), pp. 1032–1035 (2019). https://doi.org/10.1109/CCWC.2019.8666563
6. Joint use of DSRC and C-V2X for V2X communications in the 5.9 GHz ITS band - Ansari - 2021 - IET Intelligent Transport Systems - Wiley Online Library. https://ietresearch.onlinelibrary.wiley.com/doi/full/10.1049/itr2.12015. Accessed 01 Sept 2023
7. Applied Sciences — Free Full-Text — Smart Parking: A Literature Review from the Technological Perspective. https://www.mdpi.com/2076-3417/9/21/4569. Accessed 01 Sept 2023
8. Asaad, S.M., Maghdid, H.S.: A comprehensive review of indoor/outdoor localization solutions in IoT era: research challenges and future perspectives. Comput. Netw. 212, 109041 (2022). https://doi.org/10.1016/j.comnet.2022.109041

9. Paidi, V., Fleyeh, H., Håkansson, J., Nyberg, R.G.: Smart parking sensors, technologies and applications for open parking lots: a review. IET Intel. Transp. Syst. **12**, 735–741 (2018). https://doi.org/10.1049/iet-its.2017.0406
10. Mei, L., Cheng, M.: A WiFi-based positioning parking guidance system. In: Presented at the 2015 4th International Conference on Mechatronics, Materials, Chemistry and Computer Engineering (2015). https://doi.org/10.2991/icmmcce-15.2015.575
11. Mackey, A., Spachos, P., Plataniotis, K.N.: Smart parking system based on bluetooth low energy beacons with particle filtering. IEEE Syst. J. **14**, 3371–3382 (2020). https://doi.org/10.1109/JSYST.2020.2968883
12. El-Hageen, H.M.M., Ata, K.I.M., CheSoh, A.: Radio frequency identification (RFID) indoor parking control system, vol. 8 (2017)
13. Masali, M.N.: Indoor Parking Guidance System. 03
14. Liu, Y., Liu, X., Wang, S., Tian, R.: Research on parking guidance system based on computer vision. J. Phys. Conf. Ser. 2425, 012054 (2023). https://doi.org/10.1088/1742-6596/2425/1/012054
15. Lu, R., Lin, X., Zhu, H., Shen, X.: SPARK: a new VANET-based smart parking scheme for large parking lots. In: IEEE INFOCOM 2009, pp. 1413–1421 (2009). https://doi.org/10.1109/INFCOM.2009.5062057
16. Günay, F.B., öztürk, E., Çavdar, T., Hanay, Y.S., Khan, A.U.R.: Vehicular Ad Hoc network (VANET) localization techniques: a survey. Arch Comput. Methods Eng. **28**, 3001–3033 (2021). https://doi.org/10.1007/s11831-020-09487-1
17. Raghu, R., Prabhushankar, R., Rajaram, J., Vaiyapuri, M.: Efficient Dead Reckoning Approach for Localization Prediction in VANETs (2019)

TTWiFi: Time-Triggered WiFi for Mobile Robotics in Human Environments

Carl Lusty[1] , Vladimir Estivill-Castro[2](✉) , and René Hexel[1]

[1] Griffith University, Nathan 4111, Australia
`carl.lusty@alumni.griffithuni.edu.au, r.hexel@griffith.edu.au`
[2] Universitat Pompeu Fabra, Barcelona 08018, Spain
`vladimir.estivill@upf.edu`

Abstract. WiFi is a ubiquitous protocol, but exhibits flaws that become particularly critical for teams of robots in human environments. We demonstrate that our Time-Triggered WiFi (TTWiFi) protocol allows us to utilise the benefits of the hardware available in mobile robotic systems while ensuring resilience and bounded error detection in the time domain as required by teams of robots to make reliable real-time decisions. Our experiments demonstrate that TTWiFi performs equally well in static and mobile scenarios in retaining its resilience to interference.

Keywords: Wireless Communication · Mobile Robotics · IEEE 802.11

1 Introduction

In the rapidly evolving landscape of robotics, one of the most transformative advancements has been the integration of WiFi connectivity into mobile robots designed to operate in human environments [31]. This technological leap has sparked a new era of robotics, seamlessly interacting with humans and their surroundings, making them more versatile, adaptable, and valuable in various applications. WiFi plays a significant role in enabling the Internet of Robotic Things (IoRT) [23,40,50]. Whether it is the endearing Pepper robot engaging customers in retail stores [36] or tele-operated robots assisting in remote medical procedures [30], the importance of WiFi connectivity cannot be overstated. However, the ubiquity of WiFi in human environments has profound implications on efficiency, safety, and overall human-robot interaction [30,36].

Mobile robots have become increasingly ubiquitous in various human environments, from hospitals[1] and factories to public spaces and households. These robots are no longer confined to controlled, industrial settings but navigate the complexities of our daily lives. They perform tasks as diverse as delivering goods, providing companionship [18], assisting in healthcare [30], and even conducting

---

[1] Aethon's TUG autonomous mobile robot delivers medications, laboratory specimens, or other sensitive material within a hospital environment while using WiFi to communicate with elevators, automatic doors, and fire alarms.

L. A. Maglaras and C. Douligeris (Eds.): WiCON 2023, LNICST 527, pp. 14–28, 2024.
https://doi.org/10.1007/978-3-031-58053-6_2

surveillance [19]. However, WiFi faces challenges when it comes to reliability
and speed, complicating how mobile robots gather real-time information, process data, and swiftly respond to dynamic situations.

Mobile robot WiFi connectivity is so pervasive that it has been proposed and
deployed for navigation and localisation in human environments [15,43,56] where
Global Positioning System (GPS) signals are unreliable or unavailable, such as
indoor spaces[2]. Efficient wireless communication is vital for robots to collaborate
seamlessly. Although WiFi enables connectivity, severe delays or missing packets jeopardise real-time coordination amongst teams of robots or signals from
human pilots [46]. Communicating WiFi nodes often share the wireless communication medium. Thus, transmission attempts can often overlap, potentially
resulting in collisions where message payloads are lost [24]. Given this fundamental issue, many coordination algorithms have been proposed [4,24,41,42,45,48].
The growth of IoRT applications and the increasing deployment of mobile robots
in human environments has stimulated research into the reliability of communication within, to, and from mobile robots [32,33,44]. However, communication
timeliness remains a significant and open problem [17]. Therefore, applications
where robots must share information, receive commands, and promptly respond
to human input, can become safety-critical. Low latency and reliability are crucial in applications such as tele-operation, where human operators rely on near-
instant feedback to control robots remotely for tasks like surgery, search and
rescue, or hazardous material handling. WiFi connectivity also plays a pivotal
role in enhancing the quality of human-robot interaction. In scenarios where
robots are combined with mixed reality for sophisticated applications in assisting, guiding, or entertaining people, a stable and fast connection is essential
for a smooth and natural experience. The Pepper robot, for instance, relies on
WiFi to engage with customers in retail stores, answer questions, and provide
information. However, the experience when lag and dropped packets are present
eliminates the sensation of an interactive and enjoyable experience.

WiFi connectivity has also been used to extend mobile robot applications
with cloud computing and data analytics. WiFi enables mobile robots to har-
ness internet knowledge to make informed decisions and adapt to changing environments. However, with WiFi as the go-between, delays are inevitable. WiFi
offers unparalleled scalability and flexibility for robot deployment, easy integration, and makes it cost-effective to deploy robots. In robotic environments (as
opposed to many cloud services) eventual consistency is insufficient. Teams of
robots need timely information, not only of the correct order of events, but delays
that make some signals obsolete are simply unacceptable. This paper presents the
experimental design for evaluating WiFi protocols for mobile robots in human
environments. To the best of our knowledge, this is the first experimental setup
where the communicating nodes are moving. We evaluate the TTWiFi protocol [27] against off-the-shelf alternatives.

---

[2] Some commercial solutions, like Aruba's Meridian, use WiFi infrastructure for indoor
positioning (www.arubanetworks.com).

2   The Issue of Packet Loss and Packet Delay

The deployment of Wireless Local Area Networks (WLANs) in human environments is now massive. WiFi (the Institute of Electrical and Electronics Engineers (IEEE) 802.11 family) is now the most prevalent WLAN technology. However, many applications, specifically mobile robots, demand new Quality of Service (QoS) requirements for packet loss and communication timeliness [53]. Many reports highlight the significance of timeliness and reliability degradation under interference in wireless communication protocols. The community recognises that enabling real-time communications over license-free bands in open environments, encompassing multiple real-time stations, is particularly challenging [8]. Such is the demand for reliability and timeliness for mobile robotics in wireless environments that many protocols have been suggested, extending available technologies [12,52,54]. For instance, several proposals use IEEE 802.15.4 operating on the 2.4 GHz ISM band [16,34,37]. Their analyses assume unpolluted environments [8]. However, we focus here on WiFi (also known as IEEE 802.11) because of its wide availability and commonality among mobile robots deployed in human environments, as discussed in the introduction.

Variants for timely WiFi have been analysed theoretically and experimentally [10,55], with some incorporated as amendments to the IEEE 802.11 standard. We highlight the IEEE 802.11n standard as it provides longer transmission distances than other WiFi standards and its ubiquity over newer standards such as IEEE 802.11ax [13]. Since IEEE 802.11n offers open-source firmware implementations [1,49], and only two protocols are acknowledged [53] as suitable for timely communication over WiFi, we emphasize those two: the Wireless Flexible Time-Triggered (WFTT) protocol [9,11] and TTWiFi, which has been recently proposed [26,27]. However, wireless communication is so pivotal that numerous wireless protocols aim to achieve reliable real-time communication on IEEE 802.11 networks (i.e. RT-WMP [45], SchedWiFi [33], Adaptive TDMA [38], and RT-WiFi [51]). Some efforts aim at solving the problem even higher in the network stack [22,35,46]. That is, algorithms are designed at higher levels attempting to be tolerant and robust to the package losses and delays of the communication network. However, this cannot always be achieved.

Here, we report on the experimental setting where the stations move on board simple robotic platforms. The impact of packet loss has been studied for higher-level tasks, such as re-electing a leader [29]. Previous experimental research with indoor WiFi communication amongst a team of mobile robots explored WFTT behaviour when the access point changes or under a joining mesh and infrastructure networks [12]. That research emphasises the tight requirements of timely communication and reliability (detection and minimisation of packet loss). Still, it does not perform the experimental analysis we present here on single-hop broadcast performance. Moreover, no interference was evaluated [12] since swapping between two networks happens in such cases. We explore a large set of the parameters of the TTWiFi protocol under this experimental setting and contrast its performance against off-the-shelf alternatives at different levels of interference.

Definition 1. *A dependable (minimal packet loss, packet loss detection and timeliness) wireless communication protocol for mobile robotics, shall ensure alignment with the context of human environments.*

1. *The communication protocol must remain compatible with existing, widely-accessible mobile robotics platforms in human environments. Examples of such platforms include VGo [3], Giraff [2], Pepper [7], and Nao [5].*
2. *The communication protocol shall maintain functionality and coexistence within diverse wireless environments, including other IEEE 802.11 networks.*
3. *Practical implementation on physical hardware is a prerequisite for the communication protocol. This guarantees that the developed protocol holds relevance within the intended domain and can actively contribute to enhancing wireless communication, as opposed to being purely theoretical.*
4. *The reliability of the protocol's performance must be substantiated through real-world experimentation on tangible hardware across a spectrum of wireless interference scenarios. The experiments must unequivocally establish whether the protocol meets the desired latency and dependability.*

3   The TTWiFi Protocol

TTWiFi [26, 27] relies on modifications to the IEEE 802.11n MAC layer, similar to other access methods developed for dependable WiFi networks, including RT-WMP [45], WFTT [9,11], SchedWiFi [33], and RT-WiFi [51]. TTWiFi reduces the Interframe Space (IFS) timing, granting TTWiFi priority access to the wireless medium. To meet the deterministic timing requirements of Definition 1, TTWiFi deactivates the Carrier Sense (CS) mechanism of the Distributed Coordination Function (DCF) in the IEEE 802.11 standards. DCF is the first method coordinating access to the communication medium. The second method, the Point Coordination Function (PCF), is optional and involves a central Point Coordinator (PC) node that manages access to the wireless medium.

The rationale for TTWiFi is that DCF is the only mandatory, and fundamental access method within IEEE 802.11 [4], relying on CSMA/CA involving contention-based access. Thus, all nodes employ CSMA/CA as the primary mechanism to decide when to transmit on an IEEE 802.11 LAN, i.e., whether the communication medium is presently unoccupied or if another node is actively transmitting. The Carrier Sense (CS) mechanism encompasses two distinct approaches: the physical and virtual CS functions. The physical CS function listens to the communication medium to detect ongoing transmissions. The virtual CS function relies on the Network Allocation Vector (NAV), containing transmission predictions, to gauge the likelihood of another node using the medium. Mechanisms such as RTS and CTS influence these predictions. The CS mechanism registers the medium as busy when the physical or virtual CS functions determine so, requiring a node to delay its transmission. A backoff timer decreases only when the communication medium is idle. Nodes can transmit only when their CS mechanism ensures medium availability and their backoff timer reaches zero. For mobile robotics, this mechanism holds significance. First, a busy communication medium delays transmission until the medium becomes available, potentially leading to unpredictable communication delays. Second, variability in transmission timing is influenced by network load and the behaviour of other nodes using the same wireless frequency. These factors introduce dynamic and fluctuating transmission delays, causing inconsistencies in system behaviour. For instance, a remotely controlled robot relying on wireless commands could experience performance degradation and instability due to these random delays [17, 20].

TTWiFi operates as a time-triggered communication protocol, relying on precise transmission timing, thus necessitating altering the DCF to transmit without the mentioned fluctuating transmission delays. Turning off the CS mechanism makes the operation as if the medium were perpetually idle. While this action removes certain wireless collision safeguards from the DCF, TTWiFi nodes are safeguarded by the TDMA schedule, which prevents wireless collisions between synchronised nodes. Collisions between standard wireless nodes and TTWiFi nodes are minimised by the conventional wireless collision avoidance mechanisms. In such cases, standard DCF implementations will wait until TTWiFi transmissions pause before attempting retransmission, a factor that is considered in the timing allocated between TDMA slots. Other extensions, such as Enhanced Distributed Channel Access (EDCA) and Hybrid Coordination Function (HCF) Controlled Channel Access (HCCA), allow for adjustments in transmission priorities and exclusive periods for transmitting nodes.

TTWiFi employs time-triggered communication principles to determine transmission timing and promptly identify transmission failures within well-defined time constraints. Wireless communication medium access is governed by a pre-determined, cyclic Time Division Multiple Access (TDMA) transmission schedule. Consequently, the times of transmission arrivals can be inferred from their scheduled transmission times, along with the inclusion of bounded delays, e.g. the various IEEE 802.11n IFS intervals. This design ensures the detection of missed transmissions within their expected arrival times. TTWiFi is engineered to minimise single points of failure to bolster fault tolerance. As a result, it relies on Ad-Hoc wireless communication rather than a centralised Access Point (AP). TTWiFi assumes that all wireless nodes are located within transmission range, effectively sidestepping issues related to hidden nodes and exclusive groups.

Mobile robots designed for human environments employ General Purpose Operating Systems (GPOS), which poses challenges when scheduling transmission processes. GPOS robots rely on best-effort process schedulers that cannot guarantee precise timing, creating a problem for time-triggered communication, which relies on precise transmission timing. This issue can be addressed using a dedicated Real-time Operating System (RTOS) or processor for managing transmissions. Using an RTOS ensures better performance of TTWiFi, but on a GPOS, TTWiFi takes two steps to reduce OS scheduling jitter. First, when supported, we raise the priority of the TTWiFi transmission process within the OS. TTWiFi also uses process scheduling libraries compatible with multiple OSs, such as `libdispatch`, which allows scheduling tasks at specific times, enabling TDMA scheduling. Here, we show that, even when the nodes are moving, these strategies significantly mitigate the inherent uncertainties associated with GPOS. Typically, time-triggered communication protocols achieve synchronisation by using transmission times alone to deduce each node's clock drift. Due to the scheduling variability inherent in a GPOS, this approach is not feasible for TTWiFi. Thus, TTWiFi transmits a timestamp captured just before transmission to gauge clock drift among nodes. This clock synchronisation method consumes negligible additional communication bandwidth and reduces the dependence on scheduler precision, thus mitigating the effects of scheduling variability within a best-effort OS. TTWiFi accomplishes clock synchronisation through a two-phase approach. Initially, standard protocols such as the Network Time Protocol (NTP) or Precision Time Protocol (PTP) synchronise all clocks, eliminating extreme outliers. TTWiFi takes over clock synchronisation after this start-up phase, utilising its predefined TDMA communication schedule and disabling NTP and PTP to prevent uncontrolled wireless interference. During runtime synchronisation, TTWiFi evaluates clock variations among all participating nodes, establishing a unified global time that nodes use for scheduling their transmissions. TTWiFi nodes adopt Unix Time [47] as a common temporal reference (widely used in mobile robotics and general computing to measure the elapsed time since a fixed reference point). This way, TTWiFi reaches a consensus on the timing of slots in the TDMA round. Each node can compute the current communication slot by assuming the TDMA cycle commenced at the epoch time. Since the duration of our TDMA round remains constant, dividing the present time by this period yields the number of rounds since the epoch and a modulus operation determine the current offset within the TDMA round. Each node utilises the transmission time stamp and known IFS delays to assess the differences in system clock values of all other TTWiFi nodes to compensate for clock drift and periodically adjust its global clock through the Fault Tolerant Average (FTA) [25], which eliminates the impact of faulty clock values.

TTWiFi employs User Datagram Protocol (UDP)'s broadcast transmissions, offering a simple, well-supported interface on mobile robots for human environments. Unlike Transmission Control Protocol (TCP), UDP does not involve retransmissions or extensive data recovery mechanisms that affect transmission timing. Broadcast transmissions sidestep the Media Access Control (MAC) layer fragmentation timing problems. Ad-hoc frequency scanning, where nodes periodically pause transmissions to locate others for group formation, could disrupt TTWiFi's predefined transmission timing, especially when scanning nodes experience delays in sending or receiving transmissions. Since TTWiFi defines its communication frequency in advance, it turns off ad-hoc scanning.

We compare our approach with TCP as the de facto standard for wireless communication between mobile robots in human environments, and also the basis of MQTT, named as "The Standard for IoT Messaging". MQTT runs over any protocol that provides ordered, lossless, bi-directional connections, but the released implementations run on TCP. MQTT is gaining momentum, for example, in applications for robots in human environments, such as robot assistants [14].

4   Experiments with Mobile Robots

The Raspberry Pi 3 exhibits commonalities with common mobile robotics platforms for human environments; thus, its previous use for assessing TTWiFi effectiveness under a GPOS and its scheduling strategy [26,27].

TTWiFi clock synchronisation has been evaluated successfully, showing its merits [26, 27]. Moreover, TTWiFI has been shown to be robust to interference in experiments with static nodes [26,27]. Using the Raspberry Pi 3 offers several advantages for implementation and testing. Its CPU clock speed falls within the representative range of CPU speeds, and it provides numerous exposed General-Purpose Input/Output (GPIO) pins, enable measuring and debugging. Additionally, we can select a Network Interface Card (NIC) compatible with open-source firmware options, namely the Alfa Wireless Adapter AWUS036NHA [21]. Our Raspberry Pi nodes will operate using the same Raspberry Pi distribution, Raspbian GNU/Linux 8 (jessie)[6],

Fig. 1. Mobile NXT robot with a mounted Raspberry Pi 3.

coupled with version 4.4.38-v7+ of the Linux kernel. It is crucial to emphasise that TTWiFi is not bound to a specific operating system and utilises the POSIX API for portability. Moreover, we confine our implementation to a single Operating System (OS) process to mitigate any potential advantage arising from its multi-core configuration.

Until now, all experiments had employed a fixed node positioning approach, where the position and orientation of each node remained constant across different trials. While static configuration ensures consistency, for wireless communication between mobile robots, it becomes imperative to assess how mobility impacts the performance and reliability of TTWiFi. Hence, we describe a series of experiments devised to execute TTWiFi and compare it with standard baselines within a mobile experimental setup. To our knowledge, this is the first evaluation of WiFi alternatives under such dynamic conditions.

Inspired by mobile robots for human environments such as Giraff [2] and Oculus Prime, we will conduct our mobility experiments mounting the Pi 3 atop a locomotion platform (an EV3 platform common in mobile robotics localisation and map research [28]). The EV3 provides a straightforward USB interface for control and includes encoders on its motors, ensuring that movements are reproducible. Figure 1 depicts our experimental platform, set as a vertically integrated system with the battery-powered EV3 at the bottom attached to a basic track drive configuration, similar to those found in various EV3 design manuals. Atop the EV3, a 5V USB power bank supplies the Pi 3, which is mounted atop inside a standard Pi Foundation enclosure. The NIC is positioned above the Pi.

4.1   Split Group Movement Pattern

In the initial configuration, we divide the set of nodes into two groups of repeated separating and reuniting trajectories. The mobile nodes involved in this scenario are TTWiFi 2, 3, and 5, while the remaining nodes remain stationary. Figure 2a provides a visual representation of the mobile nodes, with a red line denoting the maximum distance they traverse and their respective direction. These experiments are progressively aligning with the concept of Swarm Robotics [39]. We reproduced all experiments in [27] to contrast this as a baseline for a static configuration with our mobile experiments. The first part of Table 1 shows the parameters, such as frequency (in Hz) and maximum bitrate (megabit per second (Mbit/s)) for this setting. Figure 3 shows typical results from the comparison protocols. Various nodes exhibited superior performance due to poor synchronisation, see Fig. 4. The TTWiFi results were much more consistent. Table 2 shows that the difference in well-timed packets between the static and mobile TTWiFi experiments was 0.39%.

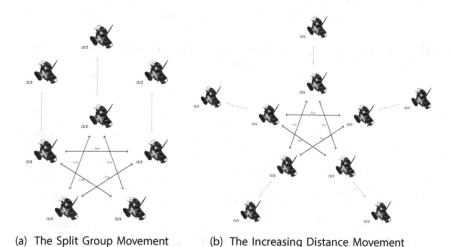

(a) The Split Group Movement   (b) The Increasing Distance Movement

Fig. 2. Movement experiments. Blue measurements denote the initial relative positioning. Red measurements denote the extents of the movement pattern. (Color figure online)

Table 1. Parameters for the two experimental settings.

Split Group Movement Pattern experiments					Increasing Distance Pattern experiments				
Hz	Max Bitrate	Clock Sync	Protocol	Moving	Hz	Max Bitrate	Clock Sync	Protocol	Moving
100	1 Mbit/s	Active (TTWiFi)	TTWiFi	Yes	100	1 Mbit/s	Active (TTWiFi)	TTWiFi	Yes
100	1 Mbit/s	Active (TTWiFi)	TTWiFi	No	100	1 Mbit/s	Active (TTWiFi)	TTWiFi	No
100	1 Mbit/s	Active (NTP)	UDP	Yes	100	1 Mbit/s	Active (NTP)	UDP	Yes
100	1 Mbit/s	Active (NTP)	TCP	Yes	100	1 Mbit/s	Active (NTP)	TCP	Yes
100	54 Mbit/s	Active (NTP)	TCP	Yes	100	54 Mbit/s	Active (NTP)	TCP	Yes

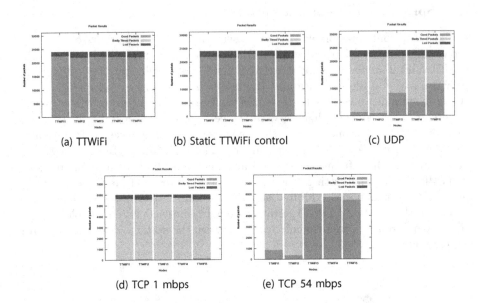

(a) TTWiFi   (b) Static TTWiFi control   (c) UDP

(d) TCP 1 mbps   (e) TCP 54 mbps

Fig. 3. Individual node experiment results for the Split Group Movement Pattern. The mobile nodes are TTWiFi2, TTWiFi3 and TTWiFi5.

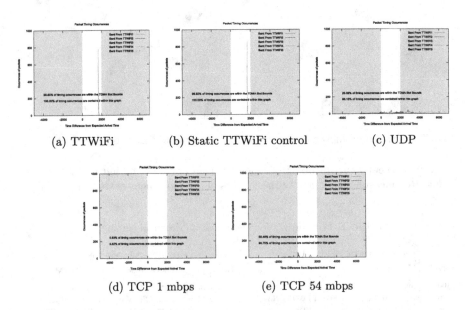

(a) TTWiFi   (b) Static TTWiFi control   (c) UDP

(d) TCP 1 mbps   (e) TCP 54 mbps

Fig. 4. Experiment packets occurance charts for the Split Group Movement Pattern. The mobile nodes are TTWiFi2, TTWiFi3 and TTWiFi5.

Table 2. Packet statistics for the protocols.

Split Group Movement Pattern experiment					Increasing Distance Movement Pattern experiment				
Protocol	Good Timing	Bad Timing	Lost Packets	% of Good Packets	Protocol	Good Timing	Bad Timing	Lost Packets	% of Good Packets
TTWiFi	110587	107	9306	92.16 % (SD: 0.87 %)	TTWiFi	107441	115	12444	89.53 % (SD: 1.51 %)
Static TTWiFi	110125	93	9782	91.77 % (SD: 2.31 %)	Static TTWiFi	107565	292	12143	89.64 % (SD: 2.75 %)
UDP	27370	81724	10906	22.81 % (SD: 17.10 %)	UDP	53449	58411	8140	44.54 % (SD: 32.85 %)
TCP 1 mbps	235	28159	1606	0.78 % (SD: 1.00 %)	TCP 1 mbps	45	26925	3030	0.15 % (SD: 0.22 %)
TCP 54 mbps	17573	12413	14	58.58 % (SD: 39.28 %)	TCP 54 mbps	21117	8869	14	70.39 % (SD: 23.82 %)

4.2 Increasing Distance Pattern

For this mobility pattern, nodes start in the standard static configuration and move directly away from each other. Once each node reaches the extent of the distance denoted in red in Fig. 2b, they reverse course and drive back to their original positions. This movement pattern repeats and forms a star shape of nodes that expands and contracts several times throughout each experiment. As with the first mobility pattern, a baseline control experiment was also conducted at the same time and in the same location using static nodes. The second part of Table 1 shows the parameters.

Table 2 shows only a slight difference between the static and mobile TTWiFi experiments of 0.11%. Based on the individual node results in Fig. 5 and the synchronisation results shown in Fig. 6, the comparison protocols behaved typically as well.

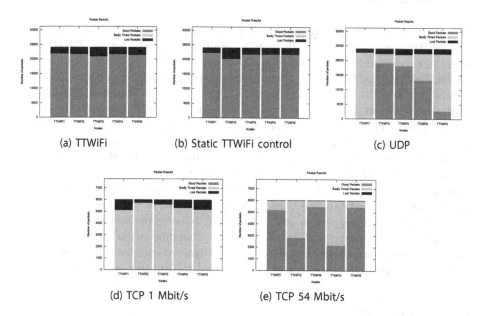

(a) TTWiFi   (b) Static TTWiFi control   (c) UDP

(d) TCP 1 Mbit/s   (e) TCP 54 Mbit/s

Fig. 5. Individual node experiment results for the Increasing Distance Movement Pattern.

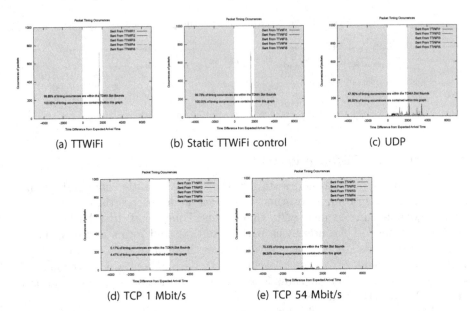

(a) TTWiFi   (b) Static TTWiFi control   (c) UDP

(d) TCP 1 Mbit/s   (e) TCP 54 Mbit/s

Fig. 6. Packets occurances for the Increasing Distance Movement Pattern.

5   Discussion

Two series of movement experiments were conducted to evaluate the impact of transmitter position changes and the movement of robots at runtime. In the first series of experiments, three nodes moved away from their initial positions as a group. This resulted in splitting the initial grouping of experiment nodes into two groups, which would later merge again. Compared to the static, no-movement control experiment we only see a slight difference in TTWiFi performance of 0.39%. The second movement pattern was to have the group of experiment nodes spread out. Each node moved away from the group, increasing its transmitter distance from all other nodes, again resulting in only a small difference (0.11%).

These minor differences between the movement patterns and their respective controls, which are well within the standard deviation observed within each set of experiments, demonstrate that there is no major detriment to the performance of TTWiFi within the movement patterns tested. These experiments demonstrate that with smaller movement patterns within communication range, TTWiFi remains a robust and temporally reliable time-triggered communication protocol, even when individual nodes change position and transmitter orientation.

6   Conclusions

WiFi connectivity plays a pivotal role for mobile robots to function optimally in human environments. Our experiments have shown that TTWiFi provides resilience against interference in both the time and value domain in scenarios critical to the reliable operation of teams of robots in human environments.

Since developers of applications for mobile robots in human environments are adopting MQTT, an avenue of further work is to evaluate an application with TTWiFi versus the same application using MQTT.

References

1. madwifi-project.org - trac (2007). http://madwifi-project.org
2. For researchers — Giraff (2014). http://www.giraff.org/for-researchers/?lang=en
3. VGo robotic telepresence for healthcare, education and business (2014). http://www.vgocom.com
4. IEEE standard for information technology-telecommunications and information exchange between systems local and metropolitan area networks-specific requirements - part 11: Wireless LAN medium access control (MAC) and physical layer (PHY) specifications. IEEE Std 802.11-2016 (Revision of IEEE Std 802.11-2012), pp. 1–3534 (2016)
5. Discover Nao, the little humanoid robot from SoftBank Robotics — SoftBank Robotics (2018). https://www.softbankrobotics.com/emea/en/robots/nao
6. Frontpage - Raspbian (2018). https://www.raspbian.org
7. Pepper, the humanoid robot from SoftBank Robotics, a genuine companion — SoftBank Robotics (2018). https://www.softbankrobotics.com/emea/en/robots/pepper
8. Bartolomeu, P., Alam, M., Ferreira, J., Fonseca, J.: Implementation and analysis of wireless flexible time-triggered protocol. Ad Hoc Netw. **58**, 36–53 (2017). https://doi.org/10.1016/j.adhoc.2016.11.016
9. Bartolomeu, P., Ferreira, J., Fonseca, J.: Enforcing flexibility in real-time wireless communications: a bandjacking enabled protocol. In: 2009 IEEE Conference on Emerging Technologies & Factory Automation, pp. 1–4 (2009). https://doi.org/10.1109/ETFA.2009.5347177
10. Bartolomeu, P., Fonseca, J.: Channel capture in noisy wireless contention-based communication environments. In: 2010 IEEE International Workshop on Factory Communication Systems Proceedings, pp. 23–32 (2010). https://doi.org/10.1109/WFCS.2010.5548640
11. Bartolomeu, P., Fonseca, J.: Towards flexible time triggered wireless communications. In: 2010 IEEE International Workshop on Factory Communication Systems Proceedings, pp. 203–206 (2010). https://doi.org/10.1109/WFCS.2010.5548603
12. Bazzi, A., Haxhibeqiri, J., Jarchlo, E.A., Moerman, I., Hoebeke, J.: Flexible Wi-Fi communication among mobile robots in indoor industrial environments. Mob. Inf. Syst. **2018**, 3918302 (2018). https://doi.org/10.1155/2018/3918302
13. Bellalta, B.: IEEE 802.11ax: High-efficiency WLANs. IEEE Wireless Commun. **23**(1), 38–46 (2016). https://doi.org/10.1109/MWC.2016.7422404
14. Diddeniya, I., Wanniarachchi, I., Gunasinghe, H., Premachandra, C., Kawanaka, H.: Human-robot communication system for an isolated environment. IEEE Access **10**, 63258–63269 (2022). https://doi.org/10.1109/ACCESS.2022.3183110
15. Ferris, B., Fox, D., Lawrence, N.: WiFi-SLAM using Gaussian process latent variable models. In: Proceedings 20th International Joint Conference on Artificial Intelligence, pp. 2480–2485. IJCAI 2007, Morgan Kaufmann, San Francisco, USA (2007)

16. Flammini, A., Marioli, D., Sisinni, E., Taroni, A.: Design and implementation of a wireless Fieldbus for plastic machineries. IEEE Trans. Industr. Electron. **56**(3), 747–755 (2009). https://doi.org/10.1109/TIE.2008.2011602

17. García-Valls, M., Casimiro, A., Reiser, H.P.: A few open problems and solutions for software technologies for dependable distributed systems. J. Syst. Archit. **73**, 1–5 (2017). https://doi.org/10.1016/j.sysarc.2017.01.007, http://www.sciencedirect.com/science/article/pii/S1383762117300310, special Issue on Reliable Software Technologies for Dependable Distributed Systems

18. Góngora Alonso, S., Hamrioui, S., de la Torre Díez, I., Motta Cruz, E., López-Coronado, M., Franco, M.: Social robots for people with aging and dementia: a systematic review of literature. Telemed. e-Health **25**(7), 533–540 (2023/09/10 2018). https://doi.org/10.1089/tmj.2018.0051

19. Habib, M.K., Baudoin, Y.: Robot-assisted risky intervention, search, rescue and environmental surveillance. Int. J. Adv. Rob. Syst. **7**(1), 10 (2010). https://doi.org/10.5772/7249

20. Hokayem, P.F., Spong, M.W.: Bilateral teleoperation: an historical survey. Automatica **42**(12), 2035–2057 (2006). https://doi.org/10.1016/j.automatica.2006.06.027, http://www.sciencedirect.com/science/article/pii/S0005109806002871

21. Inc., A.N.: AWUS036NHA 802.11b/g/n Long-Range USB Adapter (2009)

22. Jalil, A., Kobayashi, J., Saitoh, T.: Performance improvement of multi-robot data transmission in aggregated robot processing architecture with caches and QoS balancing optimization. Robotics **12**(3) (2023). https://doi.org/10.3390/robotics12030087

23. Kabir, H., Tham, M.L., Chang, Y.C.: Internet of robotic things for mobile robots: concepts, technologies, challenges, applications, and future directions. Digital Commun. Netw. (2023). https://doi.org/10.1016/j.dcan.2023.05.006

24. Kleinrock, L., Tobagi, F.: Packet switching in radio channels: Part I - carrier sense multiple-access modes and their throughput-delay characteristics. IEEE Trans. Commun. **23**(12), 1400–1416 (1975)

25. Kopetz, H., Ochsenreiter, W.: Clock synchronization in distributed real-time systems. IEEE Trans. Comput. **C-36**(8), 933–940 (1987). https://doi.org/10.1109/TC.1987.5009516

26. Lusty, C.: TTWiFi: Improving Wireless Communication Reliability for Mobile Robotics in Human Environments. Ph.D. thesis, School of Communication and Information technology, Griffith University (2023)

27. Lusty, C., Estivill-Castro, V., Hexel, R.: TTWiFi: time-triggered communication over WiFi. In: Proceedings 11th ACM Symposium on Design and Analysis of Intelligent Vehicular Networks and Applications, pp. 35–44. DIVANet 2021, Association for Computing Machinery, New York, USA (2021). https://doi.org/10.1145/3479243.3487298

28. Mac, T.T., Copot, C., Ionescu, C.M.: Design and implementation of a real-time autonomous navigation system applied to lego robots. IFAC-PapersOnLine **51**(4), 340–345 (2018). https://doi.org/10.1016/j.ifacol.2018.06.088, 3rd IFAC Conference on Advances in Proportional-Integral-Derivative Control PID

29. Madhevan, B., Sreekumar, M.: Analysis of communication delay and packet loss during localization among mobile robots. In: Berretti, S., Thampi, S.M., Dasgupta, S. (eds.) Intelligent Systems Technologies and Applications. AISC, vol. 385, pp. 3–12. Springer, Cham (2016). https://doi.org/10.1007/978-3-319-23258-4_1

30. Nertinger, S., Kirschner, R.J., Naceri, A., Haddadin, S.: Acceptance of remote assistive robots with and without human-in-the-loop for healthcare applications. Int. J. Soc. Robot. (2022). https://doi.org/10.1007/s12369-022-00931-9

31. Pahlavan, K., Krishnamurthy, P.: Evolution and impact of Wi-Fi technology and applications: a historical perspective. Int. J. Wirel. Inf. Netw. **28**(1), 3–19 (2021). https://doi.org/10.1007/s10776-020-00501-8

32. Park, P., Coleri Ergen, S., Fischione, C., Lu, C., Johansson, K.H.: Wireless network design for control systems: a survey. IEEE Commun. Surv. Tutorials **20**(2), 978–1013 (2018). https://doi.org/10.1109/COMST.2017.2780114

33. Patti, G., Alderisi, G., Lo Bello, L.: SchedWiFi: an innovative approach to support scheduled traffic in ad-hoc industrial IEEE 802.11 networks. In: 2015 IEEE 20th Conference on Emerging Technologies Factory Automation (ETFA), pp. 1–9 (2015). https://doi.org/10.1109/ETFA.2015.7301460

34. Pereira, N., Andersson, B., Tovar, E.: WiDom: a dominance protocol for wireless medium access. IEEE Trans. Industr. Inf. **3**(2), 120–130 (2007). https://doi.org/10.1109/TII.2007.898461

35. Poberezkin, E., Roozbahani, H., Alizadeh, M., Handroos, H.: Development of a robust Wi-Fi/4G-based ROS communication platform for an assembly and repair mobile robot with reliable behavior under unstable network or connection failure. Artif. Life and Robot. **27**(4), 786–795 (2022). https://doi.org/10.1007/s10015-022-00792-5

36. Roozen, I., Raedts, M., Yanycheva, A.: Are retail customers ready for service robot assistants? Int. J. Soc. Robot. **15**(1), 15–25 (2023). https://doi.org/10.1007/s12369-022-00949-z

37. Rowe, A., Mangharam, R., Rajkumar, R.: Rt-link: a global time-synchronized link protocol for sensor networks. Ad Hoc Netw. **6**(8), 1201–1220 (2008). https://doi.org/10.1016/j.adhoc.2007.11.008

38. Santos, F.: An adaptive TDMA protocol for soft real-time wireless communication among mobile computing agents. In: Proceedings of the Workshop on Architectures for Cooperative Embedded Real-Time Systems (satellite of RTSS), pp. 5–8 (2004)

39. Schranz, M., Umlauft, M., Sende, M., Elmenreich, W.: Swarm robotic behaviors and current applications. Front. Robot. AI **7** (2020). https://doi.org/10.3389/frobt.2020.00036

40. Simoens, P., Dragone, M., Saffiotti, A.: The internet of robotic things: a review of concept, added value and applications. Int. J. Adv. Rob. Syst. **15**(1), 1729881418759424 (2018). https://doi.org/10.1177/1729881418759424

41. Sobrinho, J.L., Krishnakumar, A.S.: Quality-of-service in ad hoc carrier sense multiple access wireless networks. IEEE J. Sel. Areas Commun. **17**(8), 1353–1368 (1999). https://doi.org/10.1109/49.779919

42. Song, J., et al.: WirelessHART: applying wireless technology in real-time industrial process control. In: IEEE Real-Time and Embedded Technology and Applications Symposium, pp. 377–386 (2008)

43. Tang, C., Sun, W., Zhang, X., Zheng, J., Sun, J., Liu, C.: A sequential-multi-decision scheme for WiFi localization using vision-based refinement. IEEE Trans. Mob. Comput. 1–16 (2023). https://doi.org/10.1109/TMC.2023.3253893

44. Tardioli, D., Villarroel, J.L.: Real time communications over 802.11: RT-WMP. In: 2007 IEEE International Conference on Mobile Adhoc and Sensor Systems, pp. 1–11 (Oct 2007). https://doi.org/10.1109/MOBHOC.2007.4428607

45. Tardioli, D.: Real time communications in wireless ad-hoc networks. The RT-WMP protocol. Ph.D. thesis, Universidad de Zaragoza (2010)

46. Tardioli, D., Parasuraman, R., Ögren, P.: Pound: a multi-master ROS node for reducing delay and jitter in wireless multi-robot networks. Robot. Auton. Syst. **111**, 73 – 87 (2019). https://doi.org/10.1016/j.robot.2018.10.009, http://www.sciencedirect.com/science/article/pii/S0921889017309144

47. Thompson, K., Ritchie, D.M.: UNIX Programmer's Manual. Bell Telephone Laboratories (1975)
48. Tobagi, F., Kleinrock, L.: Packet switching in radio channels: part II - the hidden terminal problem in carrier sense multiple-access and the busy-tone solution. IEEE Trans. Commun. **23**(12), 1417–1433 (1975)
49. Vanhoef, M.: modwifi (2014). https://github.com/vanhoefm/modwifi
50. O, V., et al.: Internet of robotic things intelligent connectivity and platforms. Front. Robot. AI **7**, 104 (2020). https://doi.org/10.3389/frobt.2020.00104
51. Wei, Y., Leng, Q., Han, S., Mok, A.K., Zhang, W., Tomizuka, M.: RT-WiFi: real-time high-speed communication protocol for wireless cyber-physical control applications. In: 2013 IEEE 34th Real-Time Systems Symposium, pp. 140–149 (2013)
52. Wichmann, A., Demirelli Okkalioglu, B., Korkmaz, T.: The integration of mobile (tele) robotics and wireless sensor networks: a survey. Comput. Commun. **51**, 21–35 (2014). https://doi.org/10.1016/j.comcom.2014.06.005
53. Xu, Y., Zhou, S., Cao, Q., Zheng, B., Xiong, Z., Ni, Y.: Time-triggered reservation for cooperative random access in wireless LANs. In: 2023 IEEE 97th Vehicular Technology Conference (VTC2023-Spring), pp. 1–7. IEEE (2023). https://doi.org/10.1109/VTC2023-Spring57618.2023.10199862
54. Yan, Z., Jouandeau, N., Cherif, A.A.: A survey and analysis of multi-robot coordination. Int. J. Adv. Rob. Syst. **10**(12), 399 (2013). https://doi.org/10.5772/57313
55. Zhang, J., Han, G., Qian, Y.: Queuing theory based co-channel interference analysis approach for high-density wireless local area networks. Sensors **16**(9) (2016). https://doi.org/10.3390/s16091348
56. Zhang, L., et al.: WiFi-based indoor robot positioning using deep fuzzy forests. IEEE Internet Things J. **7**(11), 10773–10781 (2020). https://doi.org/10.1109/JIOT.2020.2986685

Proximity-Driven, Load-Balancing Task Offloading Algorithm for Enhanced Performance in Satellite-Enabled Mist Computing

Messaoud Babaghayou[1], Noureddine Chaib[1], Leandros Maglaras[2(✉)],
Yagmur Yigit[2], Mohamed Amine Ferrag[3], and Carol Marsh[2]

[1] Laboratoire d'Informatique et de Mathématiques, Université Amar Telidji de
Laghouat, Laghouat, Algeria
{messaoud.babaghayou,n.chaib}@lagh-univ.dz
[2] School of Computing, Engineering and the Built Environment,
Edinburgh Napier University, Edinburgh, UK
{l.maglaras,yagmur.yigit,C.Marsh}@napier.ac.uk
[3] Technology Innovation Institute, Masdar City 9639,
Abu Dhabi, United Arab Emirates
mohamed.ferrag@tii.ae

Abstract. In an era of rapidly evolving mobile computing, integrating satellite technologies with the Internet of Things (IoT) creates new communication and data management horizons. Our research focuses on the emerging challenge of efficiently managing heavy computing tasks in satellite-based mist computing environments. These tasks, crucial in fields ranging from satellite communication optimization to blockchain-based IoT processes, demand significant computational resources and timely execution. Addressing these challenges, we propose a novel orchestration algorithm, K-Closest Load-balanced Selection (KLS), explicitly designed for satellite-based mist computing. This innovative approach prioritizes the selection of mist satellites based on proximity and load balance, optimizing task deployment and performance. Our experimentation involved varying the percentages of mist layer devices and implementing a round-robin principle for equitable task distribution. The results showed promising outcomes in terms of energy consumption, end-to-end delay, and network usage times, highlighting the algorithm's effectiveness in specific scenarios. However, it also highlighted areas for future improvements, such as CPU utilization and bandwidth consumption, indicating the need for further refinement. Our findings contribute significant insights into optimizing task orchestration in satellite-based mist computing environments, paving the way for more efficient, reliable, and sustainable satellite communication systems.

Keywords: Satellite Edge Computing · Task Orchestrationn ·
K-Closest Load-balanced Selection · Energy-efficient Offloading ·
End-to-End Delay Reduction

L. A. Maglaras and C. Douligeris (Eds.): WiCON 2023, LNICST 527, pp. 29–44, 2024.
https://doi.org/10.1007/978-3-031-58053-6_3

1 Introduction

Mobile computing has undergone a significant transformation in recent years, driven by the convergence of two key trends: the burgeoning Internet of Things (IoT) and the advent of 5G technology. This shift is steering the field away from traditional Mobile Cloud Computing towards Mobile Edge Computing (MEC), a more decentralized approach [1,8]. At the same time, satellite communication, a field with over four decades of history, is witnessing a resurgence [13]. The foundational work in this area, which includes pioneering concepts in satellite repeaters, orbital dynamics, and path-loss calculations, remains relevant even today through the increasing integration of IoT in satellite-to-satellite communications. The demand for satellite-to-satellite IoT services is rapidly growing, fueled by global enterprises and governments seeking to monitor and manage assets scattered across the globe. This has led to a significant expansion in the satellite market, with operators now offering comprehensive IoT solutions that leverage satellite technology [5]. As a result, edge computing within the satellite domain garners interest from various stakeholders, encompassing different layers from mist devices to data centres and cloud services, as seen in Fig. 1.

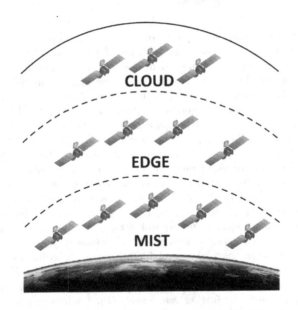

Fig. 1. The general satellite edge computing architecture.

In evolving mobile and satellite communications, the imperative for "heavy computing tasks" is critical. These tasks span a range of compute-intensive operations, from intricate calculations in satellite communication optimizations to the processing demands of blockchain-based IoT frameworks. In the field of Unmanned Aerial Vehicles (UAVs), such tasks involve video preprocessing, pattern recognition, and feature extraction, necessitating substantial computational capabilities [9]. Conversely, Yan et al. show that heavy computing arises during the mining process in integrating blockchain within IoT, requiring significant processing power [14]. The authors' research delves into efficiently handling these computationally intensive tasks within the satellite-based mist computing environment, aiming to optimize energy consumption and ensure timely task execution. This novel approach represents a pivotal step towards accommodating heavy computing tasks and fostering a more efficient satellite-based mist computing paradigm.

Undoubtedly, the meticulous preservation of privacy and security holds paramount importance in IT systems at large [2], and this significance is magnified in the domain of satellite-based mist computing [3]. These critical aspects form the bedrock upon which the success and reliability of the entire system rest. Neglecting robust privacy and security measures would expose the system to vulnerabilities, potentially allowing breaches by adversaries and malicious actors [6]. Such breaches could lead to severe consequences, undermining the efficacy and trustworthiness of the entire infrastructure. Therefore, a vigilant and proactive approach to safeguarding privacy and security is indispensable, fortifying the foundations of satellite-based mist computing and ensuring its sustained success.

Moreover, the meticulous preservation of Quality of Service (QoS), covering essential factors like latency and various types of delays, is indispensable. This necessity extends beyond general IT systems [4] and holds particular significance within the realm of satellite systems [5]. These systems' seamless operation and performance rely on consistently delivering QoS standards, underscoring the importance of maintaining and optimizing these aspects for sustained effectiveness. However, in the rapidly evolving landscape of satellite mist computing, the burgeoning potential of this paradigm is met with the inherent challenge of identifying orchestration algorithms tailored to specific application and scenario requirements. The intricate interplay between diverse factors such as energy efficiency, latency minimization, and resource optimization necessitates the continuous exploration and refinement of orchestration strategies. As the demand for satellite-based edge computing intensifies across various domains, from IoT deployments to remote sensing applications, the research community finds itself propelled to develop novel orchestration solutions that effectively address the unique demands posed by these diverse use cases. The motivation to bridge this gap and provide orchestration algorithms attuned to specific application intricacies drives ongoing research endeavours in the satellite mist computing domain. This paper makes noteworthy contributions to the domain of satellite-based mist computing through the following key elements:

1. **Innovative Orchestration Algorithm:** Our work introduces a novel orchestration algorithm, "K-Closest Load-balanced Selection" (KLS), explicitly designed for satellite-based mist computing environments. This algorithm prioritizes the selection of mist satellites based on proximity and load balancing, contributing to optimized task deployment.

2. **Fine-Tuned Parameters:** Our study investigates the impact of varying the percentage value k in the KLS algorithm. We provide insights into how parameter adjustments influence the algorithm's performance under different scenarios by testing k values of 30%, 50%, and 70%.
3. **Investigation at the Mist Level:** Our paper makes noteworthy contributions by focusing on the mist layer within the satellite-based computing environment. This investigation delves into the intricacies of task orchestration, specifically at the mist level, shedding light on the unique challenges and opportunities that arise in this crucial layer of computing architecture.

The remainder of this paper is organized as follows:

Section 2 provides an overview of related work in satellite-based mist computing. In Sect. 3, we present the system model, detailing the key entities and components within our simulated environment. Section 4 outlines the methodology, including developing and describing our novel task orchestration algorithm. Section 5 presents the simulation setup, environment, and the corresponding results. Finally, in Sect. 6, we conclude from our findings and discuss potential avenues for future research.

2   Related Work

A recent investigation conducted by Wang.F et al. [10] delves into the capabilities of Low Earth Orbit (LEO) satellites within the context of satellite-based edge computing. LEO satellites, characterized by expansive coverage and low latency, are valuable assets for delivering computing services to user access terminals. The study addresses resource allocation challenges in Edge Computing Satellites (ECS) arising from diverse resource requirements and access planes. To manage inter-satellite links (ISLs) and ECS resource scheduling, the study proposes a three-layer network architecture incorporating a software-defined networking (SDN) model. This model utilizes advanced algorithms for efficient resource allocation and ISL construction, including the Advanced K-means Algorithm (AKG) and a breadth-first-search-based spanning tree algorithm (BFST). Simulation results validate the feasibility and effectiveness of this dynamic resource scheduling approach, providing solutions to key challenges in satellite-based edge computing systems.

Zhang et al. investigated to examine the crucial integration of satellite and terrestrial networks within the realm of 6G wireless architectures [15]. These integrated networks ensure robust and secure connectivity across extensive geographic areas. The authors introduce the concept of double-edge intelligent integrated satellite and terrestrial networks (DILIGENT), emphasizing the imperative synergy between communication, storage, and computation capabilities within satellite and cellular networks. By harnessing multi-access edge computing technology and artificial intelligence (AI), the DILIGENT framework is meticulously crafted for systematic learning and adaptive network management. The article offers a comprehensive overview of academic research, standardization endeavours, and a detailed exploration of the DILIGENT architecture, accentuating its inherent advantages. Various strategies, including task offloading, content caching, and distribution, are scrutinized, and numerical results underscore the superior performance of this network architecture compared to existing integrated networks.

Wang.Y et al. explore the escalating significance of IoT within the information industry [11]. Edge computing is a promising paradigm that addresses challenges associated with network distance and the deployment of remote IoT devices. In scenarios where IoT devices are located in remote or challenging-to-access areas, the reliance on satellite communication becomes imperative. However, conventional satellites often lack universal computing capabilities and are specialized. The proposed solution involves the transformation of traditional satellites into space edge computing nodes, enabling dynamic software loading, resource sharing, and coordinated services with the cloud. The article delineates such satellites' hardware structure and software architecture and presents modelling and simulation results. The findings indicate that the space edge computing system exhibits superior performance, manifesting in reduced time and energy consumption compared to traditional satellite constellations. The service quality is influenced by factors such as satellite quantity, performance, and task offloading strategies.

Gao et al. [7] concentrate on the role of satellite networks as complements to terrestrial networks, addressing the computing needs of IoT users in remote regions and acknowledging the intrinsic limitations of satellites, including constraints in computing power, storage, and energy, an innovative strategy involves decomposing IoT user computation tasks into segments. This approach leverages multiple satellites for collaborative processing to enhance the efficiency of satellite networks. Integrating Network Function Virtualization (NFV) technology with satellite edge computing represents a burgeoning area of interest. The paper introduces a potential game-based solution for Virtual Network Function (VNF) placement within satellite edge computing. The primary goal is to minimize deployment costs for individual user requests while maximizing the provision of computing services across the satellite network. This optimization problem is formulated as a potential game, employing a game-theoretical approach to maximize overall network benefits. The proposed decentralized resource allocation algorithm, known as the possible game-based resource allocation (PGRA), seeks a Nash equilibrium to effectively address the VNF placement challenge. Experimental simulations validate the efficacy of the PGRA algorithm in solving the VNF placement problem within satellite edge computing.

In their investigation, Babaghayou et al. present a scheme called OVR (for Overseers) [1], underscoring its importance in tackling issues related to location privacy and road congestion within the Internet of Vehicles (IoV). OVR ingeniously utilizes silent periods to improve location privacy and effectively handle real-time congestion. Comparative assessments against established privacy schemes underscore OVR's exceptional privacy and QoS performance.

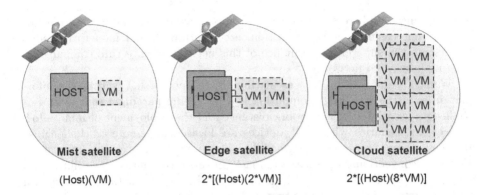

Fig. 2. The assumed types of satellites and their resources.

3   System Model

Satellite mist computing is assumed to comprise various entities, each playing a crucial role in the overall system. They are illustrated in Fig. 2 and they include:

– **Mist Satellites:** These satellites represent the mist layer and are equipped with a single host per satellite. Within each host resides a dedicated Virtual Machine (VM), where computational tasks are offloaded for processing.
– **Edge Satellites (Edge Datacenter Satellites):** Characterized as edge datacenters, these satellites are designed with heightened processing capabilities. Each edge satellite features two hosts, and each host accommodates two VMs. This architecture enhances the computational capacity for more demanding tasks.
– **Cloud Satellites:** Positioned at the highest layer, cloud satellites boast substantial computational resources. Each cloud satellite incorporates two hosts; eight VMs operate concurrently within each host. This configuration enables extensive parallel processing and scalability.
– **Tasks:** Computational workloads that necessitate offloading for efficient processing. These tasks are initiated at various points within the system and are orchestrated to suitable VMs based on the specific requirements and constraints of the satellite mist computing environment.

4   Methodology

To evaluate the performance of our proposed orchestration algorithm, which leverages the KLS approach in the mist layer, we implemented the algorithm within the satellite mist computing framework SatEdgeSim [12]. The algorithm aims to enhance task orchestration by selecting VMs strategically based on proximity, achieving load balance and efficient resource utilization. This implementation involved integrating the algorithm into the existing simulation environment, allowing for a comprehensive assessment of its impact on various performance metrics. The orchestration algorithm was tested and compared against other existing task orchestration approaches to provide insights into its effectiveness and suitability for different scenarios within the satellite mist computing paradigm.

4.1   Task Orchestration Algorithm Development

We developed a novel algorithm; that is KLS algorithm, to optimise task orchestration in the satellite mist computing framework. The pseudo-algorithm 1 is outlined below:

Algorithm 1. K-Closest Load-balanced Selection (KLS)

1: **function** KLS($task, k$)
2:      Initialize empty lists $satelliteDistances$ and $mistSatelliteIndices$
3:      **for** i in 0 to ($orchestrationHistory$ - 1) **do**
4:          **if** satDevice.getType() == TYPES.mist_Device **then**
5:              //Calculate distance between mist satellite i and task's satellite device
6:              $distance \leftarrow$ getDistance(satDevice, task.getSatDevice)/propagation_Speed
7:              Add $distance$ to $satelliteDistances$
8:              Add i to $mistSatelliteIndices$
9:          **end if**
10: **end for**
11:     Sort $mistSatelliteIndices$ based   on   corresponding   distances   in $satelliteDistances$
12:     $vm \leftarrow -1$
13:     $k \leftarrow k \times \dfrac{\text{mistSatelliteIndices.size()}}{100}$
14:     **for** i in 0 to mistSatelliteIndices.size() **do**
15:         $satelliteIndex \leftarrow$ mistSatelliteIndices.get(i)
16:         **if** offloadingIsPossible($task$, vmList.get($satelliteIndex$)) **then**
17:             **if** vm == -1 or orchestrationHistory.get($satelliteIndex$).$size()$ < orchestrationHistory.get(vm).$size()$ **then**
18:                 $vm \leftarrow satelliteIndex$
19:             **end if**
20:         **end if**
21:     **end for**
22:     **return** vm
23: **end function**

The **(KLS)** algorithm aims to efficiently orchestrate task offloading in a satellite-based mist computing environment. The following entities are integral to understanding the algorithm:

- **orchestrationHistory:** This is a data structure that maintains a historical record of task assignments to different VMs of the existing satellites.
- **satDevice.getType():** This method retrieves the type of the satellite device.

- **getDistance(satDevice, task.getSatDevice):** This function calculates the distance between a given mist satellite (*satDevice*) and the satellite device associated with the task to be offloaded (*task.getSatDevice*).
- **offloadingIsPossible(task, vmList.get(satelliteIndex)):** This function checks whether offloading the given task to a specific mist satellite (retrieved from *vmList* using *satelliteIndex*) is feasible.
- **satelliteDistances:** This list stores the calculated distances between the mist satellites and the satellite device associated with the task.
- **mistSatelliteIndices:** This list contains the indices of mist satellites eligible for task offloading.
- **vm:** This variable represents the selected mist satellite VM for task offloading.
- **k:** This variable determines the number of closest mist satellites to consider for task offloading. Its value is adjusted based on a percentage (k) of the total mist satellites.

4.2   Used Metrics

In this work, we have carefully chosen several metrics to assess the performance of our recently designed orchestration algorithm, KLS, in satellite mist computing. The metrics hold significant importance in comprehending the system's behaviour and evaluating the effectiveness of our solution within this distinct computing environment.

VM CPU Utilization Assessment: We examined the mean CPU consumption of VMs to ensure they ran within ideal bounds. This was essential to preventing resource overloads and optimizing the system's overall effectiveness.

Analysis of Average End-to-End Delay: We calculated the average time needed to complete tasks from beginning to end. This end-to-end delay is important to know if our orchestration method effectively meets the required deadlines and how well it handles time-sensitive, compute-intensive tasks.

Satellite Energy Consumption Measurement: Analyzing the energy consumption of the satellites while they processed tasks was a crucial component of our assessment. This allowed us to quantify our orchestration algorithm's sustainability and environmental impact.

Tasks Success Rate Evaluation: We examined the overall task success rate carried out using our orchestration technique. A high success rate indicates our approach's dependability and efficacy since a low success rate could negatively impact the system's functionality.

Network Usage Analysis: We measured the time spent on the network infrastructure to determine how much strain our system puts on the network infrastructure. Monitor the efficiency of the network, which involves tracking the volumes of data transmitted across various satellite mist computing system layers.

Bandwidth Consumption Monitoring: During task execution, we also calculated the bandwidth consumption. This metric is essential when determining the necessary network capacity and spotting possible bottlenecks in the system.

Total Executed Tasks per Layer: We counted the total number of tasks successfully executed at each satellite mist computing system layer. This metric provided a comprehensive view of how the workload was distributed and handled across different system layers.

4.3   Task Orchestration Algorithms

This section delves into the diverse task orchestration algorithms explored in our research. Effective task orchestration is pivotal for enhancing resource efficiency within satellite mist computing. We compare different algorithms, including our proposed KLS algorithm, to evaluate their impact on different metrics, precisely: CPU utilization, end-to-end delay, energy consumption, and overall system reliability. This analysis sheds light on the strengths and weaknesses of each algorithm, guiding their applicability in diverse scenarios within the satellite mist computing paradigm.

Round_Robin: The algorithm selects the satellite node with the least assigned tasks, fostering an evenly distributed computing workload. Its focus on underutilized resources aims to mitigate potential bottlenecks and ease the burden on heavily loaded nodes. This strategy contributes to optimal system performance and task completion rates. Additionally, it minimizes the risk of overwhelming any individual satellite node, ensuring efficient and effective resource utilization. In situations with diverse task requirements, the scheme provides a fair and practical approach to optimize task deployment in satellite-based mist computing environments.

Trade_Off: It adopts a dynamic strategy that intelligently chooses the most appropriate satellite node by striking a nuanced balance among factors such as latency, energy consumption, and resource availability. This algorithm assesses each potential satellite node, considering its type (cloud or edge device), the number of pending tasks, available CPU processing power, and task-specific attributes. Through computing a combined weighted score for each candidate, the scheme guarantees task allocation to the satellite with the most favourable trade-off among these factors. This approach enhances the efficiency and effectiveness of task orchestration, optimizing satellite resource utilization in satellite-based mist computing environments.

WEIGHT_GREEDY (WG): It represents a sophisticated strategy specifically crafted for satellite-based mist computing environments. The distinguishing feature of the "WEIGHT_GREEDY" scheme lies in its comprehensive assessment of four crucial performance indicators: transmission distance, CPU processing time, number of parallel tasks, and equipment energy consumption. Notably, the scheme's effectiveness is attributed to its meticulous weighting of these indicators, with the authors fine-tuning the ratios to be 6:6:5:3. This implies a deliberate emphasis on factors associated with task timeliness and minimal energy consumption, given their substantial weight in the proportion. In satellite edge computing, where timely task execution and energy efficiency take precedence, this weighting ensures an optimal balance between low latency and minimal power consumption demands.

K-Closest Load-Balanced Selection: The KLS scheme intelligently chooses satellite nodes based on a nuanced balance of latency, energy consumption, and resource availability. Designed explicitly to work on the mist layer devices, it prioritizes efficient orchestration in satellite-based mist computing. The scheme optimally balances these aspects by evaluating candidate nodes using factors like node type, distance, waiting tasks, and load on VMs. This dynamic approach, which considers the k percent closest mist-type satellites and loads on VMs, enhances orchestration efficiency, optimising satellite resource utilization. The emphasis on proximity-based selection and load balancing prevents resource bottlenecks, making it ideal for scenarios prioritizing energy efficiency and low-latency task execution.

5   Results and Discussion

5.1   Simulation Environment

The simulations were conducted using the SatEdgeSim framework [12], utilizing a mobility dataset generated by the Satellite Tool Kit (STK). The key parameters for the simulation environment are summarized in Table 1.

5.2   Simulation Results

The simulation results were evaluated based on several key metrics. Each metric provides insights into the performance of different orchestration algorithms. The following sub-subsections discuss the outcomes of the simulation runs:

Table 1. Simulation Environment Parameters

Parameter	Value
Number of Mist Satellites	1000 (maximum)
Number of Edge Datacenter Satellites	24
Number of Cloud Satellites	18
Duration	600 s
Task Generation Frequency	6 tasks per minute
K Values for Scheme	30%, 50%, 70%
Network Update Interval	1 s
Minimum Height	400.000 m
Earth Radius	6.378.137 m
Edge Devices Range	32.000.000 m
Edge Datacenters Coverage	36.000.000 m
Cloud Coverage	40.000.000 m

VM CPU Usage. The analysis of VM CPU usage, as shown in Fig. 3, revealed that the "Weighted Greedy" algorithm consumed a significant amount of CPU resources. Our scheme, specifically the variant with $k = 30\%$, also exhibited relatively high CPU usage. In contrast, the other orchestration schemes demonstrated lower CPU consumption.

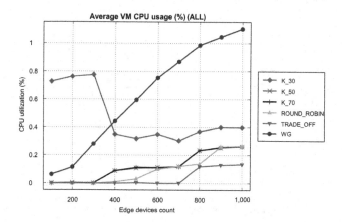

Fig. 3. The average CPU usage.

Average End-to-End Delay. In terms of average end-to-end delay shown in Fig. 4, our scheme (variant with $k = 30\%$) demonstrated superior performance. This is attributed to the scheme's emphasis on selecting close satellites to minimise communication latency. The "Weighted Greedy" algorithm followed, with other methods exhibiting varying levels of delay.

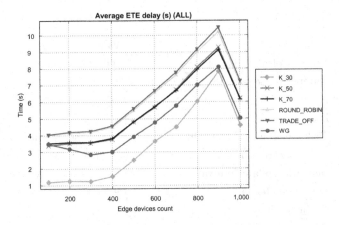

Fig. 4. The average end-to-end delay.

Satellites Energy Consumption. Our scheme (variant with $k = 30\%$) excelled in minimizing energy consumption among all orchestration algorithms, as shown in Fig. 5. The variants with $k = 50\%$ and $k = 70\%$ also performed well, along with the "Weighted Greedy" algorithm. However, the "Round Robin" and "Trade-Off" algorithms did not fare well regarding energy efficiency.

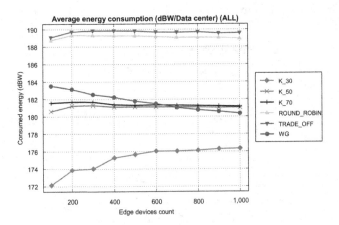

Fig. 5. The average energy consumption.

Bandwidth and Network Usage. For bandwidth usage shown in Fig. 6, the "Trade-Off" algorithm showcased the best performance, achieving a low average bandwidth per task. "Round Robin" and "Weighted Greedy" algorithms followed, while our scheme (variants with $k = 50\%$ and $k = 70\%$) demonstrated moderate performance. Surprisingly, our method (variant with $k = 30\%$) showed the highest bandwidth consumption among the tested variants.

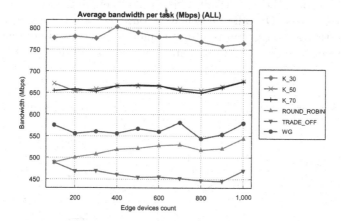

Fig. 6. The average bandwidth per task.

In the network usage metric shown in Fig. 7, our scheme (variant with $k = 30\%$) performed exceptionally well, exhibiting the lowest network usage time. The "Weighted Greedy" algorithm followed closely, with our scheme (variants with $k = 50\%$ and $k = 70\%$) showing moderate performance. "Round Robin" and "Trade-Off" algorithms demonstrated higher network usage times.

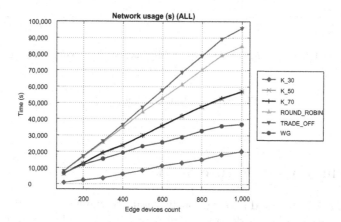

Fig. 7. The network usage.

Successfully Executed Tasks. The evaluation of successfully executed tasks revealed a unique characteristic of our KLS scheme. As it operates exclusively in the mist layer, it achieved no successful tasks in the edge data centre or cloud layers. However, our scheme (variant with $k = 30\%$) exhibited impressive results within the mist layer. Overall, our scheme's variants (30%, 50%, 70%) did not outperform other algorithms in the total number of successfully executed tasks across all layers. The obtained results are shown in Fig. 8a, Fig. 8b, Fig. 8c, and Fig. 8d.

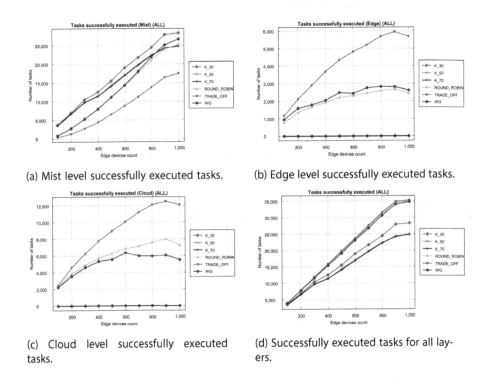

(a) Mist level successfully executed tasks.

(b) Edge level successfully executed tasks.

(c) Cloud level successfully executed tasks.

(d) Successfully executed tasks for all layers.

Fig. 8. Overall Task Execution

6   Conclusion and Future Work

In this study, we presented and rigorously evaluated the KLS algorithm, a novel task orchestration solution designed explicitly for satellite-based mist computing environments. Focused on optimizing various performance metrics, our algorithm, particularly the variant with $k = 30\%$, demonstrated promising results in reducing average end-to-end delay, minimizing satellites' energy consumption, and optimizing network usage time. However, the study also revealed particular challenges, including higher CPU usage, increased bandwidth consumption, and a lower total number of successfully executed tasks, highlighting areas for future improvement. Our comparative analysis with existing algorithms like "Weighted Greedy", "Round Robin", and "Trade-Off" uncovered varied performance characteristics across different metrics. This diversity emphasizes carefully considering specific application requirements when selecting an orchestration strategy.

Potential future directions can include optimizing CPU usage for improved efficiency and resource utilization, fine-tuning parameters like k for more balanced performance, extending the algorithm's capability across different layers, not just the mist layer, and integrating dynamic adaptation mechanisms to adjust to varying workloads and network conditions. Additionally, addressing security and privacy concerns in mist computing environments is essential to ensure that orchestration algorithms adhere to robust privacy and security standards. Lastly, real-world deployment scenarios and validations are crucial to assessing the algorithm's performance in satellite-based mist computing conditions. Future work can significantly contribute to advancing efficient and reliable orchestration strategies in dynamic satellite-based mist computing by addressing these identified limitations and exploring new paths.

References

1. Babaghayou, M., Chaib, N., Lagraa, N., Ferrag, M.A., Maglaras, L.: A safety-aware location privacy-preserving iov scheme with road congestion-estimation in mobile edge computing. Sensors **23**(1), 531 (2023)
2. Babaghayou, M., Labraoui, N., Ari, A.A.A., Ferrag, M.A., Maglaras, L.: The impact of the adversary's eavesdropping stations on the location privacy level in internet of vehicles. In: 2020 5th South-East Europe Design Automation, Computer Engineering, Computer Networks and Social Media Conference (SEEDA-CECNSM), pp. 1–6. IEEE (2020)
3. Baselt, G., Strohmeier, M., Pavur, J., Lenders, V., Martinovic, I.: Security and privacy issues of satellite communication in the avlatlon domain. In: 2022 14th International Conference on Cyber Conflict: Keep Moving!(CyCon), vol. 700, pp. 285–307. IEEE (2022)
4. Dagli, M., Keskin, S., Yigit, Y., Kose, A.: Resiliency analysis of onos and openday-light sdn controllers against switch and link failures. In: 2020 Fifth International Conference on Research in Computational Intelligence and Communication Networks (ICRCICN), pp. 149–153. IEEE (2020)
5. De Sanctis, M., Cianca, E., Araniti, G., Bisio, I., Prasad, R.: Satellite communications supporting internet of remote things. IEEE Internet Things J. **3**(1), 113–123 (2015)
6. Ferrag, M.A., Maglaras, L., Janicke, H., Smith, R.: Deep learning techniques for cyber security intrusion detection: A detailed analysis. In: 6th International Symposium for ICS & SCADA Cyber Security Research 2019, vol. 6, pp. 126–136 (2019)
7. Gao, X., Liu, R., Kaushik, A.: Virtual network function placement in satellite edge computing with a potential game approach. IEEE Trans. Netw. Serv. Manage. **19**(2), 1243–1259 (2022)

8. Mao, Y., You, C., Zhang, J., Huang, K., Letaief, K.B.: A survey on mobile edge computing: the communication perspective. IEEE Commun. Surv. Tutorials **19**(4), 2322–2358 (2017)

9. Messous, M.A., Senouci, S.M., Sedjelmaci, H., Cherkaoui, S.: A game theory based efficient computation offloading in an UAV network. IEEE Trans. Veh. Technol. **68**(5), 4964–4974 (2019)

10. Wang, F., Jiang, D., Qi, S., Qiao, C., Shi, L.: A dynamic resource scheduling scheme in edge computing satellite networks. Mob. Netw. Appl. **26**, 597–608 (2021)

11. Wang, Y., Yang, J., Guo, X., Qu, Z.: Satellite edge computing for the internet of things in aerospace. Sensors **19**(20), 4375 (2019)

12. Wei, J., Cao, S., Pan, S., Han, J., Yan, L., Zhang, L.: Satedgesim: a toolkit for modeling and simulation of performance evaluation in satellite edge computing environments. In: 2020 12th International Conference on Communication Software and Networks (ICCSN), pp. 307–313. IEEE (2020)

13. Wu, W.W.: Satellite communications. Proc. IEEE **85**(6), 998–1010 (1997)

14. Yan, Y., Dai, Y., Zhou, Z., Jiang, W., Guo, S.: Edge computing-based tasks offloading and block caching for mobile blockchain. Comput. Mater. Contin **62**(2), 905–915 (2020)

15. Zhang, J., Zhang, X., Wang, P., Liu, L., Wang, Y.: Double-edge intelligent integrated satellite terrestrial networks. China Commun. **17**(9), 128–146 (2020)

AI/ML Systems

Advanced Digital Services in Health: Global Insights on Security and Privacy Issues

Dimitrios D. Vergados and Eleni Varvarousi[(✉)]

Department of Informatics, University of Piraeus, 80, Karaoli & Dimitriou St., Piraeus, Greece
{vergados,varvaroussi}@unipi.gr

Abstract. The objective of this research is to provide an overview of digital services in the health sector. The emergence of innovative digital services has been accompanied by a multitude of issues and problems pertaining to privacy and security. To effectively tackle the issues around privacy and security in the realm of digital health, it is important to consider the principles established by international organizations. Moreover, a thorough analysis of the existing regulatory framework and unresolved issues in digital health is essential. Addressing these challenges effectively requires a unified approach that can lead to the implementation of robust solutions. Furthermore, this paper discusses the obstacles both developed and developing countries face regarding digital health, underscoring the need for a unified and international viewpoint.

Keywords: digital health · artificial intelligence · DHIS 2 · security · privacy · mobile health applications

1 Introduction

Digital health plays a crucial role in supporting the attainment of the United Nations' Sustainable Development Goals (SDGs), especially as regards SDG 3, which aims to provide universal access to healthcare and the improvement of people's health, regardless of age.

In recent years, nations have developed their own digital health policies and initiatives. The digital transformation of the health care sector is comprised of numerous technologies designed to facilitate a unified patient experience. The purpose of digital health technologies is to improve the state of one's well-being. Robotic surgery, wearable health devices, mobile health apps, remote monitoring of patients, artificial intelligence (AI) and machine learning, internet of medical things (IoMT), the use of nanotechnology for use in diagnosis or therapy, virtual reality (VR) and augmented reality (AR), blockchain systems, telemedicine, virtual health assistants and 3D printing are only a few of the many advancements in technology that have been developed in the healthcare sector. However, the utilization of disruptive technologies come with a set of challenges that are important to address and comprehend for the successful integration and maximization of the benefits of these technologies.

© ICST Institute for Computer Sciences, Social Informatics and Telecommunications Engineering 2024
Published by Springer Nature Switzerland AG 2024. All Rights Reserved
L. A. Maglaras and C. Douligeris (Eds.): WiCON 2023, LNICST 527, pp. 47–62, 2024.
https://doi.org/10.1007/978-3-031-58053-6_4

The World Health Organization (WHO) presented a Global Strategy focusing on digital health, underscoring the pivotal role of technological tools in meeting health-related objectives set by the Sustainable Development Goals. The Global Digital Health Strategy for 2020–2025 by the WHO underscores that for digital health solutions to be truly effective, they must not only be user-friendly but also foster universal and fair access to health services. Moreover, these tools should bolster health systems' capability to deliver cost-friendly, equal treatment while prioritizing the privacy and confidentiality of patient's data and the security of health-related information [1].

Additionally, the WHO emphasizes the importance of data security and highlights the need for transparency, scalability, and replicability, all while grounding these principles in equality and sustained relevance [1]. It should be highlighted that cooperation between developers, regulators, international organizations and entities is crucial to the development of innovative digital solutions for health, with a particular emphasis on privacy, data protection, data quality and transparency and the development of robust and consistent standards, among other factors. In a period where the health sector is increasingly digital and transcends geographical boundaries, fostering global synergies becomes crucial.

Digital health solutions should evolve by considering a comprehensive range of issues, including socio-economic aspects, technological advancements, cultural nuances, ethical standards, environmental considerations, legal frameworks and policy directives. These diverse considerations are instrumental in shaping truly effective and inclusive health solutions. As such, underscoring the significance of comprehensive global health solutions is pivotal, ensuring that health technologies benefit every individual in a holistic and equitable manner.

2 Digital Health

The digital health ecosystem is dynamic and complex. In general, it is possible to classify the evolution of healthcare into five distinct periods. Health 1.0 was primarily centered on the role of the doctor, Health 2.0 included electronic medical record histories, Health 3.0 shifted towards the patient emphasizing their active involvement in healthcare [2]. In the Health 4.0 framework, there's a blend of modern tools, mainly focused on the application of AI techniques [3]. Subsequently, the advent of healthcare 5.0, introduced digital health services such as wellness monitoring, emotional telemedicine, as well as smart self-management and various other innovative approaches to healthcare delivery [4].

There are several definitions concerning digital health. Particularly digital health can be defined as the integration of information technology into healthcare. This encompasses systems used in medical facilities like hospitals and clinics, as well as applications owned and used by patients [5]. After thorough research, it's evident that most of these definitions highlight the utilization of technological advancements to improve individual and community health. Furthermore, they also emphasize the enhancement of patient engagement by intelligently analyzing clinical and genetic data [6]. Several fundamental characteristics are vital to the functioning of digital health. Privacy and security, the accessibility of digital health technologies and tools, are merely a few of these. In recent years, numerous global initiatives and policies related to digital health have arisen. The World Health Organization (WHO) and the International Telecommunications Union (ITU) in the realm of global health and digital technology promote technologies and strategies, advocate policies and international standards that facilitate coordination as well as research and development. Furthermore, interactive digital tools like the Global Digital Health Index helps in benchmarking and comparing digital health advancements. Additionally, collective initiatives like the Health Data Collaborative underscore the global commitment to advancing digital health. But when examining global indicators on legislation, policy, compliance, infrastructure, leadership, governance, services, applications, strategy, investment and interoperability standards for digital health, it is evident that that there is no universal approach to digital healthcare and management, leading to notable disparities among nations. Digital health is a dynamic domain, leveraging technological advancements to revolutionize healthcare while also addressing prominent global challenges.

2.1 Artificial Intelligence in Healthcare

The integration of artificial intelligence (AI) into the domain of digital health represents a noteworthy transformation in healthcare and brings substantial changes in multiple aspects of society. This development carries far-reaching implications for diverse domains including diagnostics and imaging, predictive analytics, treatment, operation, drug development, remote monitoring and wearables, natural language processing (NLP), telemedicine, telehealth and remote diagnostics. The use of artificial intelligence and related technologies within the healthcare sector has been further expedited by the COVID-19 pandemic [7]. Owing to the prevalent use of artificial intelligence in the healthcare sector, the European Commission has introduced various initiatives. One such initiative is the establishment of the European Commission's High-Level Expert Group on Artificial Intelligence. This group has laid down guidelines to ensure trustworthy Artificial Intelligence [8]. An AI system to be secure, needs to follow among others legal, ethical principles and system robustness. Furthermore, human oversight, technological reliability, safety, data protection, accessibility, encouragement of diversity, promotion of fair treatment, accountability and responsibility are all necessary elements [9]. AI platforms ought to be reliable and secure but also safeguard people's constitutional rights. Data security and user privacy should be guaranteed by means of data management processes and ensure transparency, accessibility, openness, sustainability and accountability.

There are different methods which are frequently used in artificial intelligence means of digital health as machine learning methods, neural networks, deep learning methods. Deep learning as defined by ITU [ISO/IEC 22989] is an approach aiming at creating rich hierarchical representations through the training of neural networks with many hidden layers [10]. Deep learning has introduced sophisticated methods and tools for addressing complex health-related issues. For instance, deep learning is often used to find harmful tumors in imaging pictures or in radiomic, to process natural language (NLP) as well as in robotic process automation (RPA) [11].

Deep federated learning-based machine techniques are employed in the healthcare sector and are currently in developmentwith the use of models that maintain data at a local level and prevent exchange of information [12, 13]. This decentralized approach is particularly beneficial for privacy and data security assurance and is often selected for the retention of data. It aims at precise localization services that claim to prioritize the protection of users' privacy and security. These services use training methods that rely on resilient and privacy-preserving decentralized deep federated learning (RPDFL) strategies [14]. One notable example is its use in identifying Alzheimer's disease of individuals [15]. By leveraging this decentralized approach, medical professionals can analyze data from diverse sources without compromising patient privacy, leading to more accurate and timely diagnosis.

Furthermore, in recent years, the integration of AI in the medical sector has been notably evident in smartwatches that encompass a broad spectrum of functionalities. For example, they provide health tracking, fitness advice, seamless communication options, efficiency tools, data-driven forecasts, user-friendly interfaces, mental well-being assessments, directional aids and instant health notifications. Smartwatches have emerged as essential tools in the realm of health management, offering a range of monitoring capabilities to those facing different medical issues. For instance, according to various studies they can assist in the detection pertaining to skin cancer. These devices with the integration of advanced sensors and computational techniques, provide early detection and regular dissemination of alerts, positioning them as vital associates in preventive healthcare methods [16]. The use of AI in healthcare is significant and the issues that have been addressed up to this point just serve as examples of the challenges that relate to its utilization. In the following section some further instances of the use of artificial intelligence will be analyzed as regards the healthcare domain and the role of AI in identifying diseases.

It is important to note, however, that the use of AI in the diagnosis of illness is more prevalent in industrialized nations owing to the progress that has been made in healthcare infrastructure and resources. Furthermore, it is essential to emphasize, however, that the widespread use of information systems in developing countries helps to improve healthcare accessibility as well as disease monitoring to bridge the gap with the advantages of digital health applications.

2.2 Applications of Digital Health in Dynamic Economies

The introduction of artificial intelligence (AI) into the medical field is undergoing a transformation that is having a dramatic impact on the practice of healthcare across all its separate sectors. Therapeutic techniques, diagnostics, patient care management medical imaging technology are only some of the applications that may be used which demonstrate the technology's obvious potential for boosting patient treatment and refining medical procedures.

A notable example is the use of artificial intelligence (AI) in gastroenterology, which has expanded significantly in recent years. Applications of artificial intelligence are used for detection, diagnosis and treatment of gastrointestinal (GI) diseases that include endoscopic procedures, image analysis in radiology, predictive analytics, pathology, personalized treatment and monitoring.

The applications of AI technologies in gastroenterology are broad. For instance, the use of computer-aided detection (CADe) in the identification of polyps has promised in serving as an additional observer, hence mitigating the likelihood of polyp detection errors [17]. Furthermore, various artificial intelligence (AI) technologies are developed for the purpose of facilitating endoscopic procedures, namely colonoscopies.

Endoscopic and colonoscopic robotic surgery offers hope for many promising results, as is the case in other domains such as in digital orthopedic surgery. With the most recent advancements in robotics, the creation of new therapies for diseases and diagnoses, may improve patient accessibility to care and treatment outcomes. Furthermore, with the use of AI there is assistance in navigation, in tracking and cording of the procedure, in quicker intervention during the surgery practice. Whereas the conventional approach to clinical endoscopy relies on the doctor's expertise and training in performing biopsies, the use of artificial intelligence during gastroscopies, leads to enhanced diagnostic precision. Innovative approaches that make use of artificial intelligence during gastroscopies performed in recent years, result in increased diagnostic accuracy as well as detection of many illnesses, including stomach cancer. It's widely acknowledged that stomach cancer can rapidly advance towards a malignant state. The earliest symptoms of the phenomenon often exhibit subtlety and may evade discovery, hence emphasizing the criticality of early identification and action for enhanced results. With the use of a gastroscope based for instance on GCN (Graph Convolutional Networks), this novel detection model for early malignant lesions, according to studies, has effective results when compared to conventional medical methods [18, 19].

Moreover, AI is employed in medical and mobile health applications for various purposes, including remote patient monitoring, disease diagnosis and mental health support. At present, the market offers a wide array of healthcare applications, with a staggering number exceeding 350,000 at a global scale [20]. Furthermore, their diverse range of capabilities to aid patients in self-management contributes to their awareness as having significant potential in the treatment of acute pain and chronic diseases. The medical health applications are utilized extensively in gastroenterology to treat patients with diabetes or chronic liver disease (CLD) [21]. Furthermore, medical health apps also provide educational material for patients. In the discipline of gastroenterology, these apps are used to optimize gastrointestinal preparation prior to colonoscopy. Consequently, this ultimately results in an enhancement in the overall efficacy of this procedure and guarantees a comprehensive purification of the colon prior to the intervention. Research has shown that optimizing intestinal cleansing significantly improves the detection rate of polyps and reduces the likelihood of complications. This is of great significance due to statistical evidence indicating that 25% of individuals undergoing colonoscopy exhibit poor gastrointestinal cleaning, prior to the intervention, resulting in reduced accuracy of the obtained results [22]. The observed improvement in therapeutic outcomes may be attributed to the increase in patients' knowledge. Furthermore, it is worth noting that the mobile health apps offer significant advancement in the management of chronic illnesses. In addition, digital biomarkers assume a pivotal role in the management of cancer patients by offering enhanced prognostic information in comparison to conventional techniques.

Additionally, the prevalence of telemedicine and telehealth in gastroenterology is significant due to the chronic nature of many digestive disorders, such as liver cirrhosis. This is also the case with telemedical instruments for inflammatory bowel disease, chronic liver disease, patients undergoing liver transplantation or diabetic patients.

But as highlighted earlier, it's essential to note that the uptake and implications of artificial intelligence differ markedly between nations throughout the globe. Infrastructure, economic conditions and data accessibility are among the factors that contribute to the disparities.

According to the findings of the Organization for Economic Co-operation and Development (OECD), a total of sixty-nine (69) nations have established regulatory and legislative frameworks related to the use of artificial intelligence (AI). It is worth noting that most of these nations are high-income nations [23]. Furthermore, it should be stressed that when investigating the topic of digital health, it is essential to acknowledge the widespread adoption in developing countries as well. This is vital because of the numerous potential benefits that the digital health applications offer, not only for the global community but also for ensuring inclusion in digital health. Inclusion is a necessity, particularly considering the challenges faced in achieving the UN Sustainable Development Goals (SDGs) adopted by all UN member states in this domain.

2.3 Applications of Digital Health in Developing Nations: The District Health Information System 2

An important application of digital health in "developing nations" is seen in the implementation of health information systems, that have an important part in global digitization efforts. These systems are mostly required for effective health information management.

The District Health Information System 2 (DHIS 2) is the largest health information management system that has been designed as an innovative solution for enhancing the effectiveness of health management information systems (HMIS). The implementation of this Health Information System in several developing countries worldwide has been supported by International Organizations and the Norwegian government, underscoring the notable advancements achieved. DHIS 2 is used by 114 nations for the purpose of gathering and evaluating health data, including a population of 3.2 billion persons, which accounts for about 40% of the world's population. Furthermore, DHIS 2 is provided at no cost as a global public benefit [24]. It has been used for a wide range of health-related reasons by national health ministries, international development organizations and non-governmental organizations throughout the globe. DHIS 2 is employed in various fields, which include health management information systems (HMIS), disease surveillance and early warning, patient health records and tracking, supply chain management, program monitoring and evaluation, health workforce management, mobile health (mHealth) initiatives, health finance and budgeting, geospatial analysis and mapping, as well as integration with other systems.

The DHIS 2 platform is founded upon the principles of open data, which gives rise to several difficulties pertaining to privacy rights, confidentiality and data preservation. The susceptibility of DHIS 2 to corruption and deceit arises from several factors, including constraints in digital infrastructure, regulatory frameworks, and operational capabilities. However, it is important to note that DHIS 2 also has the capacity to contribute towards the prevention and mitigation of corruption and deception [25]. This assertion has validity because of the lack of comprehensive laws regarding data protection and privacy, particularly in nations with lower and moderate economic levels. For instance, in year 2016, a data breach took place in Sao Paulo, resulting to unauthorized disclosure of personal information and medical records related to 650,000 individuals who went through pregnancy and abortion treatment. Because of the current legislative structure in Brazil, in which abortion is illegal, women and medical practitioners affected by data breach were exposed to criminal prosecution threat [25].

The DHIS 2 platform incorporates machine learning techniques, hence presenting many difficulties pertaining to privacy and security. Moreover, with respect to the system, there is a recurring discourse around the application of data and the need to scrutinize the individuals or organizations who utilize this data [26]. The effective deployment of DHIS 2 requires an enormous and significant undertaking, demanding substantial political commitment across different levels of management. This initiative serves as a crucial element for disease surveillance and reporting systems, aiming to improve compliance, ensure longevity and safeguard the civil liberties of individuals [27].

Throughout the years, the District Health Information System (DHIS) has gradually supplied vital information for health care planning, monitoring, and reporting. The advancement of the Health Management Information System (HMIS) is focused on this component, which is significant. For instance, in South Africa the debut of DHIS in 1996/1997 as an ongoing system for monitoring health care delivery in the public health sector was an important turning point. South Africa successfully moved from DHIS 1.4 to WebDHIS, both of which are essential components of the health sector's overall Health Management Information System (HMIS). South Africa upgraded smoothly from DHIS 1.4 to WebDHIS [28]. But like any digital platform, DHIS 2 faces challenges related to security and privacy and in particular data breaches, data integrity, data transmission and software vulnerabilities.

3 Open Issues in Digital Healthcare

3.1 Privacy and Security Challenges

Security and privacy risks present serious challenges across the field of digital health. Data breaches and the unauthorized disclosure of personal data are common incidents within the digital health industry and security breaches are the primary source of threats to cybersecurity. The European Union Agency for Cybersecurity (ENISA) has conducted the examination of incidents in compliance with the Network and Information Security Directive [29]. The Cybersecurity Incident Reporting and Analysis System (CIRAS) [30], designed to facilitate incident reporting between member states presents interesting findings as regards the status among EU member states. Based on the most recent data published by the European Union Agency for Cybersecurity (ENISA), it is revealed that around 32% of incidents resulting in substantial consequences were seen within the Healthcare Sector [31]. Specifically, most instances, making up 53%, have been determined to involve medical personnel. It is noteworthy that European hospitals witnessed a significant percentage of incidents, involving 42% of the total amount of incidents. Health authorities, organizations, and agencies have been identified to be involved in 14% of the incidents, while medical companies were identified as being involved in 9% of the incidents. Most documented occurrences resulted in either data breaches or loss, accounting for 43% of the cases. Additionally, there were instances of healthcare service interruptions, which constituted 22% of the incidents. Furthermore, the European

Union Agency for Cybersecurity (ENISA), in its recent study, underscored the increasing severity of vulnerabilities found in digital wearable devices that store personal data [31].

The reliability of these devices may have a substantial influence on the health outcomes of patients, perhaps resulting in inaccurate diagnosis or inappropriate therapies. Smart health applications, utilizing smart devices pose greater security and privacy risks than conventional computing systems due to their heterogeneity, scalability, and dynamic assets. In general, these devices can collect data, store data and transmit to different systems by means of Wi-Fi connection [32]. The utilization of artificial intelligence (AI) algorithms is crucial for the comprehension and analysis of enormous amounts of information in a wide range of fields. Algorithms function at a significantly faster rate in contrast to human beings, permitting them to identify patterns, trends and irregularities which may evade manual evaluation [16]. However, the utilization of data presents substantial challenges, and it is frequently observed that there is no obvious difference among data pertaining to medical treatment and not medical treatment data [32]. Additionally, while collecting users' medical information via wireless connections and complex algorithms, developers frequently neglect to account for sensitive data security issues [33, 34]. Moreover, there's a common misconception stemming from their regular linkage with other applications or GPS tools. As a result, these methods often result in erroneous conclusions and engender the assurance of confidentiality and data privacy. Little regulation governs the digital health footprint and data analysts derive health assumptions from frequently collected data [35]. As a consequence, false assumptions are in common because they are frequently linked to other applications or GPS trackers.

Within the domain of healthcare, it is imperative to reinforce devices and systems against a variety of threats that fall into distinct categories, including but not limited to responsibility tracking, indisputable transactions, system reliability, resilience to setbacks, robustness and fault tolerance. Three fundamental principles form the basis of security requirements: confidentiality assurance, integrity maintenance and system availability guarantee. In general, potential privacy risks can be categorized as follows: apprehensions regarding location-based privacy, the prospect of impersonation, data interception, the way data is stored, inadequate testing, timely updates of devices, the absence of continuous device surveillance and the participation of anonymous users within the technological ecosystem.

Safeguarding medical data is complicated. In the past, various mechanisms such as encryption, blockchain, and biometrics have been utilized to address privacy concerns. Even though blockchain mechanisms have a significant impact on the healthcare industry and could help protect data privacy and security while ensuring information accuracy [16], contrary to this, numerous studies have shown that blockchain-based medical systems frequently lack privacy and security [36]. Transmission as well as storage, along with established security criteria should aim at maintaining data confidentiality, integrity, accessibility, and availability along with authenticity and non-repudiation and the use of security protocols.

In addition to encryption methods, the domains of machine learning (ML) and deep learning (DL) are critical components in the development of intelligent applications that place a premium on authentication of users and confidentiality. It is widely recognized that they effectively prevent unauthorized access to applications that take advantage of the features of intelligent devices and big data. Security-focused and privacy-enhancing technologies must be integrated during the design phase. Once these cutting-edge technologies have been integrated, they can be implemented in a variety of systems. To ensure that a system is resistant to threats, it is critical to implement severe security engineering practices from the outset. This fundamental stage guarantees that the following levels of the system are strengthened and resistant to potential vulnerabilities [37].

Furthermore, it is critical to incorporate ethical, governance, and regulatory considerations in an integrated way throughout the entire developmental process of artificial intelligence, encompassing its inception, conception, design, development, and ultimate integration. Ensuring the confidentiality and integrity of data within the realm of digital health is not merely an essential technological requirement; it is fundamental to maintaining the trustworthiness of healthcare infrastructures. By implementing these security precautions, resilience of healthcare systems as well as support of the confidence that patients have in them is assured. Likewise, this trust serves as the foundation for providing effective patient care and enables advancements in the field of digital health innovation.

3.2 Regulatory Framework Challenges

In accordance with international human rights obligations, the WHO resolution on digital health urges member states to "develop, as appropriate, legislation and/or data protection policies concerning issues such as data access, sharing, consent, security, privacy, interoperability, and inclusivity" [38].

Moreover, the current EU legal framework intends to increase the effectiveness and quality of protection of privacy and personal data processed in connection with electronic communications, as well as provide greater legal certainty for citizens. The objective of digital health is to become an essential element of health agendas, with the intention of providing ethical, safe, secure, reliable, fair and sustainable advantages to individuals. Furthermore, it aims to be developed with principles of transparency, accessibility, scalability, replicability, interoperability, privacy, security and confidentiality. In the event of an emergency, special rules should be considered. Regarding the privacy and security of digital healthcare as well as global strategic objectives, countries try to implement legal and ethical structures to ensure patient safety, secure health data, ensure appropriate usage and ownership of medical data, protect data privacy, facilitate data recovery, and protect intellectual property rights.

The current regulatory framework includes among others Directive 2011/24/EU, telemedicine acts, digital healthcare provisions, e-health action plans, NIS2, interoperability framework and GDPR. Furthermore, the regulatory proposal, which was unveiled in May 2022 by the European Commission, aimed to create a specialized ecosystem known as the European Health Data Space (EHDS) to accommodate health data. Ratification of the EHDS would create a framework that ensures the complete standardization of electronic patient records across the European Union and streamline the process of transferring such records between Member States. These measures aim to improve collaboration among member states, build trust in data privacy and security, and leverage the potential of cloud services.

Furthermore, ethical standards for the development of trustworthy artificial intelligence have been set up by Expert and Focus Groups such as the High-Level Expert Group on Artificial Intelligence operating under the auspices of the European Commission. Focus groups and initiatives also stress the importance of regulatory challenges aiming at harmonization among the nations. For instance, the ITU AI Focus Group on Artificial Intelligence for Health [39] prioritizes regulatory principles pertinent to AI in the healthcare sector. It emphasizes the importance of employing a comprehensive strategy that incorporates the entire product lifecycle, with risk management, meticulous design, privacy, and data security as top priorities. This statement emphasizes the importance of external validation and stakeholder engagement for the successful deployment of an AI system.

The field of digital health encounters a multitude of regulatory obstacles because of a swift in technological progress, the establishment of limits, safeguarding data privacy and security, ensuring interoperability, validating clinical efficacy, addressing global disparities, establishing reimbursement frameworks, considering ethical implications, conducting post-market monitoring, and fostering collaboration among stakeholders. The rapid rate at which technical innovations occur often surpasses the capacity of regulatory entities to assess and establish rules, resulting in deficiencies in supervision, possible hazards for patients and obstacles to innovation. Ensuring patient safety and promoting innovation within the digital health landscape necessitates the prioritization of certain key elements, such as safeguarding data privacy and security, enabling interoperability, acknowledging ethical considerations, and evaluating other pertinent issues. The European Commission's prioritization of safe, secure, and trustworthy digital health technologies, together with the implementation of the AI Act, requires sufficient time to effectively address the potential hazards and misuse of technology and safeguard civil rights. Furthermore, it is important to note that although the European Union has implemented extensive legislation regarding consumer digital privacy, the United States has not yet enacted a comprehensive legislative framework.

The United States has implemented a sector-specific approach, whereby varying levels of security are granted to health care under the Health Insurance Portability and Accountability Act (HIPAA) [40]. State governments throughout the United States are enacting privacy legislation at an accelerated rate. States such as Connecticut, Utah, California, Virginia, and Colorado are among those that have thus far enacted comprehensive legislation regarding data privacy. Additionally, protective measures are in place to ensure the confidentiality of genetic data, which is particularly delicate, in compliance with the Genetic Information Nondiscrimination Act (GINA). It should be noted that it is often stated that the regulations fail to govern significant aspects of digital consumer privacy [41]. Furthermore, the absence of standardization in eHeath interventions often gives rise to a multitude of challenges within the health sector.

Currently, there is a scarcity of effective international regulations concerning smartphone applications, including those that function as diagnostic or therapeutic tools or as medical applications [21]. It is critical to emphasize that a significant number of health applications lack adequate data security protocols, a prerequisite for safeguarding the data's confidentiality. Additionally, a mechanism that would allow end users to discern which items conform to superior security standards compared to industry standards, thereby confirming their suitability for secure utilization, has yet to be established. In addition, regarding interoperability issues, it is often observed that data is stored in separate locations that lack the necessary compatibility. Standardized interfaces and interoperability standards that are universally acknowledged are therefore essential to ensure the efficient integration of digital advancements within the medical domain [42].

Looking at digital health from a global perspective, there are numerous regulatory barriers which hinder the progress, operation, and integration of digital health systems in developing countries. In several developing countries, digital health regulations are fragmented, with numerous agencies exercising authority without clearly defined responsibilities. Therefore, a regulatory framework that is fragmented could hinder the implementation of digital health technologies. In India, for instance, there is no clear framework that outlines the functions of the multiple bodies in charge of regulating digital health, resulting in a regulatory overlap. The Central Drugs Standard Control Organization (CDSCO), the Ministry of Health and Family Welfare (MoHFW) and the Ministry of Electronics and Information Technology (MeitY) are all responsible for various issues that cause regulatory confusion, delays, or overlaps [43]. Moreover, inadequate cybersecurity and data privacy policies pose substantial threats to developing-country digital healthcare systems. In 2022, for example, Indian Healthcare experienced 1.9 million cyberattacks [44]. Regulatory barriers for digital health in developing nations include disordered regulation, the absence of insurance coverage regulatory mechanisms, the increased complexity of regulation due to the diversity of digital health tools, inadequate data protection laws and a dearth of regulatory staff expertise [45]. For example a systematic evaluation conducted in Ethiopia identified inadequate infrastructure as a significant impediment to the implementation of electronic health records [46].

Developing countries frequently have disorganized digital health regulations, which results in fragmented guidelines and legal ambiguities. Regulatory bodies are frequently overtaken by technological advancements, which complicates the regulatory process. The regulation of digital health instruments is additionally complicated by their heterogeneous character, encompassing mHealth applications, wearables and EHRs. In addition, it is difficult to determine whether these instruments qualify as medical devices. Inadequate technical expertise further impedes effective implementation and oversight [45].

Digital revolution presents several regulatory issues for developing nations. The management of regulatory assets demands a careful balance between innovation and policy compliance. Lack of technical competence makes compliance with international and local standards difficult. The lack of data protection and privacy legislation and changing cybersecurity and healthcare rules exacerbate matters. The variety of digital instruments being used, each with its own regulations, add to this complexity. Innovation and research are essential for success, but developing nations frequently lack comprehensive rules to govern their implementation and scaling. All the above mentioned issues highlight the need for stronger, clearer and more supportive regulatory structures to help these countries use digital technologies safely and effectively.

Table 1. Digital health challenges in developing vs developed nations

Developing nations		Developed nations	
Technical Assets	Regulatory assets	Technical Assets	Regulatory assets
Interoperability	Policy frameworks	Workforce training and change management	Technology adoption
Data Management	Compliance standards	Interoperability	Unregulated software apps
Limited Infrastructure	Insufficient technical knowledge	Advanced telehealth infrastructure	Ethical issues in AI and Big Data
Financial Constraints and digital divide	Inadequate data protection and privacy laws and cybersecurity healthcare regulations	Wearable health technologies	AI and machine learning regulatory framework
Data privacy and security	Regulatory divergence	Data privacy and security	Cross border data sharing
Connectivity	Innovation and research policies	Data quality and standardization	Cybersecurity requirements

4 Conclusion

Technological advances have the potential to bring about significant improvements, however, they are accompanied by several obstacles, such as data privacy concerns, difficulties in integrating new technologies into existing healthcare systems and complexities in regulatory frameworks. It is not enough to rely solely on technological solutions to protect an individual's right to privacy. Human factors, as well as policies and incentives, must be given the highest priority to achieve the desired results. To facilitate the seamless integration of technology into the healthcare sector, it is crucial to strengthen legal, ethical, and regulatory frameworks.

It is of the utmost importance that the requirements for information technology and governance are arranged to be compatible. With a unified strategy, data interoperability in healthcare systems may be addressed. It is crucial that nations should re-examine their current legal and ethical frameworks for preserving the security of health data, the appropriate use and ownership of medical data and the privacy and confidentiality of data.

Given the intricacies of the digital health domain, it is essential to approach the subject from a worldwide standpoint, recognizing the need for international collaboration to enable the secure advancement and utilization of digital health applications. Various stakeholders could maintain ongoing collaboration to foster common understanding, in conjunction with established national and international entities, to address digital health and artificial intelligence (AI)-related subjects. This collaboration is crucial for achieving convergence and harmonization of necessary legislative prerequisites as well as adopting the standards necessary to avoid privacy leakage and loss of confidentiality assurance.

Upon review of the domain of digital health, it becomes apparent both developing and developed countries face significant disparities and distinct challenges. Developing countries face a range of obstacles, such as limited technical resources and infrastructure, barriers to achieving interoperability, and complexities associated with data management. Beyond financial constraints and the digital divide, further impediments include concerns related to data security, cybersecurity and the maintenance and enhancement of connectivity. Challenges posed by regulations, inadequate data protection legislation, regulatory divergence including limited technical expertise as well as the complexity introduced by advanced digital services, present major challenges further development.

On the other hand, developed nations face a unique set of challenges, regardless of their advanced technological capabilities and regulatory frameworks. These encompass the imperative for change management to adapt to the rate of technological advancement and ethical issues pertaining to advancements in digital health. The current regulatory framework, the management of cross-border data sharing, data security and confidentiality of data are all crucial concerns. Furthermore, developed nations are faced with the simultaneous predicaments of addressing data quality and standardization concerns, ensuring interoperability among health systems and managing the unregulated nature of software applications. Both industrialized and developing countries face intricate challenges in the field of digital health. To foster a more inclusive and efficient global health ecosystem, it is vital that they mutually gain from each other's insights.

Acknowledgement. This work has been partly supported by the University of Piraeus Research Center (UPRC).

References

1. World Health Organization. Global Strategy on Digital Health 2020–2025, vol. 2021, p. 10. WHO, Geneva (2021). ISBN 978-92-4-002092-4
2. Jayaraman, P.P., Forkan, A.R.M., Morshed, A., Haghighi, P.D., Kang, Y.-B.: Healthcare 4.0: a review of frontiers in digital health. WIREs Data Min. Knowl. Discov. **10**, e1350 (2020). https://doi.org/10.1002/widm.135
3. Hathaliya, J.J., Tanwar, S.: An exhaustive survey on security and privacy issues in Healthcare 4.0. Department of Computer Science and Engineering, Institute of Technology, Nirma University, Ahmedabad, 382481, India
4. Mbunge, E., Muchemwa, B., Jiyane, S., Batani, J.: Sensors and healthcare 5.0: transformative shift in virtual care through emerging digital health technologies. Glob. Health J. **5**(4), 169–177 (2021)
5. Fatehi, F., Samadbeik, M., Kazemi, A.: What is Digital Health? Review of Definitions, vol. 275: Integrated Citizen Centered Digital Health and Social Care, Studies in Health Technology and Informatics, The European Federation for Medical Informatics (EFMI) and IOS Press (2020)
6. Paton, C.: BMBS BMedSci MBA FFCI, Textbook of Digital Health, University of Oxford, Oxford, UK
7. Wittbold, K.A., et al.: How hospitals are using AI to battle Covid-19. Harvard Business Review (2020). https://hbr.org/2020/04/how-hospitals-are-using-ai-to-battle-covid-19

8. European Commission's High-Level Expert Group on Artificial Intelligence. Ethics guidelines for trustworthy AI (2020). https://ec.europa.eu/digital-single-market/en/news/ethics-guidelines-trustworthy-ai
9. Ethics Guidelines for Trustworthy AI, High-Level Expert Group on Artificial Intelligence, European Commission, Brussels (2019)
10. Definition by ITU-T Focus Group Focus Group on Artificial Intelligence for Health, FG-AI4H DEL0.1 Common unified terms in artificial intelligence, 09/2022, International Telecommunication Union, Standardization Sector, FG-AI4H DEL0.1 for health (FG-AI4H) (2022)
11. Davenport, T., Kalakota, R.: The potential for artificial intelligence in healthcare. Future Health J. **6**(2), 94–98 (2019). https://doi.org/10.7861/futurehosp.6-2-94. PMID: 31363513; PMCID: PMC6616181
12. Mandal, K., Gong, G.: PrivFL: practical privacy-preserving federated regressions on high-dimensional data over mobile networks. In: Proceedings of the 2019 ACM SIGSAC Conference on Cloud Computing Security Workshop, pp. 57–68 (2019)
13. Wu, W., He, L., Lin, W., Mao, R.: Accelerating federated learning over reliability-agnostic clients in mobile edge computing systems. IEEE Trans. Parallel Distrib. Syst. **32**(7), 1539–1551 (2020)
14. Tian, Y., Wang, S., Xiong, J., Bi, R., Zhou, Z., Bhuiyan, M.Z.A.: Robust and privacy-preserving decentralized deep federated learning training: focusing on digital healthcare applications. In: IEEE/ACM Transactions on Computational Biology and Bioinformatics. https://doi.org/10.1109/TCBB.2023.3243932
15. Li, J., et al.: A federated learning based privacy-preserving smart healthcare system. IEEE Trans. Ind. Inform. **18**(3) (2021)
16. De Oliveira Fornasier, M.: The use of AI in digital health services and privacy regulation in GDPR and LGPD Between revolution and (dis)respect. RIL Brasília **59**(233), 201–220 (2022)
17. Zachariah, R., Ninh, A., Karnes, W.: Artificial intelligence for colon polyp detection: why should we embrace this? Tech. Innov. Gastrointestinal Endoscopy **22**(2), 48–51 (2020). https://doi.org/10.1016/j.tgie.2019.150631. https://www.sciencedirect.com/science/article/pii/S1096288319300701. ISSN 2590-0307
18. Huang, J., Jiang, Y.: Construction of gastroscope image recognition model and diagnosis system based on artificial intelligence technology. In: Proceedings of the SPIE 12703, Sixth International Conference on Intelligent Computing, Communication, and Devices (ICCD 2023), 127032E (2023). https://doi.org/10.1117/12.2682913
19. OECD.AI.OECD's live repository of AI strategies & policies
20. IQVIA. Digital Health Trends 2021. https://www.iqvia.com/insights/the-iqvia-institute/reports/digital-health-trends-2021. Accessed 24 June 2022
21. Kernebeck, S., Busse, T.S., Bottcher, M.D., Wetz, J., Ehlers, J., Bork, U.: Impact of mobile health and medical applications on clinical practice in gastroenterology. World J. Gastroentgerol. **26**(29), 4182–4197 (2020)
22. Desai, M., et al.: Use of smartphone applications to improve quality of bowel preparation for colonoscopy: a systematic review and metanalysis. Endosc. Int. Open (2019). 7Q E216-E224 [PMID 30705956]. https://doi.org/10.1067/mge.2003.294
23. OECD.AI (2021). https://oecd.ai/en/dashboards/overview
24. https://dhis2.org/in-action/#map. Accessed 07 Nov 2023
25. Hausenkamph, D.S., Cuadrado, D.C., Aarvik, P., Kirya, M.: U4 Issue 2022:9, Anti-corruption, transparency, and accountability in health management information systems, Chr. Michelsen Institute (CMI), Norway (2022)
26. Byrne, E., Sæbø, J.I.: Routine use of DHIS2 data: a scoping review. BMC Health Serv. Res. **22**, 1234 (2022). https://doi.org/10.1186/s12913-022-08598-8

27. Reynolds, E., et al.: Implementation of DHIS2 for disease surveillance in Guinea: 2015–2020. Front. Public Health **9**, 761196 (2022). https://doi.org/10.3389/fpubh.2021.761196
28. National Digital Health Strategy for South Africa 2019–2024, National Department of Health Republic of South Africa ISBN (digital) 978-1-920585-31-0. www.health.gov.za
29. Directive (EU) 2022/2555 of the European Parliament and of the Council of 14 December 2022 on measures for a high common level of cybersecurity across the Union, amending Regulation (EU) No 910/2014 and Directive (EU) 2018/1972, and repealing Directive (EU) 2016/1148 (NIS 2 Directive)
30. Cybersecurity Incident Reporting and Analysis System (CIRAS). https://ciras.enisa.europa.eu/
31. ENISA "Threat Landscape:Health Sector – January 2021 to March 2023, p. 3 (2023)
32. Kazgan, M.: Real challenge in digital health entrepreneurship: changing the human behavior. In: Wulfovich, S., Meyers, A. (eds.) Digital Health Entrepreneurship. HI, pp. 7–15. Springer, Cham (2020). https://doi.org/10.1007/978-3-030-12719-0_2
33. Iliadis, A.: Computer guts and swallowed sensors: ingestibles made palatable in an era of embodied computing. In: Pedersen, I., Iliadis, A. (eds.) Embodied Computing: Wearables, Embeddables, Ingestibles, pp. 1–20. The MIT Press, Cambridge (2020)
34. Gerke, S., Shachar, C., Chai, P.R., et al.: Regulatory, safety, and privacy concerns of home monitoring technologies during COVID-19. Nat. Med. **26**, 1176–1182. https://doi.org/10.1038/s41591-020-0994-1(2020)
35. Grande, D., Luna Marti, X., Feuerstein-Simon, R., et al.: Health policy and privacy challenges associated with digital technology. JAMA New Open **3**(7), e208285 (2020). https://doi.org/10.1001/jamanetworkopen.2020.8285
36. Ali, A., et al.: Security, privacy, and reliability in digital healthcare systems using blockchain. Electronics **10**, 2034 (2021). https://doi.org/10.3390/electronics10162034
37. Brost, G.S., Hoffmann, M.: Identifying security requirements and privacy concerns in digital health applications. In: Fricker, S.A., Thümmler, C., Gavras, A. (eds.) Requirements Engineering for Digital Health, pp. 133–154. Springer, Cham (2015). https://doi.org/10.1007/978-3-319-09798-5_7
38. WHO. Resolution A71/20 on Digital Health (2018). https://apps.who.int/gb/ebwha/pdf_files/WHA71/A71_ACONF1-en.pdf. Accessed 19 July 2019
39. ITU-T FG-AI4H Deliverable Telecommunication Standardization Sector of ITU, DEL02 -Overview of regulatory concepts on artificial intelligence for health, DEL02 (2022)
40. Glenn, T., Monteith, S.: Privacy in the digital world: medical and health data outside the HIPAA protections. Curr. Psychiatry Rep. **16**(11), 494 (2014). https://doi.org/10.1007/s11920-014-0494-4
41. Hudson, K.L., Holohan, M.K., Collins, F.S.: Keeping pace with the times-the Genetic Information Nondiscrimination Act of 2008 N. Engl. J. Med. **358**(25), 2661–2663 (2008). https://doi.org/10.1056/NEJMp0803964
42. Bork, U., Weitz, Jr.: Cloud Computing im Gesundheitswesen: Mehr Chancen als Risiken, **116** (14), 679-screens (2019). Accessed 17 Feb 2020. Dtsch Arztebl International
43. Jain, D.: Regulation of digital healthcare in India: ethical and legal challenges. Healthcare [Internet] **11**(6), 911 (2023). https://doi.org/10.3390/healthcare11060911
44. Mint. Indian healthcare sector suffers 1.9 million cyberattacks in 2022. [Internet] (2022). Cited 11 Aug 2023. https://www.livemint.com/technology/tech-news/indian-healthcare-sector-suffers-1-9-million-cyberattacks-in-2022-11669878864152.htm

45. Ahmad, Z.: Al Meslamani Technical and regulatory challenges of digital health implementation in developing countries. J. Med. Econ. **26**(1), 1057–1060 (2023). https://doi.org/10.1080/13696998.2023.2249757
46. Yehualashet, D.E., Seboka, B.T., Tesfa, G.A., et al.: Barriers to the adoption of electronic medical record system in Ethiopia: a systematic review. J. Multidiscip. Healthc. **14**, 2597–2603 (2021). https://doi.org/10.2147/JMDH.S327539

ACSIS: An Intelligent Medical System for Improving the Pre-hospital Healthcare Process

Petros Valacheas[1](✉), Sarandis Mitropoulos[2], and Christos Douligeris[1]

[1] University of Piraeus, Piraeus, Greece
petros.valacheas@gmail.com, cdoulig@unipi.gr
[2] Ionian University, Lefkada, Greece
sarandis@unipi.gr

Abstract. The purpose of this research article is to present an online intelligent pilot medical system designed to support the existing Greek pre-hospital medical care system. The proposed system effectively dispatches the available ambulances when an incident occurs and provides high quality medical services to the patients as well as transportation to the appropriate hospital. The evaluation of the proposed system, benchmarked via the paired t-test statistical tests and using the TIBCO business studio, shows a significant performance improvement on both the overall time to respond and the associated costs.

Keywords: Pre-hospital Care · Healthcare · Mobile Applications · intelligent medical systems · web IS · Business Information Systems

1 Introduction

Pre-hospital care has developed rapidly over the last decades and is now a necessary part of patient medical care [1]. An initial diagnosis in the ambulance can improve the patient's handling on arrival at the hospital [3]. Telemedicine solutions are increasingly used to speed up the process of diagnosis and care of the patient during transport to the hospital. The aim is to analyze and evaluate the health condition of a patient before the hospitalization phase. Electronic diagnostics, video conferencing and medical data analysis technologies are the main methods used [4].

Historically, the pre-hospital medical systems provided health care to patients without considering their clinical/medical condition. The most common approach was to refer them to the nearest health center or hospital. This approach resulted in considerable delays in the process of diagnosis and medical care. Too often, transporting patients to the appropriate hospital or health center for medical care was not the best possible as there was incomplete information about their condition [5].

Modern pre-hospital medical care systems have increased their ability to assess and diagnose the patient's health status, providing high quality medical care. They can also manage a fairly large number of patients who previously could not be assisted due to

L. A. Maglaras and C. Douligeris (Eds.): WiCON 2023, LNICST 527, pp. 63–81, 2024.
https://doi.org/10.1007/978-3-031-58053-6_5

insufficient equipment and know-how. The effective transport of the injured or patient to the appropriate hospital has been fully integrated into the functions of pre-hospital medical care and has ceased to be part of hospital medical care [6].

Various commercial telemedicine systems that feature state-of-the-art software are extremely bulky and expensive. Thus, they are used by very few health centers or hospitals. The rapid progress made in the field of Information and Telecommunications Technology (ICT) in recent years, enables us to design and develop quality telemedicine services for the pre-hospital health system that are accessible to all [7].

Emergency Medical Systems (EMS), as they support the first aid at the incident scene, provide some fundamental benefits to the overall healthcare services offered to the patients, as can be seen in Table 1 [3]. The Mobile Data Terminals (MDTs)[1] and the Medical Priority Dispatch Systems (MPDs)[2] are dispatching systems that help to determine the appropriate ambulance to be sent to the scene of the incident [8]. TrackerAssist, ManDown, and ePCR3[3] are remote sensing emergency care systems that can identify some critical health metrics of the patient and then notify the call center for incident reporting [9]. STREMS uses wearable sensing technology to capture the important medical data of the patient and provide a list of them for the efficient in-hospital medical care [22]. E-911 is used only for incident reporting as it cannot dispatch the appropriate ambulance [10].

The proposed ACSIS (Ambulance Consulting Services Information System) is an advanced ambulance dispatching and health care provision system which incorporates "On-time Incident Reporting", "On-time Arrival at the incident", "On-site Care", "Medical Care during Transportation", and "Transportation to the Health Center". ACSIS can be viewed as a mix of the E-911 computer aided system, MDTS and STREMS giving valuable benefits to the existing EMS systems. For example, Tracker Assist is likely a system that can track the location of individuals or assets in real-time. This can be useful for various purposes, including monitoring the movement of personnel, vehicles, or valuable items. It might have the capability to send emergency alerts or notifications when predefined conditions are met. For example, it could send an alert when a person enters or leaves a designated area. TrackerAssist may provide reporting features to generate historical location data, helping organizations analyze trends and make informed decisions. In addition, ManDown systems are typically designed to enhance the safety of personnel, especially in hazardous environments or high-risk occupations. They can detect unusual movements or conditions that may indicate a person is in distress or has fallen. ManDown systems often include fall detection features, automatically triggering alerts if someone falls or becomes immobile. These systems can send alerts to designated contacts or monitoring centers in case of a distress signal, allowing for a rapid response to emergencies. ePCR is used by emergency medical services (EMS) personnel to electronically document patient information and medical assessments during emergency incidents. It helps ensure the accuracy and legibility of patient records,

---

[1] https://thorcom.uk/products/mobilize/mobilize-mdt/ (accessed 02/12/2022).

[2] https://prioritydispatch.net/marketing-resource/ASSETS/PDFS/MPDSCatalog140114_English.pdf (accessed 02/12/2022).

[3] https://www.ems1.com/ems-products/epcr-electronic-patient-care-reporting/ (accessed 02/12/2022).

reducing errors in medical reporting. ePCR systems streamline the documentation process, allowing EMS personnel to focus on patient care. They often include templates and drop-down menus for quick data entry. ePCR systems may integrate with hospital electronic health records (EHRs) and other healthcare systems, enabling seamless sharing of patient information (Table 1) [3].

Table 1. The Respective Emergency Medical Systems per Performance criterion.

Performance Criterion	EMS Systems that support the Criterion
Timely Incident Perception	TrackerAssist, ManDown, ePCR
On-time Incident Reporting	E-911, TrackerAssist, ManDown, ePCR, eEKAB, ACSIS
On-time Arrival at the Incident	CAD, GIS, MDTs, MPDs, eEKAB, ACSIS
On-site Care (Extra operation from the e-Ekab EMS)	STREMS, ACSIS
Medical Care during Transportation (Extra operation from the e-Ekab EMS)	STREMS, ACSIS
Transfer to the Health Center	MDTs, eEKAB, ACSIS

ACSIS bridges the pre-hospital and the in-hospital health care by providing efficient and effective healthcare services to the patients. It is an add-on information system that could play a crucial role before the patient arrives at the hospital, providing inputs to the triage systems which will then take over [22].

This study aims to address the following research question: How can the Ambulance Consulting Services Information System (ACSIS) enhance pre-hospital care by incorporating advanced features such as 'On-time Incident Reporting,' 'On-time Arrival at the incident,' 'On-site Care,' 'Medical Care during Transportation,' and 'Transportation to the Health Center'? Additionally, what benefits does ACSIS offer compared to existing EMS systems, such as E-911, MDTS, and STREMS?" It explicitly outlines the research question and sets the stage for the subsequent sections to discuss the proposed ACSIS and its potential contributions to pre-hospital care.

2 Analysis and Design of ACSIS

Upon arrival of an emergency call in the call center, a process is launched for the effective selection of an ambulance to be sent to the scene of the incident. The call center operator, knowing, through the mapping application, the exact location of the available ambulances, can choose precisely the one which will be immediately dispatched. In fact, the call center can send notifications to all the available ambulances using the Firebase Cloud Messaging platform, a free notifications service provided by Google. The ambulance, after receiving the corresponding notification with the exact location, follows the route determined via Google Maps for its effective routing to the point.

At the incident location, medical care to the patient is provided in parallel with the appropriate cardiac pulse and respiration rate measurements. The nursing staff inside the ambulance is given the opportunity to make phone calls to find out the on-duty hospitals and pharmacies. A patient diagnostic functionality at the ambulance is provided to interpret the patient's symptoms. Finally, the nursing and the medical staff of the ambulance select the appropriate hospital center to which the patient will be transported. The destination is displayed on a map and the ambulance is navigated using Maps.

The ambulance taking notice (Notification) of the location of the emergency can go to it as soon as possible. GeoFire allows real-time data update, which is a very useful tool which performs "smart" calculations to retrieve selected data in specific locations. It is a key part of designing the ambulance application as it manages to update the base in real time data for the location of each vehicle. This allows the call center to be updated constantly with the current location of each ambulance, which is a crucial element for the proper dispatch of an ambulance to the emergency location [13][4].

The software development methodology that was used to plan, organize, prioritize, and proceed with the design and the implementation of the application was the Agile Scrum. For implementing ACSIS, each sprint, i.e. The smallest block of scrum which has a small team that works on an assigned task, lasted for 2 weeks [11].

The software system implemented to support and enhance the pre-hospital medical system consists of two independent applications, which are directly interconnected, of the web-based application which is the interface point with the call center operators, and of the mobile (Android) application that is handled by the ambulances. The two applications are connected on a common database located in Firebase, where the data are stored and retrieved. Their communication takes place through Firebase Cloud Messaging (FCM), which gives the capability of easy, reliable, and secure sending of messages. The mobile device sends its location via GeoFire, allowing the call center to visualize the above information in real time. The system architecture follows the Server-Client model. The server communicates with all its clients, serving requests via the HTTP protocol. Each client can be an ambulance or a call center application user. The server communicates with the database through Firebase to manage all the appropriate data for its operation (Fig. 1) [12].

The web-based application simulates the call center of the pre-hospital health system. The system has the following screens:

- Home Page (medical instructions for providing medical care to the patient)
- Display screen of the hospital centers on a map.
- HelpLine screen (incl. a table with the hospitals in which the patient can be transferred)
- Display and selection of available ambulances on a map in real time.

The screens that have been implemented for the mobile application are the following:

- Start Activity
- Login and Register Activities
- Main Activity with the following screens:
- Display and navigation to the available hospitals.

---

[4] The UML sequence diagram of ACSIS is provided in the following link: https://bit.ly/3rxfsue.

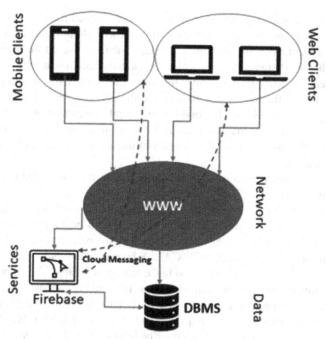

Fig. 1. ACSIS Client-Server Communication and the overall Architecture. Mobile and Web Clients communicate via the Firebase Messaging Service.

- Emergency: The nursing staff can be informed about the appropriate medical services to be offered to the patient.
- Patient Diagnosis.
- Patient's Heart Rate.
- Patient's breathing Rate Activity.

3 Demonstration of Applications' Operation

When launching the application, the user is prompted to connect to the ambulance application. Firebase adds the user details to the system and redirects the user to the main page of the application. Thus, the nursing and medical staff of the ambulance can provide medical services to the patient for immediate and timely treatment to the patient[5].

3.1 "Hospitals" Operation in Mobile Application

By clicking the Hospitals button at the top of the screen, a new application page appears with the nearest hospitals and health center's locations, where the patient can be transported - searching is possible using free text. By selecting one of the displayed hospitals,

---

[5] The image "Interface of the mobile application" is provided in the following link: https://bit.ly/3LJCnt9.

the user can use Google Maps to get directions, and estimated travel times. To display the nearest hospitals based on the specific location, the user should click on the blue icon symbolizing "Hospitals" at the bottom of the map. Then, the user of the ambulance can calculate the distance between the current location and the location to be reached, as well as the time needed to reach it. This is an extremely useful service that makes each ambulance independent of the call center. As a result, the user can determine, the available options through Google Maps[6]. Beyond the graphical representation of the available hospital centers on the map, the user in an ambulance can see their exact address on the map. This helps the user to verify the location of the hospital to which he has decided to transfer the patient.

To suppress severe symptoms, a list of actions has been documented to be followed by the ambulance nursing staff in an emergency. Pressing the "Information" button leads to the list of the available incidents. The nursing and medical staff of the ambulance can make phone calls to receive information about the on-call hospitals, to request blood from the National Blood Donation Centre, as well as to contact, if needed, the Poison Centre. By pressing the EMERGENCY CALLS button, which is located on the main screen, one can switch to a new screen to make emergency calls. The ambulance staff can also get in touch with various medical centers. The nursing and medical staff need to have direct access to information that concerns the best medical care of the patient. Using phone calls, the ambulance staff can request blood in case the patient is bleeding, search for medical advice if it is a poison incident or be informed about the on-duty hospitals. All the above operations prevent some critical medical conditions when transporting the patient to the hospital.

By pressing the MEDICAL DIAGNOSIS button, a user is led to a new page where he can select the exact symptoms of the patient, complete the year of his birth and his gender[7]. By selecting Heart Rate in the menu, located on the top-right of the application, the patient's heart rate is measured using the mobile phone camera. After 30 s the result of the measurement is displayed on the screen. This operation allows the ambulance medical and nursing staff to examine whether the pulses of the patient's heart are within or outside the normal range. The timely notification of the patient's heart rate is an important step for the effective provision of medical care in the ambulance. Using the located light sensors in the camera, the amount of blood in the body is detected at the given moment[8].

3.2 ACSIS Web Application

The ACSIS web application is used by the staff in the ambulances operating centre. By launching the web application, the location of the Call Centre and the available hospitals are shown on a map. Selecting the "Hospitals" button in the left bar, the hospitals' and

---

[6] The image "Hospital locations and route for reaching the patient" is provided in the following link: https://bit.ly/46AB5Jf.

[7] The image "Medical diagnosis button" is provided in the following link: https://bit.ly/3Q0 HUhL.

[8] The image "Screens for Heart Rate and Respiration Rate" is provided in the following link: https://bit.ly/46a8cnn.

the health centers' locations are displayed on the map. This functionality helps the call centre employee perceive the geographical zoning on the map and correlate the location of the hospital centers to the ambulance's one. This operation makes the ambulance selection for emergency handling effective.

In the past, the lack of depicting hospitals and health centers on the map often prohibited the call center from providing effective information for both the citizens and the ambulances. The "Show Hospitals" button displays the hospitals and the health centers that are located at a distance that can be used by the available ambulances. The digital display on a map of the respective locations, modernizes and speeds up the decision-making process and saves valuable time.

The call center upon arrival of an emergency is responsible for selecting and dispatching an ambulance to the scene. The need of the call center to have the full picture of the location for each ambulance led to the development of this functionality. By constantly monitoring the location of ambulances, the call center manages to efficiently optimize the available resources at its disposal and at the same time to provide the best possible medical care treatment for the patient[9].

The call center can fill in the emergency address of the patient and send a Notification to the ambulance. This feature enables the call center to speed up the dispatching of an ambulance to the scene of the incident. The traditional wireless communication with the ambulance has been recently replaced by modern cloud messaging technology. The call center can send medical assistance to the patient at no time. The Notification is sent to the mobile application of the ambulance, which undertakes to handle the part of the patient's medical care and the transport to the hospital. By clicking on Notification, the ambulance user is led to the map of the application to rush to the address of the incident. The Notification includes the exact address of the emergency incident to which the ambulance needs to be transported. The ambulance driver, by selecting the corresponding address on the map provided by Google Maps, navigates at the point knowing the estimated time it takes, the mileage and the traffic that will be encountered on the road. One primary consideration is the encryption and secure transmission of patient data. The system must employ robust encryption protocols to protect data during transmission from ambulances to healthcare centers and during any remote consultations. Discussing the specific encryption methods employed, adherence to industry standards, and strategies for preventing unauthorized access can enhance the transparency of ACSIS's security infrastructure.

4   Evaluation

4.1   Empirical Results from Cross-Sectional Research

In this section, a thorough evaluation analysis is provided regarding the performance of the EMS before and after the integration of ACSIS. The paired t-test statistical test was used to compare the corresponding results. The statistical model was applied through a survey via assumptions, which was conducted online using 30 ambulance drivers and 30 ambulance crew rescuers. Moreover, evidence regarding the health benefits in the

---

[9] The survey data are provided in the following link: https://bit.ly/3REfgUI.

adoption of ACSIS, feedback for the effective provision of in-hospital medical care of the patient and the better resource allocation of the ACSIS EMS system was achieved concerning the Cross-Sectional research.

The ambulance drivers and the ambulance rescue crew downloaded the mobile application, created their free account and used it to provide emergency medical care to the patients. The ambulance drivers received a notification via the ACSIS application and observed if they could arrive at the incident location on time. The ambulance rescue crew monitored if they could provide a quick and effective medical diagnosis of the patient's health within the ambulance. Having used the application at least once, they had to complete a questionnaire to express their satisfaction or displeasure[10].

30% of the rescuers mentioned that the ACSIS application offer benefits concerning the timely retrieval of information while 18,33% of the rescuers emphasize on the reduced costs after using ACSIS[11]. 83,33% agree that the patients were transported on time at the proper hospital to receive effective medical health care services after using the ACSIS[12]. 85% of the respondents agree that resource (ambulances, clinics, ambulance crew, time) management was improved after using ACSIS[13]. 88.33% of the ambulance drivers and ambulance crew acknowledged that the ambulance reached the spot between 3-to-5-time units. Specifically, the majority (43,33%) verified that the ambulance arrived in 4-time units. The time unit values are used to figure out the general time frame of this emergency medical care activity rather than to precisely calculate this timing value16[14]. 48.33% of the ambulance drivers and ambulance crew highlighted that the ambulance reached the spot in 1 time unit. They expressed their satisfaction on the quick arrival of the ambulance in the corresponding location and acknowledged the performance improvement using ACSIS on providing effective and on time medical services on the spot[15]. 90% of the responders agree that the traditional diagnostic procedure does not effectively assess the patient health condition on the way to the hospital[16]. 88,33% noticed an evaluation improvement on the diagnostic procedure that takes place within the ambulance. Most of the ambulance and ambulance crew highlighted that the ACSIS emergency system provides immediate medical diagnosis for the patient on the way to the hospital[17].

Specifically, there is a statistically significant difference in the arrival time of the ambulance after using ACSIS compared to the time needed before (t = 13,501, p =

---

[10] The image "The health benefit from the adoption of ACSIS between Ambulance drivers/Rescuers" is provided in the following link: https://bit.ly/3EZVbAK.

[11] The image "On time transportation and effective provision of medical care" is provided in the following link: https://bit.ly/3LHCLIG.

[12] The image "Efficient resource allocation after ACSIS" is provided in the following link: https://bit.ly/45dErQY.

[13] The image "The arrival of the ambulance times at the scene of the incident before ACSIS" is provided in the following link: https://bit.ly/46ADcwF.

[14] The image "The arrival of the ambulance at the scene of the incident after ACSIS" is provided in the following link: https://bit.ly/46vtsn9.

[15] The image "The provision of immediate diagnostics before ACSIS" is provided in the following link: https://bit.ly/3ZEBCHI.

[16] The image "The provision of immediate diagnostics after ACSIS" is provided in the following link: https://bit.ly/3PKS7xw.

[17] The statistical results are displayed in the following link: https://bit.ly/468IuQb.

0,000). Similarly, there is a statistically significant difference in the immediacy of the patient's diagnostic procedure with the use of ACSIS compared to its absence (t = - 20,433, p = 0,00). In practice, this means that the use of the application contributed significantly to the timely and immediate transportation of the patient to the hospital. Also, the automation of the procedure for the diagnosis based on the patient's symptoms with the use of ACSIS increased the possibility of correctly assessing the pathological condition[18].

In Table 2, the mean values of two emergency medical care services are compared before and after ACSIS via the paired t-test statistical test. Pair 1 is related to the arrival of the ambulance at the scene of the incident. Footnotes 16–17 show the results that were formed based on the survey. The statistical method showed that the mean value for the time units needed after ACSIS is half of the time units needed before. Also, based on the pair analysis, the diagnostic procedure has improved significantly after ACSIS. More specifically, the candidates expressed that it is almost twice more effective than the existing one. A paired t-test was employed to assess the statistical significance of the difference between the time taken for an ambulance to reach an incident location before the implementation of the ACSIS and the time taken after ACSIS adoption. Specifically, this statistical test was utilized to determine whether there was a statistically significant change in ambulance response times associated with the introduction of ACSIS. The null hypothesis (H0) posited that there would be no significant difference in the time it takes for an ambulance to reach the scene before and after ACSIS was implemented. The alternative hypothesis (H1), on the other hand, suggested that there would be a significant difference in response times before and after ACSIS adoption. Data on response times for a sample of ambulance dispatches were collected both prior to and following the implementation of ACSIS. These response times were then paired according to the specific incidents, where each pair represented the time taken before and after ACSIS utilization for the same incident location. The paired t-test was chosen for this analysis because it is appropriate for assessing the mean difference between two related groups (in this case, response times before and after ACSIS) when the data are continuous, and the assumption of normality is met. Additionally, it takes into account the dependence between the two sets of response times for the same incident locations. The results of the paired t-test indicated whether the observed difference in response times was statistically significant, which, if significant, would provide evidence for or against the effectiveness of ACSIS in reducing ambulance response times. The level of significance (alpha) chosen for the test determined the threshold for statistical significance. Overall, the paired t-test was a suitable statistical method to evaluate whether the implementation of ACSIS had a significant impact on ambulance response times and to provide valuable insights for emergency response system improvements. The results of the paired t-test provided insights into whether the observed difference in the immediacy of diagnostic procedures was statistically significant. A significant result would suggest that the implementation of ACSIS had a notable impact on expediting diagnostic assessments during ambulance transport, potentially leading to more timely and informed patient care decisions.

---

[18] The diagram "The ambulance Consulting Services application's process before ACSIS" is provided in the following link: https://bit.ly/3ZCJ0TW.

Table 2. Pairs Samples before and after ACSIS. The first question of each Pair concerns the "Before" ACSIS while the second one concerns the "After" ACSIS enforcement.

	Mean	N	Std. Deviation	p-value
How many minutes does it take for the ambulance to reach the spot before ACSIS?	4,02	60	0,965	<0.05
How many minutes does it take for the ambulance to reach the spot after ACSIS?	2,00	60	0,611	
Is diagnostic procedure immediate for assessing the patient's condition on the way to the hospital by ambulance before ACSIS?	1,73	60	0,634	<0.05
Is diagnostic procedure immediate for assessing the patient's condition on the way to the hospital by ambulance after ACSIS?	4,32	60	0,676	

4.2 ACSIS Simulation Evaluation

ACSIS was evaluated using the Tibco Business Studio, which allows the design of the components of the process to be evaluated and the simulation of the respective parameters and weights to perform a cost-effectiveness analysis [14]. To draw conclusions about the evaluation of the efficiency of ACSIS, the analysis focused on both the cost and on the time reduction through the emergency medical lifecycle. Each process consists of a logical sequence of steps which has a beginning and an end [15]. The diagram in "the ambulance Consulting Services application's process before ACSIS"[19] shows the processes that are performed to complete the transport of the patient to the hospital without the integration of ACSIS, while Fig. 3 the corresponding automated processes [14]. The first step is the initial step where an emergency incident is reported to a call center, typically through a 911 or emergency hotline. The call center operators receive information about the nature and location of the incident. Once the call center operators have gathered the necessary information, they determine the appropriate level of emergency response required. They then dispatch the nearest available ambulance or emergency response vehicle to the incident location. The ambulance is equipped with a navigation system, often using tools like Google Maps, to find the quickest and safest route to the incident location. This helps reduce response time, especially in critical situations. The ambulance arrives at the scene of the emergency, and the paramedics assess the situation and provide immediate medical attention to the patient [25]. This may involve stabilizing the patient, administering first aid, or other life-saving measures. The paramedics continue to provide medical care to the patient as needed. This care can range from basic first aid to advanced life support, depending on the severity of the situation. Based on the patient's condition and the hospital's availability, the system automatically selects the most suitable hospital for the patient. The ambulance's navigation system guides the crew to the chosen hospital using tools like Google Maps. During transport to the hospital, paramedics and nursing staff may have access to medical guidance

---

[19] The image "Available Ambulances" is provided in the following link: https://bit.ly/3terCJ0.

or protocols via digital devices or communication with a medical control center. This ensures that the patient receives appropriate care end route to the hospital. Paramedics continue to assess the patient's condition during transport, updating the patient's status and vital signs. This information is vital for the hospital staff to prepare for the patient's arrival.

The ambulance arrives at the selected hospital, and the patient is transferred to the hospital's care. The hospital staff takes over the patient's treatment and may perform further diagnostic tests and medical procedures. The described process for handling emergency incidents, from the arrival of the incident in the call center to the patient's arrival at the hospital, is highly useful for several reasons, like rapid response, efficient resource allocation, efficient navigation and ambulance routing, medical guidance, automatic appropriate hospital selection, effective coordination and communication, patient data management, quality assurance, reduced human error and, enhanced accountability.

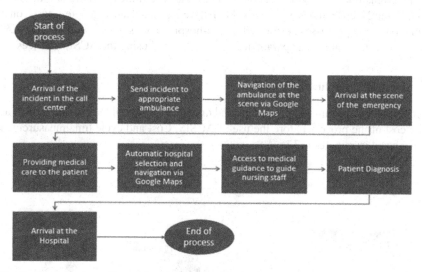

Fig. 3. The ambulance Consulting Services application's process after ACSIS enforcement.

The quality management approach requires to clearly understand the requirements, create a value-add process, and improve the overall process. The ASCIS evaluation presented hereby follows the ISO 9001:2015 qualified process approach, which involves the Plan-Do-Check-Act (PDCA) cycle and risk-based thinking [16]. The methodology for assigning time and cost parameters to the EMS simulated Tibco processes is conceptually supported by the Pairs Sample Statistical test as described previously. The cross-sectional statistical method that was used to compare the differences in the mean values before and after ACSIS, proved that it can enhance the EMS activity by 2 or 3 times. Particularly, the arrival time of the ambulance at the scene of the incident decreased by 50% compared with the time needed before ACSIS. Moreover, the ambulance drivers and the ambulance crew clearly expressed their satisfaction for the improved diagnostic procedure of the patient within the ambulance. They expressed that the medical diagnosis of the patient after ACSIS is almost 3 times more immediate. We assume that the automated emergency medical services will follow the same statistical flow and as a result they will improve 2 or 3 times compared to the emergency medical services offered before ACSIS.

To be more specific, the emergency processes that take place and handle the arrival of the ambulance on the spot are estimated to be twice as fast after ACSIS. The provision of medical care processes is estimated to be three times more efficient after ACSIS. In addition, we assume that the cost of the Tibco simulation will remain the same before/after ACSIS as the resources (ambulances, hospitals, ambulance crew and call center employees) will stay unchanged. In terms of the cost parameter for both simulations, we consider 12 call centers and 40 call center employees with a labor cost per day of 30 Euros. We also presume to have 1200 ambulances with an hourly cost of 160 Euros each. Therefore, we consider 1200 Euros for operating the call center and 200.000 Euros as an estimated cost for the ambulances.

The evaluation process of the parameters for the cost - time estimation of the ACSIS system using Tibco includes two stages. At first, we estimated the parameters based on the simulation of the processes performed by pre-hospital care systems without the ACSIS services and at second, these parameters were estimated using the ACSIS services.

4.3   Simulation Evaluation Results

Tibco calculated the minimum, average, and maximum values of the execution time, and of the cost of the process before the use of ACSIS. Cost and cycle time measurements are displayed in minutes in Fig. 4.

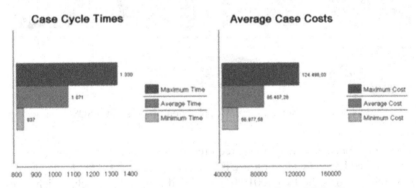

Fig. 4. Average Case Cycle Times and Case Costs after ACSIS enforcement.

It is obvious that the use of ACSIS has decreased spectacularly the total cost required for the response to an incident. In Fig. 5, it appears that before integrating applications the average cost relative with the average time of completion of the processes is estimated at 220,000 euros for 1100 min. After integrating the applications, the average cost in relation to the completion time of processes is set at 85,000 euros with an average time of 880 min.

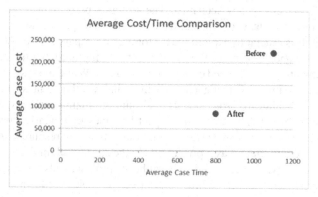

Fig. 5. Average Cost/Time comparison of before and after ACSIS enforcements.

5   Discussion and Future Work

The ambulance is transformed into a modern independent medical care unit that is an integral part of the pre-hospital health system. The ambulances are not any more fully dependent on the call center directions regarding the fast and reliable dispatch in the scene of the incident and the transportation of the patient to the nearest hospital. The medical diagnosis of the patient within the ambulance, the heart and respiration rate measurements in the ambulance play a vital role in assessing the patient's medical condition and helping to provide the optimal health services by the ambulance team. There are also some research limitations that we need to highlight. The proposed system does not thoroughly examine economic feasibility, despite acknowledging a reduction in accompanying costs. The lack of a comprehensive analysis of staffing and training needs, especially for non-medical personnel, raises concerns about the long-term sustainability and practicality of implementing the system on a broader scale. The low accessibility to networks in rural and barren areas can be an obstacle for the efficient operation of ACSIS. Moreover, poor ambulance availability can limit the effective provision of pre-hospital emergency care in these areas. It is also vital to ensure the protection of the patient's data concerning both the medical and location-based information [22].

While ACSIS presents a promising advancement in pre-hospital care, it is crucial to acknowledge and address potential limitations and challenges that may arise during its implementation across diverse healthcare contexts. One key consideration is the variability in healthcare infrastructures and resources among different regions. The effectiveness of ACSIS may be influenced by the level of technological infrastructure available in a particular area, potentially posing challenges in areas with limited access to advanced technologies. Moreover, cultural and regulatory differences across healthcare systems may impact the seamless integration of ACSIS. Adhering to diverse medical protocols, privacy regulations, and data security standards is essential. Ensuring compliance with these requirements is imperative for the successful adoption and sustained use of ACSIS in various healthcare settings. Another potential challenge lies in the adaptability of ACSIS to different emergency scenarios. The system's performance may vary based on the nature of incidents, geographical locations, and the specific healthcare needs of the population. It is crucial to explore the customization capabilities of ACSIS to cater to the unique demands of each healthcare context. Furthermore, the financial implications of implementing ACSIS need careful consideration. While the system aims to be a cost-effective alternative to existing telemedicine solutions, the initial setup costs, training programs for healthcare professionals, and ongoing maintenance expenses should be thoroughly evaluated. This economic aspect becomes particularly important when introducing ACSIS in healthcare systems with limited financial resources. Additionally, user acceptance and training play a pivotal role in the successful implementation of any healthcare technology. The readiness of healthcare professionals, emergency responders, and other stakeholders to embrace and effectively use ACSIS must be assessed. Addressing potential resistance to change and ensuring comprehensive training programs will be essential for the smooth integration of ACSIS into daily pre-hospital care practices. In conclusion, a thoughtful examination of these potential limitations and challenges will contribute to a more nuanced understanding of the practical implications of ACSIS in diverse healthcare contexts. By proactively addressing these issues, stakeholders can work towards maximizing the benefits of ACSIS and fostering its successful integration into pre-hospital care systems worldwide [23]. While our study provides valuable insights into the potential benefits of ACSIS within the Greek healthcare system, it is essential to acknowledge the potential limitations in generalizability to other healthcare systems with distinct operational dynamics. The Greek healthcare system has its unique characteristics, including specific regulatory frameworks, infrastructure, and patient demographics, which may differ significantly from other global healthcare contexts. The operational dynamics of pre-hospital care can vary widely between countries due to differences in healthcare policies, emergency response systems, and technological infrastructures. Therefore, the successful implementation of ACSIS in the Greek healthcare system does not automatically guarantee its seamless integration into other healthcare systems. Cultural and regulatory differences also play a crucial role in the generalizability of ACSIS. Compliance with local privacy laws, medical protocols, and ethical standards is paramount. The degree to which ACSIS can accommodate these variations without compromising its functionality and effectiveness should be explored in future research. To enhance the external validity of our findings, future studies could consider multi-country comparisons, taking into account a diverse range of healthcare systems. Such comparative analyses would provide a more comprehensive understanding of how ACSIS performs across different contexts and could identify specific challenges and opportunities unique to each setting. For instance, a comparative study could explore the implementation of ACSIS alongside similar ambulance dispatching and healthcare provision systems in countries with varying healthcare infrastructures, regulatory frameworks, and technological landscapes. By evaluating the experiences of these systems, we can draw meaningful comparisons that highlight the specific strengths and challenges of ACSIS in relation to its counterparts. Such a comparative approach allows for the identification of best practices, lessons learned, and potential areas of improvement. It also facilitates a more comprehensive understanding of the factors influencing the success or challenges faced by telemedicine solutions in different global settings. Additionally, it provides a basis for developing recommendations that are not only tailored to the Greek healthcare system but are also informed by a broader international perspective [12].

Various areas can certainly be improved. One area where the system could be extended, is the creation or updating of the electronic Medical Record of the patient within the ambulance. The medical diagnosis of the patient could be recorded and used to analyze and evaluate the health progress of the patient in the hospital. This operation could improve the medical services that are provided to the patient when at the hospital [20]. Another area where the system can be improved is security. The need to connect ambulances remotely to a wireless communication network (VPN) which would allow them to stay connected for the duration of providing emergency services, is an important feature for its effective operation. VPN offers a complete encryption and secure service over the network.

Finally, ACSIS could expand the clinical Triage systems and improve the overall health care services offered to the patients [21, 22]. The basic idea is that a Triage system can start cooperating with ACSIS still from the ambulance stage. In recent years, a key aspect of societal progress has centered around the availability of healthcare facilities [23]. Consequently, the strategic placement of ambulance stations and dispatching methods has gained significant importance. One widely adopted approach is the Emergency Medical System (EMS), which aims to optimize the allocation of a limited number of ambulances across emergency stations to effectively serve areas with the highest demand. Moreover, the challenge has grown more complex due to escalating medical expenses, surging demand, and urban traffic congestion [24]. These variables exert an influence on ambulance response times and should be taken into account when determining their optimal locations [25]. Regrettably, the prevalent technologies and methods employed by the majority of EMS agencies could impede this shift, as they continue to rely on outdated and less effective EMS approaches that were in use during the 1990s. As an example, numerous ambulances still utilize radio communication to connect with hospitals [26]. This research offers several noteworthy contributions. Initially, it delves into the organizational framework of regional medical unions. Within these unions, specialists collaborate with general practitioners to formulate treatment strategies and assume a central role in the treatment process [27]. Further research proposals could include the following: (1) investigating the management of identified system weaknesses, particularly addressing the omission of personnel-related cost analysis, to enhance the overall reliability and practicality of the research; (2) exploring the impact of the system on real-world healthcare practices; (3) investigating the most effective way to manage patients' digital data in terms of security and confidentiality compliance.

Acknowledgment. This work has been co-financed by Greece and the European Union (European Regional Development Fund-ERDF) through the Regional Operational Program "Attiki" 2014–2020.

Appendix

(See Tables 3 and 4).

Table 3. The simulation of the ACSIS process.

	Activity	Property values
1	Emergency call in the call center.	The duration of the procedure follows the normal distribution with an average value of 5 and a deviation of 2.
2	Ambulance information from the call center.	The duration of the procedure follows the normal distribution with an average value of 10 and a deviation of 2.
3	Send the route that the ambulance must follow to reach the point of the incident.	The duration of the procedure follows the normal distribution with an average value of 20 and deviation 2.
4	Arrival of the ambulance at the scene of the emergency.	The duration of the procedure follows the normal distribution with an average value of 4 and a deviation of 2.
5	Providing medical care to the patient at the scene.	The duration of the procedure follows the normal distribution with an average value of 15 and a deviation of 2.
6	Selection of the hospital center for the transfer of the patient.	The duration of the procedure follows the normal distribution with an average value of 10 and a deviation of 2.
7	Phone communication of the ambulance staff with the specialized medical staff of the hospital to suppress the patient's symptoms.	The duration of the procedure follows the normal distribution with an average value of 15 and a deviation of 2.
8	Assess the patient's health to determine its severity incident.	The duration of the procedure follows the normal distribution with an average value of 10 and a deviation of 2.
9	Arrival of the patient in the hospital.	The duration of the process follows the normal distribution with an average value of 10 and a deviation of 2.

Table 4. The second simulation case using ACSIS

	Activity	Property values
1	Emergency at the call center.	The duration of the procedure follows the normal distribution with an average value of 5 and a deviation of 2.
2	Automated procedure for sending the incident to the appropriate ambulance.	The duration of the procedure follows the normal distribution with an average value of 1 and a deviation of 1.
3	Automated ambulance navigation process at the emergency incident via a route specified by Google Maps.	The duration of the procedure follows the normal distribution with an average value of 4 and a deviation of 1.
4	Ambulance arrival at the scene.	The duration of the procedure follows normal distribution with mean value 2 and deviation 1.
5	Automated process of providing medical care to the patient on the spot incident.	The duration of the procedure follows the normal distribution with an average value of 3 and deviation 1.
6	Automated hospital selection process for patient transfer.	The duration of the procedure follows the normal distribution with an average value of 3 and a deviation of 1.
7	Automated process of providing medical advice to the nurse ambulance staff.	The duration of the procedure follows the normal mean distribution value 4 and deviation 1.
8	Automated diagnostic process of the patient based on the symptoms.	The duration of the procedure follows the normal distribution with an average value of 3 and a deviation of 1.
9	Automated process of patient arrival at the hospital.	The duration of the procedure follows the normal distribution with an average value of 5 and a deviation of 1

References

1. Handberry, M., et al.: Changes in emergency medical services before and during the COVID-19 pandemic in the United States, January 2018–December 2020. Clin. Infectious Dis. **73**(Supplement_1), S84–S91 (2021)
2. Gagnon, M., Ngangue, P., Payne-Gagnon, J., Desmartis, M.: M-health adoption by healthcare professionals: a systematic review. J. Am. Med. Inform. Assoc. **23**(1), 212–220 (2016)
3. Mitropoulos, S., Mitsis, C., Valacheas, P., Douligeris, C.: An online emergency medical management information system using mobile computing. Appl. Comput. Inform. **17**(2) (2021)
4. Becker, J., Hugelius, K.: Driving the ambulance: an essential component of emergency medical services: an integrative review. BMC Emerg. Med. **21**(1), 1–8 (2021)
5. Olave-Rojas, D., Nickel, S.: Modeling a pre-hospital emergency medical service using hybrid simulation and a machine learning approach. Simul. Model. Pract. Theory **109**, 102302 (2021)
6. Marshall, C., Lewis, D., Whittaker, M.: mHealth technologies: a feasibility assessment and a proposed framework. Technical Report. [Internet] (2013)

7. Bergrath, S., et al.: Implementation phase of a multicentre prehospital telemedicine system to support paramedics: feasibility and possible limitations. Scand. J. Trauma Resuscitation Emergency Med. **21**(1) (2013)

8. Mpillis, A., Zouka, M., Nicopolitidis, P., et al.: Towards the definition of an intelligent triage and continuous monitoring system for hospital emergency departments and clinics. Stud. Health Technol. Inform. **264**, 1641–1642 (2019). https://doi.org/10.3233/SHTI190574

9. Andersson, H., et al.: Using optimization to provide decision support for strategic emergency medical service planning–three case studies. Int. J. Med. Inform. **133**, 103975 (2020)

10. Al Amiry, A., Maguire, B.J.: Emergency medical services (EMS) calls during COVID-19: early lessons learned for systems planning (a narrative review). Open Access Emerg. Med. 407–414 (2021)

11. Srivastava, A., Bhardwaj, S., Saraswat, S.: SCRUM model for agile methodology. In: 2017 International Conference on Computing, Communication and Automation (ICCCA), pp. 864–869. IEEE (2017)

12. Gibson, C., Ventura, C., Collier, G.D.: Emergency medical services resource capacity and competency amid COVID-19 in the United States: preliminary findings from a national survey. Heliyon **6**(5) (2020)

13. Valacheas, P.: Platform to automate and improve the efficiency of pre-Hospital medical system [Internet]. Dione.lib.unipi.gr (2020). Cited 16 October 2021

14. Bijani, M., et al.: Major challenges and barriers in clinical decision-making as perceived by emergency medical services personnel: a qualitative content analysis. BMC Emerg. Med. **21**, 1–12 (2021)

15. Aringhieri, R., Bruni, M., Khodaparasti, S., van Essen, J.: Emergency medical services and beyond: addressing new challenges through a wide literature review. Comput. Oper. Res. **78**, 349–368 (2017)

16. ISO 9001:2015. https://www.iso.org/standard/62085.html. Accessed 17 Jan 2023

17. Luo, W., Yao, J., Mitchell, R., Zhang, X., Li, W.: Locating emergency medical services to reduce urban-rural inequalities. Socioecon. Plann. Sci. **84**, 101416 (2022)

18. Bass, R., Lawner, B., Lee, D., Nable, J.: Medical oversight of EMS systems. In: Emergency Medical Services: Clinical Practice and Systems Oversight, Clinical Aspects of EMS (2015)

19. Vidul, H., Pranave, V., Archana, A.: Telemedicine for emergency care management using WebRTC. In: 2015 International Conference on Advances in Computing, Communications, and Informatics (ICACCI), August, pp. 1741–1745. IEEE (2015)

20. Lastrucci, V., et al.: The indirect impact of COVID-19 pandemic on the utilization of the emergency medical services during the first pandemic wave: a system-wide study of Tuscany Region, Italy. PLoS One **17**(7), e0264806 (2022)

21. Billis, A., Logaras, E., Zouka, M., et al.: Functional and non-functional requirements of a s mart triage system for Emergency Departments: the case of IntelTriage project. In: Conference: SEEDA-CECNSM 2019. IEEE (2019)

22. Mavropodi, R., Fourlis, A., Mitropoulos, S., et al.: The architecture of an intelligent incident response system in health environments. In: Conference: SEEDA-CECNSM 2019. IEEE (2019)

23. Ghobadi, M., Arkat, J., Farughi, H., Tavakkoli-Moghaddam, R.: Integration of facility location and hypercube queuing models in emergency medical systems. J. Syst. Sci. Syst. Eng. **30**, 495–516 (2021)

24. Croatti, A., et al.: On the integration of agents and digital twins in healthcare. J. Med. Syst. **44**(9), 1–8 (2020)

25. Huh, J.-H., Kim, T.-J.: A location-based mobile health care facility search system for senior citizens. J. Supercomput. **75**(4), 1831–1848 (2019)

26. Xu, B., et al.: Healthcare data analysis system for regional medical union in smart city. J. Manag. Anal. **5**(4), 334 (2018)
27. Wu, X., Dunne, R., Yu, Z., Shi, W.: STREMS: a smart real-time solution toward enhancing EMS prehospital quality. In: 2017 IEEE/ACM International Conference on Connected Health: Applications, Systems and Engineering Technologies (CHASE) (2017)

Study of Dimensionality Reduction and Clustering Machine Learning Algorithms for the Analysis of Ship Engine Data

Theodoros Dimitriou[1], Emmanouil Skondras[1], Christos Hitiris[2], Cleopatra Gkola[3], Ioannis S. Papapanagiotou[1], Dimitrios J. Vergados[3], Georgia Fasoula[4], Stratos Koumantakis[5], Angelos Michalas[2(✉)], and Dimitrios D. Vergados[1]

[1] Department of Informatics, University of Piraeus, Piraeus, Greece
`{theodim,skondras,jpapapanagiotou,vergados}@unipi.gr`
[2] Department of Electrical and Computer Engineering, University of Western Macedonia, Kozani, Greece
`{c.hitiris,amichalas}@uowm.gr`
[3] Department of Informatics, University of Western Macedonia, Kastoria, Greece
`{c.gkola,dvergados}@uowm.gr`
[4] Internet Business Hellas, Athens, Greece
`geo.fasoula@ibhellas.gr`
[5] MAS S.A., Athens, Greece
`skoumantakis@maseurope.com`

Abstract. Machine Learning (ML) is being successfully applied to ship engine management with proven economic and environmental benefits by engine performance optimization, timely fault detection and appropriate service planning. However, the data preparation for usage in ML algorithms provides several advantages including faster training and improved performance of the algorithm, improved visualization of the dataset, noise reduction, dataset simplification, avoidance of the curse of dimensionality and improved resource utilization. In this paper, two key techniques of the ML algorithms, that can be applied for data preparation and organization of ship engine data are studied, namely the dimensionality reduction and the data clustering. Dimensionality reduction involves the reduce of the number of input variables or features in a dataset, by retaining as much valuable information as possible. On the other hand, clustering ML techniques help to uncover insights and reduce data complexity through the organization of the data into clusters. Evaluation results demonstrate the usefulness of both techniques.

Keywords: Unsupervised Machine Learning · Dimensionality Reduction · Data Clustering · Ship Engine Data

1 Introduction

The problem of handling a high volume of data in Machine Learning (ML) [1] is a critical challenge. As the information stored to ML datasets grows exponentially, it becomes increasingly difficult to efficiently process, store, and analyze the data. This high volume

L. A. Maglaras and C. Douligeris (Eds.): WiCON 2023, LNICST 527, pp. 82–96, 2024.
https://doi.org/10.1007/978-3-031-58053-6_6

of data can lead to issues such as extended training times, increased computational and storage requirements, and the risk of overfitting, where models may fit noise rather than true patterns. Effective data management and feature selection become critical to mitigate these challenges and ensure that machine learning models can operate effectively and make accurate predictions in the face of vast datasets.

Dimensionality reduction [2] and clustering [3] are considered as two critical parts of the ML science. In particular, dimensionality reduction involves the reduction of the number of input variables or features in a dataset, while retaining as much valuable information as possible. This process offers several advantages for the ML algorithms. Indicatively, the smaller datasets resulting from dimensionality reduction are faster to process. This situation leads to faster training of the ML algorithms, as well as it improves their performance in data prediction tasks. Also, it has to be noted that it is challenging to visualize data in high-dimensional spaces. Dimensionality reduction techniques can transform the data into lower dimensions, making it easier to visualize and interpret, which can aid in data analysis. Furthermore, high-dimensional data often contains noise and irrelevant features. Dimensionality reduction helps eliminate or reduce the impact of these noisy features, leading to cleaner and more relevant data.

Another important advantage of the dimensionality reduction is referred as "avoidance of the curse of dimensionality". Specifically, high-dimensional data can suffer from the "curse of dimensionality", where the data become sparse, and distances between data points lose their meaning. Dimensionality reduction can mitigate this problem by preserving the most important dimensions. Last but not least, improved memory and storage utilization are accomplished through the dimensionality reduction. In particular, reduced dimensionality means less resources are required to store the data. Common dimensionality reduction techniques include the Principal Component Analysis (PCA) [4] and the Recursive Feature Elimination (RFE) [5].

Data clustering is also a significant tool in ML. Similar to dimensionality reduction, data clustering is also a useful technique in ML, providing several advantages. Indicatively, data clustering helps uncover hidden patterns and structures within a dataset by grouping similar data together. This can lead to insights and discoveries that might not be apparent when examining the data as a whole. Furthermore, data clustering reduces the complexity of a dataset by dividing it into distinct clusters. This simplification can make it easier to understand, visualize, and analyze large datasets. Also, outlier values that exist into a dataset can be identified through the application of data clustering. This is valuable in a variety of problems including the detection of engines malfunction.

Clustering can also be used as a feature engineering technique. Instead of using the original features, cluster labels can be used as new features, potentially improving model performance in classification or regression tasks. Examples of clustering algorithms include the K-Means [6] and the Density-Based Spatial Clustering of Applications with Noise (DBSCAN) [7].

In both dimensionality analysis and data clustering, the choice of the appropriate algorithm depends on the specific characteristics of the dataset and the goals that the analysis should satisfy.

The main contribution of this work, is that based on the analysis performed, the most effective ML algorithms for performing dimensionality reduction and clustering in datasets containing ship engine data will be selected. These algorithms will be applied for the analysis of real ship engine data that will be produced from sensors installed in specific ships, in future work.

The remainder of the paper is organized as follows: Sect. 2 performs an overview of existing ML algorithms for dimensionality reduction and clustering. Subsequently, in Sect. 3 the performance of each algorithm is evaluated. Finally, Sect. 4 concludes our work.

2 Application of Machine Learning Algorithms for Dimensionality Reduction and Data Clustering

Dimensionality reduction and data clustering are two of the most important categories of the unsupervised ML algorithms.

Dimensionality reduction improves the performance of ML algorithms through the mitigation of overfitting, achieves faster training and predicting, enhances the data visualization, reduces the noise data in a dataset, helps the avoidance of the curse of dimensionality, as well as decreases the memory and storage requirements. As a result, it optimizes the data, making them more manageable and relevant while preserving essential information, ultimately leading to more efficient and effective machine learning models.

Data clustering offers several advantages, since it helps the discovery of hidden patterns of data and simplifies complex datasets. Also, data clustering assists to the exploration of unlabeled data, and helps preprocess data by addressing missing values and outliers. Moreover, it improves data understanding and aids in data-driven decision-making processes.

2.1 Dimensionality Reduction Algorithms

In this subsection, two well-known ML algorithms for performing dimensionality reduction are described, namely the Principal Component Analysis (PCA) and the Recursive Feature Elimination (RFE) algorithms.

The Principal Component Analysis (PCA) Algorithm. The PCA algorithm is used to decompose a multivariate dataset into a sequence of - mutually orthogonal components that explain, to the greatest extent, the variation in the dataset. PCA performs linear dimensionality reduction using Singular Value Decomposition (SVD) of the data, projecting it into a lower dimensional space than the original. PCA is implemented in scikit-learn library [8] as a transformer object that uses the fit method to extract the mutually orthogonal components [9, 10], and then it can be used on new data to project them onto those components.

Code Listing 1 shows how to use the PCA algorithm of the scikit-learn library, and how to check the ratio of explained variance and the unique values of the components.

- In lines 1 and 2, the PCA class from the decomposition module of the scikit-learn library, and the NumPy (np) library is imported, which is widely used for numerical computations in Python.
- Line 3 defines a two-dimensional input dataset as a NumPy array, with eight points and two attributes.
- Line 4 creates an instance of the PCA class, with the number of components equal to 2 (n_components = 2). Before the instance is assigned to the model variable, it is trained with the fit method, which takes the input data as a parameter and returns the trained model.
- Line 5 requests the display of the percentage of explained (interpreted) variation for each component, which are shown in line 6. Specifically, the first and second components show percentages of explained variation of 97.619048% and 2.380952% respectively of the total variation. Both components together account for 100% of the total variance since the example dataset contains only these two features.
- Finally, line 7 requests the display of the unique values of each component, which are displayed in line 8.

Code Listing 1. Usage Example of the PCA algorithm.

```
1: >> from sklearn.decomposition import PCA
2: >> import numpy as np
3: >> data = np.array([[4,-4],[2,-2],[1,0],[0,-1],[0,1],[-1,0],[-2,2],[-4,4]])
4: >> model = PCA(n_components=2).fit(data)
5: >> model.explained_variance_ratio_
6: array([0.97619048, 0.02380952])
7: >> model.singular_values_
8: array([9.05538514, 1.41421356])
```

The Recursive Feature Elimination (RFE) Algorithm. The RFE algorithm is a recursive process that ranks features according to some measure that expresses their importance. In each iteration, the importance of each feature is assessed. Then, the attribute with the least importance is removed from the attributes considered. Another possibility is to remove an entire group of features at each iteration (instead of just a single feature), in order to speed up the process. Repeating the process removing one feature at a time is necessary. This is because in some cases the relative importance of each attribute may change when it is evaluated against a different subset of attributes during the stepwise elimination process. RFE was exploited in the present project, with the aim of investigating the performance relationship of features of ship engine data, using a number of features as input for training to select a subset of the most important features as output.

Code Listing 2 shows how to use the scikit-learn library's RFE algorithm to select the most important features from a dataset using a Support Vector Regression (SVR) linear regression model.

- Line 1 imports the RFE class to the algorithm, line 2 produces an indicative dataset using the make_regression class of the sklearn.feature package and line 3 imports the LinearRegression model class.
- Line 4 uses the make_regression function to create the X, Y dataset which includes 100 samples of 15 features, setting the random state parameter equal of 5.
- Line 5 initializes the estimator to be used in RFE, creating a linear support vector regression model using the LinearRegression class.
- Line 6 initializes the variable of the model, by an instance of the RFE class, which takes as arguments the estimator, along with the number of features to select which in this case is equal to 4.
- Line 7 fits the model to the dataset (X, Y) using the fit method.
- Line 8 retrieves the ranking of the features by reading the model.ranking_ property, which returns an array of integers representing the ranking of each attribute. A rank of 1 indicates that the feature is selected. The output is presented at line 9, which shows that the fourth, the sixth, the seventh and the fifteenth features are selected since they have a rank equal to 1. The remaining features are not selected.

Code Listing 2. Usage Example of the RFE algorithm.

```
1:  >> from sklearn.feature_selection import RFE
2:  >> from sklearn.datasets import make_regression
3:  >> from sklearn.linear_model import LinearRegression
4:  >> X, Y = make_regression(n_samples = 100, n_features = 15, random_state=5)
5:  >> estimator = LinearRegression()
6:  >> model = RFE(estimator, n_features_to_select=4)
7:  >> model.fit(X, Y)
8:  >> model.ranking_
9:  array([10, 6, 9, 1, 5, 1, 1, 12, 11, 7, 4, 2, 3, 8, 1])
```

2.2 Clustering Machine Learning Algorithms

In this subsection, two well-known ML algorithms for performing Clustering of data are studied, namely the K-Means and the Density-Based Spatial Clustering of Applications with Noise (DBSCAN) algorithms.

The K-Means Algorithm. The K-Means algorithm is a popular unsupervised learning algorithm used for data clustering. The algorithm creates a set of groups (clusters) and categorizes in each group the data it receives as input based on the similarity between them. The steps of the K-Means algorithm, follow below:

1. Definition of the number of groups (clusters) to be created: In this step, the number (k) of clusters to be produced is determined by the user.
2. Initialization: k points are randomly selected from the data, as initial centers of the groups (centroids).
3. Placement-categorization of data into clusters: For each of the input data, its distance from the center of each cluster is calculated and it is placed in the cluster where the smallest distance is observed.
4. Update centers: Cluster centers are recalculated as the average of the data values placed in each cluster.
5. Iteration: Steps 3 and 4 are repeated until the centers of the clusters no longer change and convergence of the algorithm has been achieved

Code Listing 3 shows the use of the K-Means implementation of the scikit-learn library.

- In lines 1 and 2, the necessary libraries (KMeans and numpty) are imported into the program.
- In line 3, the dataset is defined on which the K-Means algorithm will be applied, in order to group the data present there by creating clusters. The given dataset includes 16 samples with 2 feature values per sample.
- In line 4, initially the appropriate values to the initialization parameters of the KMeans class are set. In particular, for the parameter n_clusters we set the value 4, so that 4 clusters will be created in which the samples present in the dataset will then be grouped. Also, for the random_state parameter we set the value 5, which means that every time a new sample is introduced into a cluster, then the centroid of the cluster will be recalculated as the average value of the samples present in the cluster. For the parameter n_init we set the value auto, which means that the number of executions of the algorithm will depend on the number of samples present in the dataset. Subsequently, the dataset that the algorithm is applied to the KMeans object to perform clustering.
- In line 5, we request the clusters in which each one of the 16 samples of the dataset is grouped. The result of this command is shown in line 6.
- In line 6, we notice that the first 4 samples of the dataset (i.e. [0, 1], [1, 2], [2, 1] and [1, 0],) are grouped in cluster 0, the next 4 samples of the dataset (i.e. [0, 9], [1, 10], [2, 9] and [1, 8]) are grouped into cluster 3, the next 4 samples of the dataset (i.e. [8, 9], [9, 10], [10, 9] and [9, 8]) are grouped into cluster 1, and the final 4 samples of the dataset (i.e. [8, 1], [9, 2], [10, 1] and [9, 0]) are grouped into cluster 2.

- In line 7 we ask the algorithm to show us the centroids of the four clusters created. The result of this command is shown in line 8.
- In line 8, we notice that the center of cluster 0 is equal to [1., 1.]. We recall that cluster 0 contains four samples namely the [0, 1], [1, 2] and [1, 0]. Based on these samples, we confirm that the center of cluster 0 has been correctly calculated, as the average value obtained from the three samples of that particular cluster. The centers of the rest clusters are evaluated similarly.
- In line 9, we request the algorithm to categorize into the clusters four new samples, namely the [1, 1], the [1, 9], the [9, 9] and the [9, 1]. The result of this command is shown in line 10.
- In line 10, we notice that the algorithm categorized sample [1, 1] into cluster 0, sample [1, 9] into cluster 3, sample [9, 9] into cluster 1 and sample [9, 1] into cluster 2.

Code Listing 3. Usage Example of the K-Means algorithm.

```
1:  >> from sklearn.cluster import KMeans
2:  >> import numpy as np
3:  >> data = np.array([[0,1],[1,2],[2,1],[1,0],    [0,9],[1,10],[2,9],[1,8],
                        [8,9],[9,10],[10,9],[9,8],   [8,1],[9,2],[10,1],[9,0]])
4:  >> algorithm = KMeans(n_clusters=4, random_state=5,
        n_init="auto").fit(data)
5:  >> algorithm.labels_
6:  array([0, 0, 0, 0, 3, 3, 3, 3, 1, 1, 1, 1, 2, 2, 2, 2], dtype=int32)
7:  >> algorithm.cluster_centers_
8:  array([[1., 1.], [1., 9.], [9., 9.], [9., 1.]])
9:  >> algorithm.predict([[1,1],[1,9],[9,9],[9,1]])
10: array([0, 3, 1, 2], dtype=int32)
```

The Density-Based Spatial Clustering of Applications with Noise (DBSCAN) Algorithm. The DBSCAN algorithm detects and clusters the data located in high-density areas, while ignoring the data located in low-density areas since it considers them as noise.

The DBSCAN algorithm starts by randomly selecting a value from the dataset. Next, the distance of neighboring values from the selected value is examined. If the density of neighboring values is high enough (greater than the minimum acceptable density defined by the user), then a cluster is created, in which the selected value and neighboring values are placed. Conversely, if the density of neighboring values is not high enough, the algorithm continues by looking at the next value present in the dataset.

The DBSCAN algorithm continues this process by incrementally examining all values present in the dataset. Finally, the values that do not belong to any cluster are classified as noise. Code Listing 4 shows the use of the DBSCAN algorithm of the scikit-learn library.

- In lines 1 and 2, the necessary libraries (DBSCAN and numpty) are imported into the program.
- Line 3 defines the dataset on which the DBSCAN algorithm will be applied, in order to group the data into clusters. The given dataset includes 5 samples with 2 feature values per sample.
- In line 4, we initialize the DBSCAN algorithm. In particular, the eps parameter expressing the maximum acceptable distance between two neighbors is set to 2. The min_samples parameter expresses the minimum required number of samples that must be present in a cluster and in our case, it is set equal to 2.
- In line 5, the DBSCAN algorithm is applied to the dataset using the fit command.
- In line 6, we request the clusters in which each one of the samples of the dataset is grouped. The result of this command is shown in line 7.
- In line 7, the labels of the clusters to which the samples are grouped are displayed. We notice that 2 clusters were created. In the first cluster, with label 0, the first 2 samples of the dataset, namely the [2, 1] and the [1, 2], are included. Moreover, the samples [5, 4] and [4, 5] are grouped into the second cluster with label 1. Finally, the third sample [3, 3] cannot be grouped to any cluster, because this sample is characterized as noise by the DBSCAN algorithm and thus it appears to be placed into a cluster with label -1.

Code Listing 4. Usage Example of the DBSCAN algorithm.

```
1: >> from sklearn.cluster import DBSCAN
2: >> import numpy as np
3: >> data = np.array([[2,1],[1,2],[3,3],[5,4],[4,5]])
4: >> model = DBSCAN(eps=2, min_samples=2)
5: >> model.fit(data)
6: >> model.labels_
7: array([ 0,  0,  -1,  1, 1])
```

---

3 Performance Analysis

In this section, the dimensionality reduction algorithms (PCA and RFE) and the clustering algorithms (K-Means and DBSCAN) are evaluated using the Condition Based Maintenance of Naval Propulsion Plants (CBM) dataset [11, 12]. The CBM dataset contains 11934 records with data about ship engines. Each record consists of the 16 features presented in Table 1. For the evaluation of the algorithms, only the 14 features will be considered, since the features 9 (gas turbine compressor inlet air temperature) and 12 (gas turbine compressor inlet air pressure) obtain the same value in the entire records and, thus, they are considered as non-important for our analysis.

It has to be noted that the CBM dataset has not been analysed yet in the existing literature, in situations where dimensionality reduction or data clustering is applied. Thus, our analysis provides useful insights about the structural characteristics of the dataset.

Table 1. The features included to the CBM dataset.

No.	Feature Name	Abbreviation	Measurement Unit
1	Lever position	lever_position	[1–9]
2	Ship speed	ship_speed	Knots
3	Gas Turbine (GT) shaft torque	gt_shaft	Kilonewton/meter
4	GT shaft rate	gt_rate	Rounds per Minute
5	Gas Generator (GG) rate	gg_rate	Rounds per Minute
6	Starboard Propeller Torque	sp_torque	Kilonewton
7	Port Propeller Torque	pp_torque	Kilonewton
8	High Pressure (HP) Turbine exit temperature	hpt_temp	Celsius degrees
9	GT Compressor inlet air temperature	gt_c_i_temp	Celsius degrees
10	GT Compressor outlet air temperature	gt_c_o_temp	Celsius degrees
10	HP Turbine exit pressure	hpt_pressure	Bar
11	GT Compressor inlet air pressure	gt_c_i_pressure	Bar
12	GT Compressor outlet air pressure	gt_c_o_pressure	Bar
13	GT exhaust gas pressure	gt_exhaust_pressure	Bar
14	Turbine Injection Control	turbine_inj_control	Presentence (%)
15	Fuel flow	fuel_flow	Kilograms/second
16	Lever position	lever_position	[1–9]

3.1 Evaluation of Dimensionality Reduction Algorithms

This subsection presents the results of the execution of the PCA and the RFE algorithms using the CBM dataset.

Therefore, an instance of the PCA class using the CBM training dataset was created and the explained variance of each component of the resulting new vector space basis was extracted as a result in the explained_variance_ratio_ variable, as shown in Table 2. As an indication of the effectiveness of PCA, the first component explains 99.96569% of the total variance in the CBM data set, with the next two components in order of rank, explaining 0.03% and 0.002% respectively, and with the others following.

In addition, the cumulative variance of the training dataset interpreted by the components is shown in Fig. 1. We observe that the first component explains almost all (99.96569%) of the variance, with subsequent components contributing minimally and from the 4th component onwards, the contribution is practically zero.

Table 2. The explained variance of each component in the new vector space basis.

Component	Explained variance
1	0.999656935554048
2	0.000320778697501
3	2.10E−05
4	1.15E−06
5	8.59E−08
6	4.34E−08
7	1.43E−08
8	1.40E−09
9	2.67E−11
10	3.77E−13
11	1.47E−13
12	3.97E−14
13	1.73E−16
14	1.58E−39

The execution of the RFECV [13] that finds the optimal number of features for RFE using cross-validation, it is obtained that the optimal number of dimensions is also quite different for the two target decay features. For the prediction of the gas turbine compressor decay coefficient "gt_c_decay" using the Extra Trees Regressor algorithm, the optimal number of dimensions is 7 (Fig. 2), while for the gas turbine decay coefficient "gt_t_decay" the optimal number of dimensions is 11 (Fig. 3).

Accordingly, in performing the RFE, using as desired number of attributes equal to 7 for the gas turbine compressor decay coefficient (gt_c_decay) and 11 for the gas turbine decay coefficient (gt_t_decay), it was observed that the order of ranking the importance of the attributes is different for each of the two target decay attributes, as shown in Table 3. For the prediction of gt_c_decay the 7 most important features are: gt_c_o_temp, gg_rate, gt_exhaust_pressure, gt_shaft, hpt_pressure, gt_rate, hpt_temp. Similarly, for the prediction of gt_t_decay the 11 most important features are: gt_c_o_pressure, fuel_flow, gg_rate, turbine_inj_control, gt_shaft, gt_rate, hpt_temp.

To further evaluate the results of the RFE algorithm, the importance of each feature is evaluated as extracted during the training of the ML algorithms Random Forest Regressor [14], the Extra Trees Regressor [15] and the Decision Tree Regressor [16]. The importance of each feature is ranked based on its contribution for predicting the gt_c_decay feature. Figure 4 shows the rankings produced by the three ML algorithms, indicating that the same seven features of the case of RFE are considered as the most important features.

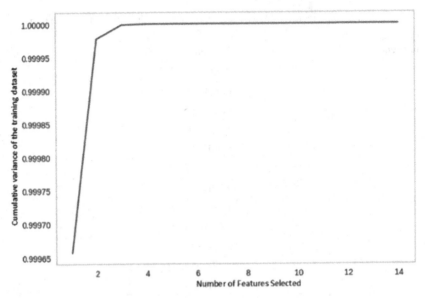

Fig. 1. Cumulative variance of the training dataset as interpreted by the components.

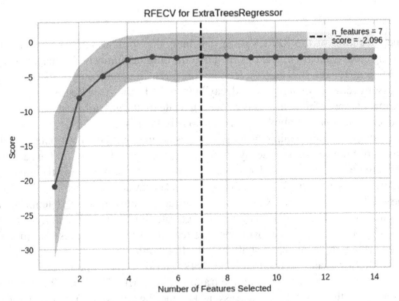

Fig. 2. The cross-validation method for predicting the gas turbine compressor decay factor gt_c_decay.

According to the experimental results, it has to be noted that both PCA and RFE can be considered as appropriate algorithms for performing dimensionality reduction in ship engine data.

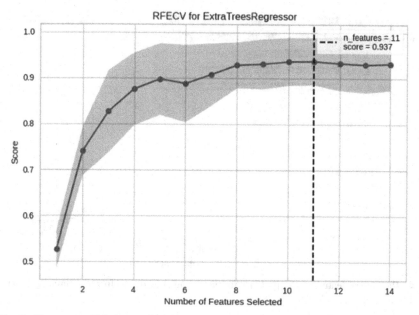

Fig. 3. The cross-validation method for predicting the gas turbine decay factor gt_t_decay.

Table 3. Rank of feature importance for the gt_c_decay and the gt_t_decay.

Name	gt_c_decay rank	gt_t_decay rank
lever_position	13	14
ship_speed	14	13
gt_shaft	4	5
gt_rate	6	6
gg_rate	2	3
sp_torque	8	11
pp_torque	9	12
hpt_temp	7	7
gt_c_o_temp	1	10
hpt_pressure	5	9
gt_c_o_pressure	12	1
gt_exhaust_pressure	3	8
turbine_inj_control	10	4
fuel_flow	11	2

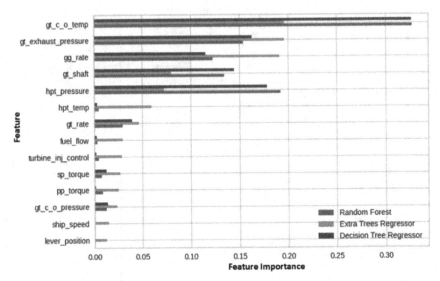

Fig. 4. Ranking of features by importance for predicting gt_c_decay, from the three decision tree algorithms.

3.2 Evaluation of Clustering Algorithms

For the evaluation of the K-Means and the DBSCAN algorithms, an indicative subset of values of the lever_position and the fuel_flow features of the CBM dataset is used.

Regarding the initialization of the two clustering algorithms, the n_clusters parameter of the K-Means is initialized with a value equal to 2, so that 2 clusters will be created in which the samples present in the dataset will be grouped. Also, the random_state parameter is initialized with a value equal to 5, which means that every time a new sample is grouped into a cluster, then the centroid of the cluster will be recalculated as the average value of the samples present in the cluster. Furthermore, the DBSCAN algorithm has been applied by setting the eps parameter equal to 2, which is the maximum acceptable distance between two values in order to be considered as neighbors. Also, the min_samples parameter of the DBSCAN is also set to be equal to 2, and thus each cluster created will include at least 2 samples.

Figure 5 presents the results obtained after the application of the two algorithms. As it can be observed the K-Means algorithm created two clusters. The first cluster contains three samples and the second cluster contains the remaining two samples. It is obvious that the algorithm grouped the samples into the two clusters based on the distances among the values of the samples. Accordingly, the DBSCAN algorithm also created two clusters. However, in this case each cluster contains two samples, while one sample is considered as outlier (or noise) by the DBSCAN algorithm and it is not grouped to any cluster. Since DBSCAN can detects outlier values, it can be considered as more appropriate than the K-Means for the analysis of ship engine data, because in such cases outlier values may indicate failure in engine components.

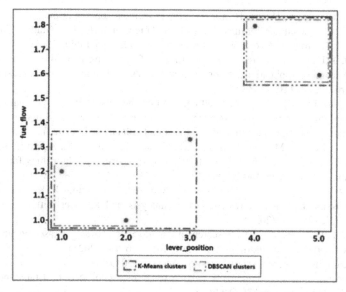

Fig. 5. The clusters created using the K-Means and the DBSCAN algorithms.

4   Conclusion

In this work, useful algorithms for performing dimensionality reduction as well as data clustering are studied. In particular, dimensionality reduction offers important advantages to ML algorithms, such as faster training of these algorithms, simplification of complex datasets and improved memory and storage utilization. Regarding this category of ML algorithms, two alternative techniques studied, namely the PCA and the RFE algorithms. On the other hand, the advantages offered by data clustering techniques include the uncover of insights and the reduction of data complexity through the organization of the data into clusters. During the study of this category of algorithms, two alternative techniques also studied, namely the K-Means and the DBSCAN algorithms. The functionality of both dimensionality reduction and data clustering algorithms are evaluated through experiments, where the usefulness of both algorithm categories demonstrated. Based on the analysis performed, future work includes the application of the most effective dimensionality reduction and clustering ML algorithms in data generated from ship engines' operation.

Acknowledgements. This research has been co-financed by the European Regional Development Fund of the European Union and Greek national funds through the Operational Program Competitiveness, Entrepreneurship and Innovation, under the call RESEARCH-CREATE-INNOVATE (project code: T2EDK-C.873).

References

1. Dogan, A., Birant, D.: Machine learning and data mining in manufacturing. Expert Syst. Appl. **166**, 1–22 (2021)

2. Zhang, G., Wang, Z., Huang, H., Li, H., Sun, T.: Comparison and evaluation of dimensionality reduction techniques for the numerical simulations of unsteady cavitation. The acoustic signature of a propeller-hydrofoil system in the far field. Phys. Fluids **35**(7) (2023)

3. Ezugwu, A.E., et al.: A comprehensive survey of clustering algorithms: State-of-the-art machine learning applications, taxonomy, challenges, and future research prospects. Eng. Appl. Artif. Intell. **110**, 1–43 (2022)

4. Park, J., Oh, J.: Analysis of collected data and establishment of an abnormal data detection algorithm using principal component analysis and K-nearest neighbors for predictive maintenance of ship propulsion engine. Processes J. **10**(11), 1–13 (2022)

5. Habibi, A., Delavar, M.R., Sadeghian, M.S., Nazari, B., Pirasteh, S.: A hybrid of ensemble machine learning models with RFE and Boruta wrapper-based algorithms for flash flood susceptibility assessment. Int. J. Appl. Earth Obs. Geoinf. **122**, 1–18 (2023)

6. Ikotun, A.M., Ezugwu, A.E., Abualigah, L., Abuhaija, B., Heming, J.: K-means clustering algorithms: a comprehensive review, variants analysis, and advances in the era of big data. Inf. Sci. **622**, 178–210 (2023)

7. Xu, X., Cui, D., Li, Y., Xiao, Y.: Research on ship trajectory extraction based on multiattribute DBSCAN optimisation algorithm. Pol. Marit. Res. 136–148 (2021)

8. Scikit-learn library. https://scikit-learn.org. Accessed 30 Oct 2023

9. Decomposing signals in components, Scikit learn. https://scikit-learn.org/stable/modules/decomposition.html. Accessed 30 Oct 2023

10. Principal Component Analysis (PCA) class, Scikit learn. https://scikit-learn.org/stable/modules/generated/sklearn.decomposition.PCA.html. Accessed 30 Oct 2023

11. The Condition Based Maintenance of Naval Propulsion Plants (CBM) dataset. https://www.kaggle.com/datasets/elikplim/maintenance-of-naval-propulsion-plants-data-set. Accessed 30 Oct 2023

12. Coraddu, A., Oneto, L., Ghio, A., Savio, S., Figari, M., Anguita, D.: Machine learning for wear forecasting of naval assets for condition-based maintenance applications. In: IEEE International Conference on Electrical Systems for Aircraft, Railway, Ship Propulsion and Road Vehicles (ESARS), pp. 1–5 (2015)

13. Recursive Feature Elimination with Cross-Validation (RFECV) scikit-learn class. https://scikit-learn.org/stable/modules/generated/sklearn.feature_selection.RFECV.html. Accessed 30 Oct 2023

14. Graw, J.H., Wood, W.T., Phrampus, B.J.: Predicting global marine sediment density using the random forest regressor machine learning algorithm. J. Geophys. Res. Solid Earth **126**(1), 1–14 (2021)

15. John, V., Liu, Z., Guo, C., Mita, S., Kidono, K.: Real-time lane estimation using deep features and extra trees regression. In: Bräunl, T., McCane, B., Rivera, M., Yu, X. (eds.) PSIVT 2015. LNCS, vol. 9431, pp. 721–733. Springer, Cham (2016). https://doi.org/10.1007/978-3-319-29451-3_57

16. Colditz, R.R.: An evaluation of different training sample allocation schemes for discrete and continuous land cover classification using decision tree-based algorithms. Remote Sens. **7**(8), 9655–9681 (2015)

Supervised Machine Learning Algorithms for the Analysis of Ship Engine Data

Theodoros Dimitriou[1], Emmanouil Skondras[1], Christos Hitiris[2], Cleopatra Gkola[3], Ioannis S. Papapanagiotou[1], Dimitrios J. Vergados[3], Stavros I. Papapanagiotou[4], Stratos Koumantakis[5], Angelos Michalas[2(✉)], and Dimitrios D. Vergados[1]

[1] Department of Informatics, University of Piraeus, Piraeus, Greece
`{theodim,skondras,jpapapanagiotou,vergados}@unipi.gr`
[2] Department of Electrical and Computer Engineering, University of Western Macedonia, Kozani, Greece
`{c.hitiris,amichalas}@uowm.gr`
[3] Department of Informatics, University of Western Macedonia, Kastoria, Greece
`{c.gkola,dvergados}@uowm.gr`
[4] Internet Business Hellas, Athens, Greece
`sip@ibhellas.gr`
[5] MAS S.A., Athens, Greece
`skoumantakis@maseurope.com`

Abstract. Supervised Machine Learning (ML) algorithms are used for making predictions or decisions based on labeled data. In this paper, an overview about existing supervised ML algorithms is performed. In particular, the algorithms that are studied comprehend the Linear Regression (LR), the Ridge Regression (RR), the Decision Tree (DT), as well as Ensemble algorithms. Subsequently, a comparative analysis of the algorithms is performed using a dataset containing data about ship engines. Effective management of ship engines is important for their robust operation, which can then bring significant economic and environmental benefits. Inferences about the condition of engines and predictions about their performance could prove crucial for specifying optimal cruise parameters, early fault detection and timely service planning. The analysis demonstrates the strength and the weaknesses of each algorithm in terms of predicting decay factors of the ship engine by taking into consideration the data included to the aforementioned dataset.

Keywords: Supervised Machine Learning (ML) · Linear Regression (LR) · Ridge Regression (RR) · Decision Tree (DT) · Ensemble algorithms · ship engine data · engine decay prediction

1 Introduction

Supervised machine learning (ML) [1] is a fundamental and powerful approach for solving a wide range of problems in data analysis and prediction, and it forms the basis for many real-world applications of artificial intelligence. Specifically, supervised

L. A. Maglaras and C. Douligeris (Eds.): WiCON 2023, LNICST 527, pp. 97–109, 2024.
https://doi.org/10.1007/978-3-031-58053-6_7

ML algorithms are a class of algorithms used in the field of artificial intelligence and data science for making predictions or decisions based on labelled training data. In supervised learning, the algorithm learns a mapping from input data to output labels by observing and generalizing from a set of example data points where both the input and the corresponding output (target) are known. In general, supervised learning is widely used in various applications, including natural language processing, image recognition, recommendation systems, fraud detection, and healthcare diagnostics.

Some key points about supervised ML algorithms include the data preparation, the classification, and the regression. Specifically, regarding the data preparation, it should be noted that in supervised learning, the dataset is split into two subsets, namely the training data and the validation data. The training data are used to train the model and the validation data are used to evaluate its performance. Accordingly, in classification, the algorithm assigns a category (or label) to input data. Examples include spam email detection (categorizing emails as spam or not) and image classification (identifying objects in images). Finally, regression models predict a continuous numerical value as output. For example, predicting house prices based on features like size, location, and number of bedrooms.

Common metrics used for the evaluation of the performance of supervised learning models include accuracy, precision, recall, F1-score, Mean Squared Error (MSE), and R-squared (for regression) [2, 3]. Also, supervised learning models can suffer from overfitting (fitting the training data too closely) or underfitting (failing to capture the underlying patterns). Techniques like cross-validation and regularization are used to restrict these issues.

Additionally, choosing the right hyperparameters (parameters that are not learned from the data) is essential for optimizing the performance of supervised learning models. Techniques like grid search and random search are often used for hyperparameter tuning. Finally, the scalability of a supervised learning algorithm depends on the size and complexity of the dataset. Some algorithms, like k-nearest neighbours, can be slow for large datasets, while others, like linear models, can scale better.

In this paper, existing supervised ML algorithms are studied. More specifically, the Linear Regression (LR) [4], the Ridge Regression (RR) [5], the Decision Tree (DT) [6] are described, as well as Ensemble [7] algorithms, such as the Bagging Regression (BR) [8], the Random Forest Regression (RFR) [9], the Extra Trees Regression (ETR) [10], the k-Nearest Neighbour (kNN) Regression [11] and the Artificial Neural Network (ANN) [12]. Furthermore, a comparative analysis of the algorithms is performed using the Condition Based Maintenance of Naval Propulsion Plants (CBM) dataset [13] containing data about ship engines. In particular, the CBM dataset contains 11934 records, consisting of the 16 features presented in Table 1.

The main contribution of this work, is that based on the analysis performed, the most effective supervised ML algorithms for the case of shipping data will be selected. The intelligent management of ship engines is an important factor in achieving their optimum efficiency and performance. A key requirement therefore is the use of digital data, models and systems that allow reliable measurement of specific engine performance parameters, their evaluation and the use of the results to make decisions on the operation and maintenance of these engines.

Table 1. The features included to the CBM dataset.

No.	Feature Name	Measurement Unit
1	Lever position (lp)	[1–9]
2	Ship speed (v)	Knots
3	Gas Turbine (GT) shaft torque (GTT))	Kilonewton per meter (kN/m)
4	Revolutions per minute gas turbine shaft (GT rate of revolutions (GTn))	Rounds/Minute (rpm)
5	Gas Generator rate of revolutions (GGn)	Rounds/Minute (rpm)
6	Starboard Propeller Torque (Ts)	Kilonewton (kN)
7	Port Propeller Torque (Tp)	Kilonewton (kN)
8	High Pressure (HP) Turbine exit temperature	Celsius degrees (°C)
9	Air temperature at the gas turbine compressor inlet valve (GT Compressor inlet air temperature)	Celsius degrees (°C)
10	Air temperature at the outlet valve of the gas turbine compressor (GT Compressor outlet air temperature)	Celsius degrees (°C)
11	HP Turbine exit pressure	Bar
12	Air pressure at the gas turbine compressor inlet valve (GT Compressor inlet air pressure)	Bar
13	Air pressure at the gas turbine compressor outlet valve (GT Compressor outlet air pressure)	Bar
14	Gas turbine exhaust gas pressure (GT exhaust gas pressure)	Bar
15	Turbine Injection Control (TIC)	Presentence (%)
16	Fuel flow (mf)	Kilograms per second (Kg/s)

The remainder of the paper is organized as follows: Sect. 2 performs an overview of existing supervised ML algorithms. Subsequently, in Sect. 3 the performance of each algorithm is evaluated. Finally, Sect. 4 concludes our work.

2 Overview of Supervised Machine Learning Algorithms

In this section, existing supervised machine learning algorithms are described including the Linear Regression (LR), the Ridge Regression (RR), the Decision Tree (DT), as well as Ensemble algorithms. Furthermore, the application of these algorithms using the Python sci-kit library [14] is introduced.

2.1 The Linear Regression (LR) Algorithm

The Linear Regression (LR) algorithm is used to predict the value of a variable based on the values of other variables. The variable we want to predict is called dependent variable, while those used to predict other variables are called independent variables.

The algorithm estimates the coefficients of a linear equation, which includes independent variables X that predict the value of the dependent variable Y. LR fits a straight line or surface to minimize the deviations between predicted and actual output values. There are simple linear regression calculations that use the "least squares" method to determine the best possible line that shows the shortest distance from a set of data pairs. Then, the dependent variable Y is estimated from the independent variables X.

LR models are relatively simple and provide an easy-to-interpret mathematical formula that can produce predictions. LR models have become a proven way to predict the future. Since linear regression is a long-established statistical procedure, the properties of linear regression models are well understood and can be trained very quickly.

Code Listing 1 presents an example of the LR algorithm.

- In lines 1 and 2, the necessary libraries are entered. Specifically, the LR model from the scikit-learn and the NumPy libraries is imported.
- In line 3, the data set (dataset X), which includes 2 samples with 2 characteristic values per sample, is specified.
- Line 4 computes the dependent variable Y for each sample of X by performing the inner product of the array X with the vector [2, 4] and adding the constant 5. The inner product yields the output of the values of the array X in the equation:

$$Y = 2 * x_1 + 4 * x_2 + 5 \tag{1}$$

where x_0 and x_1 are the characteristic values of X.

- In line 5, a Linear Regression object is initially created. Then, via the command model = LinearRegression().fit(X, y), the object is fitted to the given training data (data array X and label values Y).
- In line 6, the prediction is made with the value [8, 9] as input data.
- In line 7, you return the result (array([57.]) which certifies the correct training of the model as for the input data [8, 9] the function $Y = 2*x_1 + 4*x_2 + 5 = 57$.
- Line 8 calculates the prediction coefficient by considering the values of the training data and the given labels. The value of the prediction coefficient ranges between 0 and 1, with 1 shown by line 9 indicating a perfect fit.

Code Listing 1. Usage example of the LR algorithm.

```
1: >> from sklearn.linear_model import LinearRegression
2: >> import numpy as np
3: >> X = np.array([[1, 2], [4, 8]])
4: >> Y = np.dot(X, np.array([2, 4])) + 5  # Y = 2*x₁ + 4*x₂ + 5
5: >> model = LinearRegression().fit(X, Y)
6: >> model.predict(np.array([[8, 9]]))
7: array([57.])
8: >> model.score(X, Y)
9: 1.0
```

2.2 The Ridge Regression (RR) Algorithm

The Ridge Regression (RR) algorithm aims to avoid overfitting the model by adding a penalty term to the Objective Least Squares (OLS) function. This penalty term is proportional to the square of the magnitude of the coefficients in the regression equation, which encourages the algorithm to select coefficients with smaller magnitudes. By reducing the size of the coefficients, vertex regression can effectively reduce the complexity of the model and improve its generalization performance to new, unseen data. The RR algorithm can be used in a variety of applications where linear regression is an appropriate modelling technique and where there is a need to control model overfitting.

Code Listing 2 presents an example of the RR algorithm.

- Lines 1 imports the Ridge class from the scikit-learn library.
- Line 2 creates an instance of the Ridge Regression model, with a normalization parameter 'alpha', set to 0.5. The larger the value of alpha, the stronger the normalization effect.
- Line 3 fits the RR model to the data (i.e. learns the relationship between the feature matrix 'X' and the target variable 'y').
- Lines 4 and 5 return the coefficients of the RR function resulting from the training stage.
- In line 6, the constant term of the RR function is returned. In this case is 0.5357142857142847, as shown in line 7.

Code Listing 2. Usage example of the RR algorithm.

```
1: >> from sklearn.linear_model import Ridge
2: >> model = Ridge(alpha=0.5)
3: >> model.fit([1, 2], [2, 3], [3, 4], [4, 5], [2, 4], [5, 6])
4: >> model.coef_
5: array([0.61904762, 0.61904762])
6: >> model.intercept_
7: 0.5357142857142847
```

2.3 The Decision Tree (DT) Algorithm

The Decision Tree (DT) algorithm implements a function that maps a vector of feature values to a single output value, the decision. In order to arrive at its decision, a decision tree performs a sequence of checks, starting from the root and following the appropriate branch, until it reaches a leaf. Each internal node of the tree corresponds to a check on the value of one of the input attributes. The branches from the node are labelled with the possible values of the attribute, and the leaf nodes specify which value should be returned by the function. Input and output values can be discrete or continuous.

Code Listing 3 presents an example of the DT algorithm and the application of cross-validation to evaluate model performance.

- In lines 1 and 2, the decision tree class DecisionTreeRegressor and the cross_val_score model evaluate function and are imported to the program.
- In line 3, the dataset X, which includes 5 samples with 2 characteristic values per sample, is specified.
- Line 4 defines the dependent variable Y for each sample of X.

- In line 5, the DecisionTreeRegressor model is created and in line 6, the model is trained by taking into consideration the dataset X and the dependent variable Y for each sample of X.
- In line 7, 10-fold cross-validation is applied, which evaluates the performance of the decision tree on the data set. The cross_val_score function that is implemented, it takes as parameters the model, the input data array, the target variable vector, and the number of subsets to split the data set into. As output, the function returns a vector of the subset in line 8, which can be used to estimate the overall model return, but also the standard deviation between individual returns.
- Line 9 uses the model to perform a prediction. In this case, the model takes as input the samples that exist to X.
- Line 10 shows the result of the prediction. In this case, we confirm that the model has successfully trained since the result is similar to the content of the dependent variable Y.

Code Listing 3. Usage example of the DT algorithm.

```
1: >> from sklearn.tree import DecisionTreeRegressor
2: >> from sklearn.model_selection import cross_val_score
3: >> X = [[1,0], [2,3], [3,4], [4,3], [5,0]]
4: >> Y = [0, 3, 4, 3, 0]
5: >> model = DecisionTreeRegressor(random_state=0, max_depth=2)
6: >> model.fit(X, Y)
7: >> cross_val_score(model, X, Y, cv=2)
8: array([0.88461538, 0.77777778])
9: >> model.predict(X)
10: array([0., 3., 4., 3., 0.])
```

2.4 The Ensemble Algorithms

The category of the Ensemble algorithms employ a set of prediction algorithms (called "base algorithms" or "base models"). These algorithms combine multiple machine learning techniques to solve a problem, achieving a reduction in bias and variance relative to the individual machine learning models involved [15]. In the following subsections, the Ensemble algorithms are implemented using the indicative dataset $X = [[1, 0], [2, 3], [3, 4], [4, 3], [5, 0]]$, which includes 5 samples with 2 characteristic values per sample. Also, the dependent variable $Y = [0, 3, 4, 3, 0]$ for each sample of X is used. Both X and Y can be considered as an indicative part of the CBM dataset that will be analysed in the next section.

The Bagging Regression (BR) Algorithm. A common implementation of ensemble ML algorithms is called "pooling", where for base models the same algorithm is employed multiple times, but each copy of the algorithm is trained with a different and random subset of the dataset. The two most common subcategories of the pooling implementation are the Pasting and the Bootstrap AGGregating" (Bagging). In the Pasting algorithm, random subsets of the dataset are created. Accordingly, in the Bagging algorithm, the subsets of the dataset are created by reshuffling. Bagging generally performs better than Pasting, which is why it is preferred. However, if possible, cross-validation can be used to compare the two algorithms [16]. In Bagging sampling, when the number of samples of each classifier equals the total of samples, due to sample reshuffling, on average about 63% of the samples in each classifier are selected, with the remaining 37% not used at all for training, so can be used to verify each classifier. This remaining subset, which is different for each classifier, is called out-of-bag.

Code Listing 4 shows how the Bagging Regression (BR) is used with Support Vector Regression (SVR) as the base estimator. The model is trained on an artificial dataset constructed by the make_regression function. Then, evaluates its performance on a sample input.

- In lines 1 and 2, the BaggingRegressor and the DecisionTreeRegressor classes are imported to the program.
- In line 3, the BaggingRegressor algorithm is initialized with base estimator an instance of the DecisionTreeRegressor, with 5 instances of the base estimators (n_estimators = 5) and seed equal to 5 for the random number generator (random_state = 5). Also, in this line, the algorithm is trained by calling fit, which takes as parameters the input dataset X and the target variable vector Y.
- In line 4, the trained algorithm is called in order to make a prediction by taking as input the new sample [2, 4].
- In line 5, the result of the algorithm's prediction for the sample [2, 4] is presented.

Code Listing 4. Usage example of the BR algorithm.

```
1: >>> from sklearn.ensemble import BaggingRegressor
2: >>> from sklearn.tree import DecisionTreeRegressor
3: >>> model = BaggingRegressor(estimator=DecisionTreeRegressor(), n_estimators=5,
          random_state=5).fit(X, Y)
4: >>> model.predict([[2, 4]])
5: array([3.4])
```

The Random Forest Regression (RFR) Algorithm. A special class of model collection algorithms called Random Forests employ for base models, trees, as well as random sampling with the Bagging algorithm or less commonly with Pasting. However, the algorithm differs in its tree implementation in terms of feature selection of each branch, where the optimum is not sought from all features, but the optimum from a random subset of features.

Code Listing 5 shows how the Random Forest Regression (RFR) is used. The model is trained on an artificial dataset constructed by the make_regression function and then evaluates its performance on a sample input.

- In line 1, the RandomForestRegressor class is imported to the program.
- In line 2, the RandomForestRegressor algorithm is initialized, with a maximum tree depth equal to 2 (max_depth = 2) and a seed of 5 for the random number generator (random_state = 5). Also, in this line, the algorithm is trained by calling fit, which takes as parameters the input dataset X and the target variable vector Y.

- In line 3, the trained algorithm is called in order to make a prediction by taking as input the new sample [2, 4].
- In line 4, the result of the algorithm's prediction for the sample [2, 4] is presented.

Code Listing 5. Usage example of the RFR algorithm.

```
1: >>> from sklearn.ensemble import RandomForestRegressor
2: >>> model = RandomForestRegressor(max_depth=2,
        random_state=5).fit(X, Y)
3: >>> model.predict([[2, 4]])
4: array([3.35])
```

The Extra Trees Regression (ETR) Algorithm. A variant of Random Forests called Extremely Randomized Trees or Extra-Trees, randomly chooses the separation threshold at each distinction of the tree, resulting in much faster training, since finding this threshold is computationally demanding. Random Forests, despite its simplicity, is one of the most powerful ML algorithm available today [16].

Code Listing 6 shows how Extra Trees Regression (ETR) is used through a reference part of the CBM dataset, where the included data are split into training and test data subsets. The model is then trained with the training subset and evaluated with the test subset.

- In lines 1 and 2, the ExtraTreesRegressor class and the train_test_split function are imported to the program.
- Line 3 splits the dataset into training and test sets using the train_test_split function, with a random_state specified to make the split reproducible.
- In line 4, the ExtraTreesRegressor algorithm is initialized, with 10 instances of base estimators (n_estimators = 10) and with a seed of 5 for the random number generator (random_state = 5). Also, in this line, the algorithm is trained by calling fit, which takes as parameters the input dataset X_train and the target variable vector Y_train.
- Line 5 evaluates the performance of the ExtraTreesRegressor algorithm on the test set by calling the model.score method with the X_test and Y_test as inputs.
- Line 6 outputs the result of evaluating the algorithm's performance on the test data.

Code Listing 6. Usage example of the ETR algorithm.

```
1: >>> from sklearn.ensemble import ExtraTreesRegressor
2: >>> from sklearn.model_selection import train_test_split
3: >>> X_train, X_test, Y_train, Y_test = train_test_split(X, Y, test_size=0.4, random_state=2)
4: >>> model = ExtraTreesRegressor(n_estimators=10, random_state=5).fit(X_train, Y_train)
5: >>> model.score(X_test, Y_test)
6: 0.86375
```

The k-Nearest Neighbor (kNN) Regression Algorithm. The k-Nearest Neighbor (kNN) Regression algorithm prediction result for the value of a feature i depends on the k closest (neighboring) values present in the training data set. Specifically, the distance of the value of feature i from all existing values is calculated and the k closest values are selected. This calculation is carried out using formula (2), where t expresses the timestamp of receiving the values x1 and x2 for feature i. Formula (3) calculates the target value, where the set Nk(x) contains the indices of the k nearest neighbors of the input value x for feature i, the parameter yi expresses the label specified for feature i [17].

$$d(x_1, x_2) = \left(\sum_{i=0}^{t}(x_{1i} - x_{2i})^2\right)^{\frac{1}{2}} \tag{2}$$

$$f_{kNN}(x) = \frac{1}{k}\sum_{i \in N_k(x)} y_i \tag{3}$$

Code Listing 7 shows the use of the kNN Regression algorithm of the scikit-learn library.

- In line 1, the KNeighborsRegressor class is imported to the program.
- Line 2 creates initializes the kNN algorithm and assigns the value 3 to the n_neighbors variable. Thus, it is specified that the model will consider the 3 nearest neighbors (the three closest values) whenever it is asked to make a prediction for a new input value.
- In line 3, the algorithm is trained using the dataset X and the corresponding outputs specified to the vector Y.
- In line 4, the trained algorithm is called in order to make a prediction by taking as input the new sample [2, 4].
- In line 5, the result of the algorithm's prediction for the sample [2, 4] is presented.

Code Listing 7. Usage example of the kNN Regression algorithm.

```
1: >>> from sklearn.neighbors import KNeighborsRegressor
2: >>> model = KNeighborsRegressor(n_neighbors=3)
3: >>> model.fit(X, Y)
4: >>> model.predict([[2, 4]])
5: array([3.33333333])
```

The Artificial Neural Network (ANN) Algorithm. A multilayer feedforward neural network (multilayer perceptron) was also used to predict engine damage values. The implementation of the Artificial Neural Network (ANN) was done with the Tensorflow library [15], through the Keras programming interface [19]. In contrast to the implementations of algorithms in the scikit-learn library, an ANN algorithm in Tensorflow arises as a composition of individual modules, with the aim of building an appropriate architecture for each application.

The layers of neural nodes inserted into the model to construct the ANN are instances of the tf.keras.layers.Dense class [20], which implements a standard densely connected neural network with the formula: output = activation(dot(input, kernel) + bias), where activation is the per-element activation function passed as the activation argument, dot is the inner product operation, kernel is a matrix of weights generated by layer and bias is a vector of constant terms generated by layer (only valid if use_bias is True).

The use of Dropout levels is a popular deep ANN normalization technique that has proven to be highly successful improving the accuracy of even advanced models by

1–2% [16]. This is a special class of layers that are inserted between normal layers and in each iteration, only during the training phase, they disable random neural nodes of the model, as a result of which they do not participate at all in the current iteration. A node can be disabled in one iteration but active in another, with the probability of being disabled being determined by the dropout rate hyperparameter.

Code Listing 8 presents an example of the RR algorithm.

- In lines 1–3, the Sequential, Dense and Dropout classes are entered into the program respectively.
- In line 4, we initialize and assign to the model variable an object of the tf.keras.Sequential class, in which we will "build" our neural network by adding the levels of the neurons.
- In line 5, we add the first layer of densely connected neurons of type tf.keras.layers.Dense, in which we define the number of neurons (units = 6), the activation function (activation = 'sigmoid') and the number of inputs (input_dim = 14). The last parameter automatically creates a level of type tf.keras.Input and is only needed when creating the first level, if we have not explicitly specified an input level.
- In line 6, we add a level of type Dropout with a probability of turning off neurons, during the training phase, equal to 0.2.
- In line 7, we add another layer of neurons with one neuron for the output of the ANN.

Code Listing 8. Usage example of the ANN algorithm.

```
1: >>> from keras.models import Sequential
2: >>> from keras.layers import Dense
3: >>> from keras.layers import Dropout
4: >>> model = Sequential()
5: >>> model.add(Dense(untis=6, input_dim=14, activation='sigmoid'))
6: >>> model.add(Dropout(rate=0.2))
7: >>> model.add(Dense(untis=1, activation='sigmoid'))
```

---

3 Performance Analysis

In this section, the supervised ML algorithms are evaluated using the CBM dataset. As mentioned to Section 1, the CBM dataset contains 11934 records and each consists of 16 features. However, for the evaluation of the algorithms, only the 14 features will be considered, since the features 9 (gas turbine compressor inlet air temperature) and 12 (gas turbine compressor inlet air pressure) obtain the same value in the entire records and, thus, they are considered as non-important for our analysis.

Figure 1 presents the average absolute error of gas turbine compressor decay factor accomplished by each ML algorithm. As it is observed, the three most efficient algorithms belong to the ensemble methods and are Extra Trees Regressor, the Random Forest and the Bagging Regressor. This is followed by the decision tree algorithm Decision Tree Regressor and with lower yields, KNN Regressor, Linear Regressor, Ridge Regressor and Artificial Neural Network.

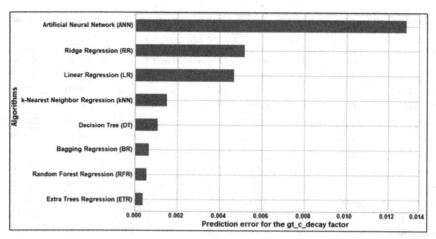

Fig. 1. Average absolute error of gas turbine compressor decay factor based on the CBM data set.

We observe that the algorithms of model collection methods (ensemble) show the best performances. This be justified by considering that the ensemble methods combine multiple machine learning models, achieving a reduction in bias and variance relative to the individual base models they include. In this case, all three ensemble algorithms are based on decision tree estimators, so it is expected that they will have improved performance over the next in line algorithm, that of the single decision tree Decision Tree Regressor. The Decision Tree Regressor and kNN show close performance, outperforming the next two linear regression algorithms Linear Regressor and Ridge Regressor. This is true as the Decision Tree Regressor and kNN algorithms can learn non-linear relationships. ANN accomplishes the worst performance, because the construction and parameterization of the network is particularly complex and in case it is selected as a prediction model, further investigation will be needed for its implementation.

Regarding the prediction of every other feature of the dataset, similar results are shown to the predictions of engine decay (Table 2). The three most efficient algorithms belong to ensemble methods. This is followed by the decision tree algorithm Decision Tree Regressor and, with lower yields, KNN Regressor, linear regression algorithms, and finally the ANN. In this table, we also observe that for the features gt_shaft and gg_rate all prediction algorithms show large errors in predicting their values. Furthermore, concerning the gt_rate feature, we observe that the Linear. Regressor, Ridge Regressor, KNN Regressor and the ANN show large errors in predicting its values, while the rest algorithms succeed sufficient prediction results. For the rest features, sufficient prediction results are succeeded by the most algorithms.

Table 2. Comparative results about the prediction of each characteristic of the CBM dataset.

Name	Linear Regressor	Ridge Regressor	KNN Regressor	Bagging Regressor	Random Forest	Extra Tree Regressor	Decision Tree Regressor	Artificial Neural Network
level_position	0.010	0.011	0.007	0.000	0.000	0.000	0.000	4.150
ship_speed	0.033	0.035	0.022	0.000	0.000	0.000	0.000	13.948
gt_shaft	131.513	178.364	18.994	7.568	6.419	4.369	11.51	27119.9
gt_rate	16.139	19.619	3.368	0.111	0.099	0.063	0.127	2130.34
gg_rate	52.955	85.180	9.334	2.020	1.867	1.458	2.402	8191.31
sp_torque	0.000	0.000	0.338	0.003	0.002	0.002	0.003	225.245
pp_torque	0.000	0.000	0.338	0.003	0.002	0.002	0.004	225,245
hpt_temp	2.280	3.768	2.416	0.581	0.491	0.332	0.872	733.297
gt_c_o_temp	1.514	1.588	0.455	0.263	0.232	0.153	0.388	644.734
hpt_pressure	0.005	0.006	0.000	0.000	0.000	0.000	0.000	1.347
gt_c_o_pressure	0.056	0.063	0.010	0.008	0.007	0.005	9.013	11.264
gt_exhaust_pressure	0.000	0.000	0.000	0.000	0.000	0.000	0.000	0.0299
turbine_inj_control	2.308	2.242	0.894	0.088	0.069	0.046	0.092	32,649
fuel_flow	0.003	0.004	0.002	0.000	0.000	0.000	0.000	0.127

4 Conclusion

In this paper, an overview about existing supervised ML algorithms performed. The Linear Regression (LR), the Ridge Regression (RR), the Decision Tree (DT), as well as Ensemble algorithms were studied. Ensemble algorithms include the Bagging Regression (BR), the Random Forest Regression (RFR), the Extra Trees Regression (ETR), the k-Nearest Neighbor (kNN) Regression and the Artificial Neural Network (ANN). Furthermore, a comparative analysis of these algorithms performed using the CBM dataset. In particular, a dataset containing data about ship engines used, resulting to the evaluation of each algorithm in terms of predicting decay factors of the ship engine. Based on the analysis performed, future work includes the application of the most effective supervised ML algorithms for the analysis of ship engine data that will be produced from sensors installed in specific ships.

Acknowledgements. This work has been partly supported by the University of Piraeus Research Center (UPRC).

References

1. Rawson, A., Brito, M.: A survey of the opportunities and challenges of supervised machine learning in maritime risk analysis. Transp. Rev. J. **43**(1), 108–130 (2023)
2. Jafar Zaidi, S.A., Chatterjee, I., Brahim Belhaouari, S.:COVID-19 tweets classification during lockdown period using machine learning classifiers. In: Applied Computational Intelligence and Soft Computing, Hindawi, pp. 1–8 (2022)

3. Aram, S.A., et al.: Machine learning-based prediction of air quality index and air quality grade: a comparative analysis. Int. J. Environ. Sci. Technol. 1–16 (2023)

4. Kim, T., Sharda, S., Zhou, X., Pendyala, R.M.: A stepwise interpretable machine learning framework using linear regression (LR) and long short-term memory (LSTM): city-wide demand-side prediction of yellow taxi and for-hire vehicle (FHV) service. Transp. Res. Part C: Emerg. Technol. **120** (2020)

5. Suhail, M., Chand, S.: Performance of some new ridge regression estimators. In: 13th International Conference on Mathematics, Actuarial Science, Computer Science and Statistics (MACS), pp. 1–4. IEEE (2019)

6. Costa, V.G., Pedreira, C.E.: Recent advances in decision trees: an updated survey. Art. Intell. Rev. **56**(5), 4765–4800 (2023)

7. Zhang, Y., Liu, J., Shen, W.: A review of ensemble learning algorithms used in remote sensing applications. Appl. Sci. **12**(17), 1–20 (2022)

8. Tekouabou, S.C.K., Cherif, W., Silkan, H.: Improving parking availability prediction in smart cities with IoT and ensemble-based model. J. King Saud Univ.-Comput. Inf. Sci. **34**(3), 687–697 (2022)

9. El Mrabet, Z., Sugunaraj, N., Ranganathan, P., Abhyankar, S.: Random forest regressor-based approach for detecting fault location and duration in power systems. Sensors **22**(2), 1–19 (2022)

10. Wang, K., Zhang, D., Shen, Z., Zhu, W., Ye, H., Li, D.: Novel ship fuel consumption modelling approaches for speed and trim optimisation: using engine data as auxiliary. Ocean Eng. **286**, 1–12 (2023)

11. Viale, L., Daga, A.P., Fasana, A., Garibaldi, L.: Least squares smoothed k-nearest neighbors online prediction of the remaining useful life of a NASA turbofan. Mech. Syst. Signal Process. **190**, 1–15 (2023)

12. Veza, I., et al.: Review of artificial neural networks for gasoline, diesel and homogeneous charge compression ignition engine. Alex. Eng. J.. Eng. J. **61**(11), 8363–8391 (2022)

13. The Condition Based Maintenance of Naval Propulsion Plants (CBM) dataset. https://www.kaggle.com/datasets/elikplim/maintenance-of-naval-propulsion-plants-data-set. Accessed 30 Oct 2023

14. Scikit-learn library. https://scikit-learn.org. Accessed 30 Oct 2023

15. Russell, S., Norvig, P.: Artificial Intelligence: A Modern Approach. Hoboken (2020)

16. Géron, A.: Hands-On Machine Learning with Scikit-Learn, Keras, and TensorFlow: Concepts, Tools, and Techniques to Build Intelligent Systems, 2nd edn. O'Reilly Media, Inc. (2019)

17. Poloczek, J., Treiber, N.A., Kramer O.: KNN regression as geo-imputation method for spatio-temporal wind data. In: de la Puerta, J., et al. (eds.) International Joint Conference SOCO'14-CISIS'14-ICEUTE'14. AISC, vol. 299, pp. 185–193. Springer, Cham (2014). https://doi.org/10.1007/978-3-319-07995-0_19

18. The Tensorflow library. https://www.tensorflow.org. Accessed 30 Oct 2023

19. The Keras programming interface. https://keras.io. Accessed 30 Oct 2023

20. The Dense class of the Keras programming interface. https://www.tensorflow.org/api_docs/python/tf/keras/layers/Dense. Accessed 30 Oct 2023

Machine Learning and Explainable Artificial Intelligence in Education and Training - Status and Trends

Dimitris Pantazatos[1] (ORCID), Athanasios Trilivas[2], Kalliopi Meli[3],
Dimitrios Kotsifakos[2](✉) (ORCID), and Christos Douligeris[2]

[1] National Technical University of Athens, Athens, Greece
dpantazatos@netmode.ntua.gr
[2] University of Piraeus, Piraeus, Greece
{a.trilivas,kotsifakos,cdoulig}@unipi.gr
[3] University of Patras, Patras, Greece
kmeli@upatras.gr

Abstract. Nowadays, the need to explain the decisions or predictions made by Artificial Intelligence (AI) is emerging more than ever as AI applications are more complex. The research field of eXplainable Artificial Intelligence (XAI) tries to fulfill this need. XAI provides a way to help humans understand how an AI's predictions and decisions come. The scope of this work is to examine the role of XAI in the field of Education, especially in Educational Data Mining in Vocational Education and Training.

Keywords: Artificial Intelligence · Machine Learning · Explainable AI · Educational Data Mining · VET

1 Introduction

In the past few decades, there has been a significant shift in machine learning practitioners' focus towards enhancing their models' predictive capabilities. This shift has gradually replaced simpler, inherently interpretable machine learning models with more complex and performant networks. However, the complexity of these modern "black box" models presents challenges regarding their interpretability, a significant concern for developers, users, and legal entities who are responsible for their deployment in production environments.

For developers, the complexity of these models poses difficulties in understanding, debugging, and asserting the post-deployment of the models' intended functions. On the other hand, users often need help to receive justifications for the decisions made by these models based on their data. Furthermore, legal regulators face hurdles in ensuring that such models, especially when deployed within critical infrastructures, comply with regulatory mandates such as GDPR, which necessitates model transparency and the right to explanation.

L. A. Maglaras and C. Douligeris (Eds.): WiCON 2023, LNICST 527, pp. 110–122, 2024.
https://doi.org/10.1007/978-3-031-58053-6_8

To mitigate these challenges, eXplainable Artificial Intelligence (XAI) has emerged. XAI proposes techniques that provide insights into the machine's inner workings and deep learning models. Among the spectrum of XAI techniques, the most versatile and universally applicable are those categorized as post-hoc and model-agnostic [1]. These algorithms can be applied after the model's training phase (post-hoc) and are not dependent on the specific type of model used (model-agnostic), making them broadly applicable across various models. XAI methods can furnish explanations on two levels: global explanations that shed light on the model's behavior using the training data as a whole and local explanations that detail how models arrive at specific decisions for individual input examples.

This work describes how XAI facilitates a relatively straightforward understanding for education experts of predictive algorithms and decision-making processes employed by educational platforms. Typically, these platforms provide decision-making outputs without accompanying explanations, leaving educators in the dark about the reasoning behind these outputs. XAI can bridge this gap by elucidating the factors and mechanics behind algorithmic decisions, fostering a transparent and trustful adoption of AI in educational settings.

This work is structured as follows: Sect. 2 provides the reader with the basic terminology related to AI and Machine Learning (ML) algorithms. Section 3 describes what XAI means and how it is used in various fields, while Sect. 4 explains how XAI is currently used in education, especially in applications that require data mining. Section 5 presents a use case in Vocational Education and Training (VET) while Sect. 6 concludes the paper and provides ideas for future work.

2   Artificial Intelligence and Machine Learning

This section will provide a brief introduction to Artificial Intelligence (AI) and Machine Learning (ML) and their use in educational settings.

2.1   Artificial Intelligence

Several definitions have been proposed for what AI means. John McCarthy [2] proposed that AI can be considered as the science and engineering of making intelligent machines and is related to using computers to understand human intelligence. Nevertheless, as John McCarthy points out, we must consider that AI does not have to confine itself to biologically observable methods.

However, this definition is one of many. AI is used in many senses (even outside of Computer Science), so the definition varies occasionally. According to Pei Wang [3], many people do not consider it a big problem, as many scientific concepts get sufficient definitions only after the research has grown. In addition, he also thinks that there is no correct working definition of AI, as each has theoretical and practical values, but some definitions can be considered better than others. In the scope of this work, we will stick to the definition that John McCarthy provides, as it describes in quite a few sentences the meaning of AI in our period.

2.2   Machine Learning

ML can be considered a field of AI that uses data from various sources and algorithms (e.g., Linear/Logistic Regression) to imitate how humans learn [4]. This procedure aims to help computers to understand and gradually improve their accuracy. According to Olladipupo [5], ML algorithms are mainly categorized based on the desired outcome of the algorithm. The most known categories of ML algorithms are:

- Supervised learning: The ML algorithm generates a function that maps inputs to desired outputs (labeled examples are available)
- Unsupervised learning: ML is based on a specific set of inputs (not labeled examples).
- Semi-supervised learning: Supervised and Unsupervised techniques are used in this case.
- Reinforcement learning: In this case, the ML algorithm interacts with the environment. As a result, the algorithm uses a policy of how to act given an observation of the world. Every action impacts the environment, and the environment provides feedback that guides the learning algorithm (a case of a grid with a reward system).

Other types of ML techniques are Transduction and Learning to Learn. Transduction is an inference that makes predictions about new data points using specific training examples without abstracting a general rule first [6]. Learning to Learn (or Meta-learning) follows a different approach as a model is trained to learn from other learning tasks [7]. However, these models are outside the scope of this work as they are not widely used in education-related cases.

2.3   Machine Learning in Education

ML has been used in education, as in many cases there is a need to thoroughly analyze the student's performance and to predict their academic development. As a result, there is a need to extract valuable information from data related to education.

Wu [8] presents a use case based on a relatively simple dataset containing 1000 and 8 different variables such as gender, race, parental level of education, lunch, test preparation course, math score, reading score, and writing score. The variables related to scores are ordinal, while the others are nominal. The paper examined correlations based on these variables using linear regression (single-wise and stepwise). Another application of this dataset was to make a simple classifier based on K-nearest Neighbors (KNN) and Logistic Regression (LR). Using these simple supervised methods, she proved that personal study habits are more important than family influence.

Another work that shows the potential of ML in educational data mining is that from Ya Zhou et al. [9], which examines the effectiveness of ML in education Big Data. In this work, the authors stress the need for an intelligent education solution. They present four main practical methods in educational data mining, namely Clustering, Prediction, Relationship Mining, and Model Construction. These methods can be implemented using relatively simple and known ML methods like Multivariate Regression, and K-means.

Kishan Das Menon et al. [10], present other methods for educational data mining, such as Naive Bayes (which is a supervised learning algorithm) and IDE3 (an algorithm used for decision tree generation). They used these algorithms alongside Linear/Logistic

Regression and KNN to provide a mechanism for predicting students' performance and to counsel students for college enrolment more effectively. To test their proposed mechanism, they used a dataset that consisted of details of 132 students of all majors in their university. The dataset included the students' marks/grades from Class XI/Pre-University to the marks of the latest available semester.

Hilbert S., Coors S. et al. [11] conclude that education, especially after the COVID-19 pandemic, will eliminate the one-size-fits-all approach as learning is required to suit the needs of the individual to be more effective. As a result, data collected from different resources must be analyzed more efficiently and accurately. Nevertheless, as they also point out, this requires not only ML models suitable for this cause but also researchers in the educational sciences to be aware of these techniques.

3 Definition of XAI

The previous section examined how ML can be used in educational data mining. The view from the previous section is that researchers and educational experts have many ways to analyze their data. Nevertheless, how do these experts know that the results are accurate and suitable for their purpose? XAI aims to answer this question by providing the tools and methodology to explain how this output was provided. In this section, essential aspects of XAI will be presented to better understand how XAI can be used in the case of educational data mining.

3.1 Why Do We Need XAI?

During the last two decades, ML algorithms have become increasingly popular as they provide a way to create accurate decision support systems. These systems are based on relatively complex techniques such as Deep Neural Networks (DNNs). DNNs' complexity is based on their sizeable parametric space, utilizing many layers and parameters. These aspects of DNNs make them considered black-box models [12].

As these kinds of black-box models are used on most prediction systems, the demand for transparency is constantly increasing among various stakeholders [13].

This demand can also be based on the ethical aspects of the usage of AI. It makes sense that humans tend not to trust solutions they cannot oversee. In addition, if the user understands how a model works and how the output has been created, they can check if the model is accurate. So, the need for implementing ML models that are transparent is more than necessary. According to Alejandro Barredo Arrieta et al. [14], when an ML model is based on transparency and interpretability, it can improve its implementation ability for three reasons:

- Integrity in decision-making.
- Confidence that only useful variables will be used in the model.
- Accuracy of the prediction.

From the points stressed above, we can conclude that XAI should be considered a necessary part of a successful ML application in terms of user experience and trust.

3.2 Basic Aspects of XAI

As shown in the previous paragraph, the nature and complexity of most decision systems based on AI created the need to explain these applications' output. According to Philips et al. [15], four main principles are needed for a successful XAI solution. These principles are mentioned below:

- Explanation: Systems deliver supporting evidence or reason(s) for all outputs.
- Meaningful: Systems provide explanations that are understandable to individual users.
- Explanation Accuracy: The explanation correctly reflects the system's output-generating process.
- Knowledge Limits: The system only operates under the conditions it was designed for or when it reaches sufficient confidence in its output.

Regarding the implementation of an XAI solution, there are a lot of possible solutions. Among various XAI techniques, we will mainly focus on Shapley Additive explanations (SHAP), which can be described in more detail in the work of Lundeberg et al. [16].

SHAP is one of the most prominent model-agnostic XAI methods. It originates in game theory and determines feature importance by considering how much classification decisions vary when specific features are used and when they are removed.

The SHAP values deliver insights into a model's decision-making on two levels: globally and locally. Global explanations using SHAP values highlight which features are pivotal across all predictions, offering a broad understanding of the model's behavior. On the other hand, local explanations focus on individual predictions, detailing how specific features affect each decision made by the model [17]. This dual capacity of SHAP values, complemented by intuitive visualizations, provides developers with a clear window into their model's interpretative framework. Model-agnostic SHAP methods leverage a Kernel Explainer module, which approximates feature importance via a weighted linear regression trained on an input sample. Apart from Kernel Explainer, other explainers are also available, but they only apply to specific models.

The SHAP solutions are the standard for implementing XAI on ML algorithms, as they provide an extensive Python library. Apart from SHAP, according to Angelov et al. [18], other methods are Class Activation Maps (CAMs), Global Attribution Mappings (GAMs), Concept Activation Vectors (CAVs), Local interpretable model-agnostic explanations (LIME), Layer-wise relevance propagation (LRP) and others. The central aspect of these solutions is that they are relatively new and are under active development, as all solutions are related to XAI.

3.3 XAI Use Cases

As it has emerged from the previous sections, XAI can be implemented in various ways and contexts. As a result, there are a lot of applications of XAI that are worth mentioning. Some of the fields that XAI currently implements are cases related to Justice, Natural Language Processing (NLP), Financing, Anomaly detection, and others. Other subjects and impact areas that are mentioned by L. Longo et al. [19] are:

- Threat Detection and Triage.
- Explainable Object Detection.

- Protection Against Adversarial ML.
- Open-Source Intelligence (OSINT).
- Trustworthy (autonomous) Medical Agents.
- Autonomous Vehicles.

As mentioned in the same work, several challenges (technical, legal, and practical) are almost identical for all cases. The following section will present some topics related to XAI in education.

4 XAI in Education

In the previous section, the fundamental aspects of XAI were presented concisely. This section will examine how XAI is implemented in educational data mining. Even though XAI is implemented in the same way in ML applications in education, there are also unique needs emerging from a pedagogical point of view.

H. Khoravi et al. [20] introduced the ED-XAI framework to present this distinction. This framework consists of six dimensions. These six dimensions can be considered questions that must be answered to build a successful XAI solution. These questions are:

- Who are the main stakeholders (e.g., teachers)?
- What are the main benefits?
- What potential pitfalls need to be considered?
- What approaches are used for presenting explanations?
- What are AI models commonly used?
- How can educational AI tools be effectively designed?

These questions have more than one answer. The answers depend on the context in which this application will be used. Four different applications are presented based on ED-XAI are also presented in [20]. In both cases, trust can be considered the common XAI benefit, while the main stakeholders are educators and students. Regarding the models that were used, they were mostly related to NLP and Classification. Finally, incomplete explanations and inaccurate models were the main drawbacks regarding the pitfalls of needlessly complex models.

On the work of Clancey and Hoffman [21], the XAI systems have much in common with Intelligent Tutoring Systems (ITS). ITS was first created during the 1960s and 1980s. Although XAI and ITS have some shared values and issues (especially trust should be considered a common issue in both technologies), ITS is a more generic way of implementing solutions that would teach learners to solve problems by themselves.

Conati et al. [22] also examine the role of ITS in the development of XAI. However, they seem to compare XAI more to Open Learner Models (OLMs), which, according to Bull and Pain [23], are models that allow learners to access their material with different levels of interactivity. OLMs can be scrutable, cooperative, negotiable, or editable.

Nowadays, there are ITS systems that provide OLM functionalities. OLMs could be a form of XAI for an ITS but suited to user needs. One interesting work regarding adaptive to user needs XAI can be considered the work by Embark [24]. In this work, an intelligent education system was examined. The scope of this educational system was to provide more personalized learning material to the learners based on data collected by Internet of Things (IoT) and Internet of Bodies (IoB) devices. In this case, XAI was used to filter/select features that students can choose to take a complete view of their performance and to seek help when needed.

Finally, XAI can use a few resources or is intended for experienced users. According to Alonso [24], even kids under 12 could use an XAI application implemented in Scratch, a visual programming language commonly used in primary education that helps students get familiar with programming. In this case, they implemented XAI in NLP applications. The following section will examine how XAI can be integrated into a Vocational Education and Training (VET) case related to the Network Management course.

5   Enhancing Network Management Training with Explainable AI

XAI is more significant in VET than in general education due to its tailored and practical application. In VET, students are focused on acquiring specific skills and knowledge directly relevant to their chosen professions. XAI's ability to provide transparent, comprehensible insights into AI decision-making aligns seamlessly with this objective. By understanding the 'why' behind AI's recommendations and errors, VET students can hone their skills more effectively, address their weaknesses, and develop a deeper understanding of the subject matter. Moreover, in vocational fields where safety, ethics, and real-world applicability are paramount, XAI ensures students are well-prepared to navigate AI-driven workplaces, make informed decisions, and uphold ethical standards. XAI's capacity to enhance learning outcomes, facilitate skill development, and prepare students for practical, career-focused challenges makes it uniquely valuable in Vocational Education and Training (VET). In the following sections, we will examine a scenario of xAI in a VET course.

5.1   The Network Management Course Use Case

The following use case exemplifies how xAI techniques can be harnessed to enhance the learning experience, improve transparency, and empower instructors and students in critical fields like IT infrastructure management. By examining the practical application of xAI within this context, we can appreciate its transformative potential in Vocational Education and Training (VET).

The use of AI applications in Learning Management Systems (LMS) like Moodle is something that has been introduced previously. Manhica et al. highlight the use of AI for student performance assessment and the most used AI algorithms in LMS like Moodle [25].

The trainer in the proposed case can use the Moodle prediction plugin for this course [26]. This plugin harnesses the power of machine learning algorithms to predict student performance based on an array of data inputs, including quiz scores, forum participation, assignment submissions, and more. While the plugin offers valuable insights, it tends to need more transparency, leaving instructors and students needing clarification about the factors driving its predictions. One relevant work based on this case is from Ogata et al., they propose a system where both students and the AI system explain their decision-making processes, enhancing metacognitive skills and providing insights into learners' challenges [27]. The proposed scenario can also utilize a mechanism based on the same principles.

To bridge this transparency gap and elevate the overall learning experience, the adoption of explainable AI (xAI) techniques becomes imperative. Several xAI techniques prove to be highly effective in this context:

- Feature Importance Analysis: A xAI technique that analyses feature importance within the predictive model. In this context, it can identify which factors exert the most substantial influence on student performance predictions. This revelation empowers instructors with a clear understanding of the elements driving the projections.
- Decision Tree Visualization: Another approach related to xAI entails the creation of decision trees that visually represent the logic behind the prediction model's conclusions. These decision trees can serve as enlightening tools for instructors and students, shedding light on the intricate factors contributing to performance assessments.
- Local Explanations: xAI techniques extend their power by providing localized explanations. These explanations are tailored to individual students, offering insights specific to their strengths and weaknesses. For instance, if a student grapples with subnetting concepts, the xAI system can pinpoint this issue and deliver customized resources or guidance focused solely on subnetting.
- Model Agnostic Techniques: Model agnostic techniques such as Local Interpretable Model-agnostic Explanations (LIME) or Shapley Additive explanations (SHAP) enhance model interpretability. These techniques work seamlessly with a broad spectrum of predictive models and provide intricate insights into their predictions, rendering them more transparent and understandable.

Regarding the last two methods, one interesting work is by Adnan [28]. In this work, the author proposes an xAI model that provides an early global and local interpretation of students' performance at various course stages. The model offers interpretations at 20%, 40%, 60%, 80%, and 100% of course length, providing insights into student performance in a human-understandable way and aiding instructors in offering timely personalized feedback and guidance. Various traditional and ensemble ML algorithms (e.g., Logistic Regression) were trained on demographic, clickstream, and assessment features to determine the best-performing algorithm, which was then provided to the xAI model to interpret students' study behavior at various percentages of course length. Another work worth mentioning is the work of Shamy et al., where they explained black-box machine learning models in the context of student performance prediction in MOOCs [29]. They discovered that all the evaluated methods could (partially) detect the prerequisite relationship between weeks while relying on only behavioral features.

The advantages of incorporating xAI in the VET setting are far-reaching:

- Transparency and Accountability: xAI techniques introduce transparency into the prediction process. Instructors gain a precise understanding of why particular predictions are made, establishing accountability within the educational ecosystem [30]. This transparency empowers instructors to make informed decisions regarding interventions and support for students who may be struggling.

- Customized Support: Instructors can deliver targeted support by providing individualized student explanations. When students comprehend their shortcomings, they can receive more effective assistance. For example, xAI analysis can reveal a student grappling with specific networking protocols. In that case, instructors can recommend additional study materials or one-on-one tutoring tailored to that concern.
- Course Design Enhancement: xAI insights are pivotal in shaping course design adjustments. If certain course materials or assessment methodologies consistently yield poor performance predictions, instructors can recalibrate them to better align with student needs. This iterative approach to course improvement invariably enhances the overall learning experience. According to V. Shamy, university-level educators are interested in having concrete explanations as they could transform these insights into actionable course design decisions. Still, more has to be done to make explanations more user-friendly [31].
- Enhanced Student Engagement: Students are more likely to become deeply engaged in their studies When they understand the direct correlation between their actions and performance predictions. xAI provides students with a clear roadmap to success, empowering them to take ownership of their education and strive for continuous improvement.
- Data-Driven Decision-Making: Instructors and educational institutions can make data-driven decisions regarding resource allocation, interventions, and curriculum development. This data-driven approach leads to more efficient utilization of resources and a higher quality of education, ultimately benefiting both students and educators.

The proposed mechanism can be implemented based on these aspects:

- Integration of XAI Techniques: XAI techniques like SHAP (Shapley Additive exPlanations) or LIME (Local Interpretable Model-agnostic Explanations) can be utilized to interpret the model's predictions. For global explanations, SHAP values can be aggregated across all predictions to understand overall feature importance. For local explanations, generated SHAP values for individual predictions can be used.
- Development of an Interface: An interface within Moodle that presents the predictions and their explanations in a user-friendly manner has to be developed. The explanations must be clear and understandable for non-technical users, potentially using visualizations like bar charts or decision plots.
- Ethical and Privacy Considerations: The ethical implications of predicting student performance, including the potential impact on students and the risk of bias in the model, must be considered. In addition, data privacy is maintained in compliance with regulations such as GDPR, and students have consented to use their data for these purposes.
- Testing and Iteration: Test the integrated system within a live Moodle environment with a pilot group before rolling it out widely. User feedback and iteration on the model and interface to improve accuracy and usability are also necessary.
- Documentation and Training: The system has to provide documentation and training for educators on how to interpret and act on the predictions and explanations.

Incorporating xAI techniques into VET, especially in courses like network management, can significantly enhance the educational experience. XAI promotes transparency, personalization, and data-driven decision-making, ultimately better-preparing students for successful careers in IT infrastructure management. The following section will offer some extensions of the presented proposal.

5.2 Proposed Extensions

Some extensions that would be considered as added value for the proposed scenario can be these:

- Sequential Pattern Explanation Framework: An XAI algorithm tailored to decipher the sequence of student interactions could be constructive in network management courses. This framework could elucidate how the chronological progression through course materials influences student performance, providing insights into optimal learning paths. For instance, it could reveal if studying specific network protocols before practicing with management tools could lead to a deeper understanding and better practical exam scores.
- Demographic Impact Analyzer: An analyzer that leverages XAI to assess the influence of demographic factors on course outcomes would enable educators to tailor the network management curriculum to accommodate diverse educational backgrounds, learning paces, and prior technical experience, fostering a more personalized educational approach.
- Bias Detection and Explanation Engine: An XAI algorithm designed to identify and explain biases within predictive models would ensure equitable education, highlighting if specific model predictions inadvertently favor or disadvantage student segments and clarifying the underlying reason. For example, the work of Arias-Duar et al. seems promising, especially for examining biases in predictive and classification problems, even with noisy data [32].
- Predictive Model Feedback Loop: A predictive feedback loop would enable a dynamic interaction where educators can input their expertise into the XAI system. Disagreements with the model's explanations can be addressed, and this feedback will be instrumental in refining the model, ensuring that the course evolves in line with educator insights and industry relevance.
- Curriculum Alignment Insights: Lastly, an XAI application that could align the course's learning analytics with established network management competencies and industry standards could be highly innovative. This alignment would ensure that the course content remains current and relevant and that educators understand how AI-derived insights correspond with educational benchmarks.

By incorporating these proposed extensions, the corresponding course presented in the previous section could significantly benefit from enhanced interpretability and relevance, empowering educators and students with actionable insights and fostering a deeper understanding of complex network systems.

6   Conclusion

In this paper, we argued that integrating XAI within educational applications, particularly for VET, is pivotal in fostering trust and transparency between the software and its users. The successful application of XAI goes beyond the complexity of underlying machine learning models and educational contexts. The simplicity of implementing XAI, when underpinned by robust architecture and design principles oriented towards explainability, is instrumental in realizing its benefits. The adaptability of the proposed XAI approach in the VET use case demonstrates its potential for broader educational applications. The exploration of diverse educational scenarios will further enrich this dynamic field, contributing to the refinement and enhancement of XAI strategies in education. The ongoing studies and experiments in this field are expected to lead to significant breakthroughs, making sure that the tools used in educational technology advance in step with the rapid developments in AI and machine learning.

Acknowledgment. This work has been co-financed by Greece and the European Union (European Regional Development Fund-ERDF) through the Regional Operational Program "Attiki" 2014–2020.

References

1. Ali, S., et al.: Explainable artificial intelligence (XAI): what we know and what is left to attain trustworthy artificial intelligence. Inf. Fusion **99** (2023). https://doi.org/10.1016/j.inffus.2023.101805
2. Mccarthy, J.: What is artificial intelligence? (2007). https://dl.acm.org/doi/pdf/10.1145/1283920.1283926
3. Wang, P.: On defining artificial intelligence. J. Artif. Gener. Intell. **10**, 1–37 (2019). https://doi.org/10.2478/jagi-2019-0002
4. IBM: What is machine learning? https://www.ibm.com/topics/machine-learning. Accessed 19 Nov 2023
5. Ayodele, T.O.: X types of machine learning algorithms. New Adv. Mach. Learn. **3**, 19–48 (2010)
6. Vapnik, V.N.: The Nature of Statistical Learning Theory. Springer, New York (2000). https://doi.org/10.1007/978-1-4757-3264-1
7. Baxter, J.: Theoretical models of learning to learn. In: Thrun, S., Pratt, L. (eds.) Learning to Learn, pp. 71–94. Springer, Boston (2020). https://doi.org/10.1007/978-1-4615-5529-2_4
8. Wu, J.: Machine learning in education. In: Proceedings - 2020 International Conference on Modern Education and Information Management, ICMEIM 2020, pp. 56–63. Institute of Electrical and Electronics Engineers Inc. (2020). https://doi.org/10.1109/ICMEIM51375.2020.00020
9. Zhou, Y., Song, Z.: Effectiveness analysis of machine learning in education big data. In: Journal of Physics: Conference Series. IOP Publishing Ltd. (2020). https://doi.org/10.1088/1742-6596/1651/1/012105
10. Kishan Das Menon, H., Janardhan, V.: Machine learning approaches in education. In: Materials Today: Proceedings, pp. 3470–3480. Elsevier Ltd. (2020). https://doi.org/10.1016/j.matpr.2020.09.566

11. Hilbert, S., et al.: Machine learning for the educational sciences (2021). https://doi.org/10.1002/rev3.3310

12. Castelvecchi, D.: Can we open the black box of AI? Nature **538**, 20–23 (2016). https://doi.org/10.1038/538020a

13. Preece, A., Harborne, D., Braines, D., Tomsett, R., Chakraborty, S.: Stakeholders in explainable AI (2018)

14. Barredo Arrieta, A., et al.: Explainable Artificial Intelligence (XAI): concepts, taxonomies, opportunities, and challenges toward responsible AI. Inf. Fusion **58**, 82–115 (2020). https://doi.org/10.1016/j.inffus.2019.12.012

15. Jonathon P., Hahn, C.A., Fontana, P.C., Broniatowski, D.A.: Draft NISTIR 8312 - four principles of explainable artificial intelligence (2020). https://doi.org/10.6028/NIST.IR.8312-draft

16. Lundberg, S.M., Allen, P.G., Lee, S.-I.: A unified approach to interpreting model predictions (2017)

17. Molnar, C.: Interpretable machine learning a guide for making black box models explainable (2019)

18. Angelov, P.P., Soares, E.A., Jiang, R., Arnold, N.I., Atkinson, P.M.: Explainable artificial intelligence: an analytical review. Wiley Interdiscip. Rev. Data Min. Knowl. Discov. **11** (2021). https://doi.org/10.1002/widm.1424

19. Longo, L., Goebel, R., Lecue, F., Kieseberg, P., Holzinger, A.: Explainable artificial intelligence: concepts, applications, research challenges and visions. In: Holzinger, A., Kieseberg, P., Tjoa, A.M., Weippl, E. (eds.) CD-MAKE 2020. LNCS, vol. 12279, pp. 1–16. Springer, Cham (2020). https://doi.org/10.1007/978-3-030-57321-8_1

20. Khosravi, H., et al.: Explainable artificial intelligence in education. Comput. Educ.: Artif. Intell. **3** (2022). https://doi.org/10.1016/j.caeai.2022.100074

21. Clancey, W.J., Hoffman, R.R.: Methods and standards for research on explainable artificial intelligence: lessons from intelligent tutoring systems. Appl. AI Lett. **2** (2021). https://doi.org/10.1002/ail2.53

22. Conati, C., Porayska-Pomsta, K., Mavrikis, M.: AI in Education needs interpretable machine learning: lessons from open learner modelling (2018)

23. Bull, S., Pain, H.: "Did I Say What I Think I Said, and Do You Agree with Me?": Inspecting and Questioning the Student Model. AACE (1995)

24. Alonso, J.M.: Explainable Artificial Intelligence for Kids (2019)

25. Manhica, R., Santos, A., Cravino, J.: The use of artificial intelligence in learning management systems in the context of higher education: systematic literature review. In: 2022 17th Iberian Conference on Information Systems and Technologies (CISTI), pp. 1–6. IEEE (2022). https://doi.org/10.23919/CISTI54924.2022.9820205

26. Zhang, Y., Ghandour, A., Shestak, V.: Using learning analytics to predict students performance in moodle LMS. Int. J. Emerg. Technol. Learn. **15**, 102–114 (2020). https://doi.org/10.3991/ijet.v15i20.15915

27. Ogata, H., Flanagan, B., Takami, K., Dai, Y., Nakamoto, R., Takii, K.: EXAIT: educational eXplainable artificial intelligent tools for personalized learning (2024)

28. Adnan, M., Uddin, M.I., Khan, E., Alharithi, F.S., Amin, S., Alzahrani, A.A.: Earliest possible global and local interpretation of students' performance in virtual learning environment by leveraging explainable AI. IEEE Access. **10**, 129843–129864 (2022). https://doi.org/10.1109/ACCESS.2022.3227072

29. Swamy, V., Radmehr, B., Krco, N., Marras, M., Käser, T.: Evaluating the explainers: black-box explainable machine learning for student success prediction in MOOCs (2022)

30. Holmes, W., et al.: Ethics of AI in education: towards a community-wide framework. Int. J. Artif. Intell. Educ. **32**, 504–526 (2022). https://doi.org/10.1007/s40593-021-00239-1

31. Swamy, V., Du, S., Marras, M., Kaser, T.: Trusting the explainers: teacher validation of explainable artificial intelligence for course design. In: ACM International Conference Proceeding Series, pp. 345–356. Association for Computing Machinery (2023). https://doi.org/10.1145/3576050.3576147

32. Arias-Duart, A., Pares, F., Garcia-Gasulla, D., Gimenez-Abalos, V.: Focus! Rating XAI methods and finding biases. In: 2022 IEEE International Conference on Fuzzy Systems (FUZZ-IEEE), pp. 1–8. IEEE (2022). https://doi.org/10.1109/FUZZ-IEEE55066.2022.9882821

5G/6G Networks

Comparative Analysis of Terahertz MAC Protocols for Wireless Data Center

Muhammad Absaruddin[1]([⊠]), Saim Ghafoor[1], and Mubashir Husain Rehmani[2]

[1] Department of Computing, Atlantic Technological University, Donegal, Ireland
{L00177821,saim.ghafoor}@atu.ie
[2] Department of Computer Science, Munster Technological University, Cork, Ireland

Abstract. Over the last few years, generation of Internet data by the users has drastically increased. As this data is accessed, processed, shared, and delivered through the data centers (DC), therefore bandwidth requirement for DC is increasing. Although, wired technologies are being used, but at the cost of high maintenance, limited flexibility, and high energy consumption. Wireless Terahertz (THz) links can help to overcome these challenges of wired technologies and can also provide high data rates upto Terabits-per-second (Tbps) with low latency due to very high bandwidth availability. However, THz band itself has some challenges including high spreading, molecular, and material penetration losses. In the same way, the challenges for a DC includes its unique environmental and traffic characteristics which are in form of blockages, and different packet sizes (small and long flows) and traffic patterns. With these factors communication in DC can become challenging, so to ensure reliable and efficient communication it is necessary to understand the effect of these factors in the existing THz Medium Access Control (MAC) protocols. In this paper, we compare the existing THz MAC protocols, considering the unique environment and characteristics of DC like blockages and different packet sizes which will provide the basis to design and develop new THz MAC protocols. These protocols are implemented and evaluated on NS-3, and results show that the performance decreases when the unique requirements of THz band and DC environment are considered.

Keywords: Blockages · MAC protocol · Packet flows · Terahertz wireless links · Wireless data center

1 Introduction

In today's world as more and more people and devices are connecting to the Internet, the generation of data has also increased. Cisco [1] reported that in 2023, the devices which will be connected to the Internet will be approximately three

This research was supported by President's Research Bursary Scholarship Award offered by Atlantic Technological University, Donegal, Ireland.

L. A. Maglaras and C. Douligeris (Eds.): WiCON 2023, LNICST 527, pp. 125–138, 2024.
https://doi.org/10.1007/978-3-031-58053-6_9

times the population of humans, and 4.8 zetta-bytes of data will be generated annually. As this data is accessed, processed, shared, and delivered through the data centers (DC), therefore, DC need to support high bandwidth. Additionally, bandwidth requirement of these DC is also increasing with exponential growth which is double down each year [2]. Therefore, higher data rate has become the requirement of these DC. In present DC, wired technologies are being used in the form of copper and fiber optics cable which are costly, takes up lots of space and affects cooling [3]. Additionally, with the use of traditional topologies in wired DC, there is a hotspots and oversubscription problem. In a hotspot problem, a server in the DC significantly receive more network traffic comparing to other server nodes. An oversubscription problem occurs in communication between the server racks when the maximum demand for bandwidth exceeds the available bandwidth [4]. Therefore, to solve the problems of wired DC and provide higher data rate upto Tbps, THz wireless communication can be considered as a potential technology for future DC.

Considering DC specific environment, THz wireless links can be used in between inter-rack and intra-rack communication. By using THz wireless links, cables (wires) can be reduced which can help in reducing cabling complexity, and reduction in cooling as well as airflow will not be blocked. There are some other benefits too of using THz wireless link like flexible and new topologies can be designed which can help to reduce the deployment cost and provide energy efficient design for DC [5]. Additionally, the hotspot and oversubscription problem can be solved by using THz wireless links in the high demand area with more bandwidth availability. Moreover, THz bands have huge bandwidth availability due to which they can provide high data rates. Whilst the THz has many advantages, it has some challenges as well which include high spreading and molecular absorption loss, high scattering and reflection losses, and material penetration losses (blockages due to materials) [6,7]. Similarly, the challenges for a DC include its unique environmental and traffic characteristics [8]. Due to these issues, the use of THz wireless links in DC can become challenging.

In the context of a DC, the efficiency and reliability of data transfer is important, so it is necessary to understand the complications posed by the environmental and traffic characteristics of the DC which are blockages and different packet size respectively. Within the DC there is presence of racks, and cables which makes the DC environment dynamic and unique. Since THz band cannot penetrate a lot of materials and are sensitive to obstacles. Therefore, using THz band in this unique environment can bring up issues whilst designing communication protocols especially at the MAC layer for a DC. Through blockages, the signal gets attenuated which affects the received signal power, due to which the overall Quality of Service (QoS) can be degraded, and communication can become challenging. In addition to the unique environment, the nature of DC traffic can also bring up a problem whilst designing a THz MAC protocol specific to DC. The DC traffic characteristics includes two types of flow; short and long flows, amongst them short flows used for latency sensitive applications, for example query traffic often require packets with smaller size [9]. Moreover, in a DC majority of traffic is short flow which consists of packets with smaller size [10,11], so by not using optimal size for short flow in a DC can bring up latency, throughput and longer cycle time concerns. These blockages and small packet size can degrade the overall performance of the MAC protocol. Hence, to ensure reliable and efficient communication in a DC it is necessary to first analyse the effect of these characteristics in existing THz protocols, before proposing a MAC protocol specific for DC. Primarily, the function of MAC protocol is to ensure that if nodes (devices) want to communicate with each other, how they can access the medium, what rules they can follow to access the medium. Unlike the traditional MAC protocols which mainly focused on contention of nodes to access the channel, in THz band, as there is huge bandwidth available, so nodes do not aggressively contend to access the channel. But the focus in THz MAC protocols is coordination and scheduling. More specifically, through coordination in THz MAC for DC, blockages issue can be mitigated by using an alternate path for communication link [5]. Similarly, scheduling mechanisms can be used for packets with small size from which the packets can be transmitted quickly, increasing the throughput, and lowering delay.

Currently, for the DC environment, only one work is available [12] who have presented two THz MAC protocols as HCU and HTS-MAC. They mainly proposed a hybrid model with (carrier sense multiple access) CSMA and TDMA with two way handshaking mechanism for HCU MAC, and TDMA with one way handshake mechanism for HTS-MAC. However, the architecture and implementation details are not sufficiently mentioned like TDMA slot structure, guard time, timeslots etc. The unique environmental characteristics of DC scenario are also not considered including channel propagation, link losses and blockages. Terahertz MAC protocols have been proposed for applications like cellular net- work, Wireless Personal Area Network (WPAN), and Wireless Local Area Network (WLAN) [13]. In [13], two versions of an adaptive directional antenna MAC protocol (ADAPT) as ADAPT-1 and ADAPT-3 are presented. ADAPT-3 with three way handshake and ADAPT-1 with one way handshake. They have considered the centralized network architecture and addressed issues like synchronization, low channel utilization and collision avoidance. In ADAPT-3, they have used adaptive modulation coding scheme, and adaptive sector time and addressed co-ordination problem among the nodes. Whereas in ADAPT-1 they have partially used adaptive sector time to improve channel utilization. The recent THz MAC protocol (TAN-MAC) is proposed [14], however for airborne networks with ultra high range of 10 km, and with main focus on mobility and velocity of nodes. Therefore, in our analysis we are not considering this protocol, because of its non-suitability for DC environments.

To the best of our knowledge, nobody has analyzed the performance of existing THz MAC protocols for the suitability of a DC considering the environmental and traffic characteristics of the DC. Hence, we aim to bridge this gap by providing the performance comparison of THz MAC protocols in data center environment. The main contribution of our work includes the comparative analysis of existing receiver-initiated carrier sensing based THz MAC protocols [13] in the

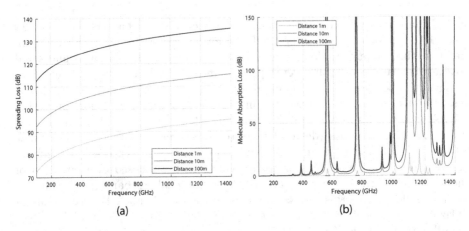

Fig. 1. Terahertz Channel Characteristics. (a) Spreading Loss directly proportional to distance and frequency. (b) Molecular Absorption Loss increasing with frequency.

context of DC, we will analyze how THz MAC behaves in DC environment while considering the two important factors, the environmental characteristics (blockages) and traffic characteristics (small packet size). This performance analysis will provide the basis to design and develop new THz MAC protocols considering DC specific constraints.

The remainder of this paper is organized as follows: We have provided the description of THz Channel Characteristics and Data Center Environment in Sect. 2. In Sect. 3, we have discussed the mechanism of MAC protocols. Section 4 provides the description of performance evaluation with simulation results. Finally we have drawn the conclusion in Sect. 5.

2   THz Channel Characteristics and Data Center Environment

In this section, we discuss the channel characteristics of Terahertz band. Additionally, to compare the performance, and suitability of THz MAC protocols in order to work in a DC scenario its necessary to understand its unique environmental factors and characteristics. Therefore, in this section, we also discuss the unique environment of data center, and unique requirement for THz MAC for wireless DC.

2.1   Channel Characteristics of THz Band

In electromagnetic spectrum, THz band ranges between 0.1 to 10 THz (100 GHz–10000 GHz), and it is in between microwave and infrared band. The key challenge include its high path loss which is due to spreading and molecular absorption loss, and it increases with increasing distance and frequency as shown in Fig. 1.

Due to this spreading loss, transmission of signal is affected, and it also creates the distance problem due to which directional antennas are used in THz to increase the coverage range [6].

Similarly, molecular absorption loss is occurred as THz signals gets absorbed through water vapours (H_2O) in the atmosphere. Additionally, THz signals are also absorbed by molecules of (0_2) oxygen in the atmosphere [15]. Since the molecular absorption loss is very less for the selected frequency i.e. 0.021868 dB, and it can be seen in Fig. 1, therefore it can be neglected.

Spreading loss can be calculated as [6],

$$Spreading\ Loss = \left(\frac{4\pi f d}{c}\right)^2 \tag{1}$$

where; c is the speed of light, f is the central frequency, and d the distance between transmitter and receiver.

Molecular absorption loss can be calculated as [6],

$$Molecular\ Loss = e^{kf \cdot d} \tag{2}$$

where; kf is the absorption coefficient at specific frequency, and is calculated using High resolution transmission molecular (HITRAN) database, and d is the distance.

To calculate the received power we have used the channel model as described in [6].

$$P_r(d) = \int_B PSD_t(f)|H_c(f,d)|^2 G_t(f)G_r(f)df, \tag{3}$$

where channel frequency response $H_c(f,d)$ is calculated using losses, G_t, G_r are the gain of antennas, and PSD_t represents one sided power spectral density of transmitted signal.

2.2 Data Center Unique Environment

1. **Blockages:** In a DC environment, there are blockages in form of racks and cables as discussed by Cheng et al. [8]. In their DC environment, servers were arranged on the metallic racks, and the rack consist of mesh type structure door to maintain the cooling inside the racks. Moreover, the racks also consist of cables. They performed their measurement by considering different propagation scenarios. They concluded that in the DC, pillars of server racks can be utilized as a reflecting material to assist communication, and optical lenses can be helpful to provide gain in both LoS and NLoS communication. On the other hand, power cables can cause a signal loss of 20 dB. Similarly, mesh door of servers racks can also cause signal attenuation of 5.7 dB. These losses are computed from mean path loss of LoS, OLoS, NLoS, ONLoS [8]. Mean path loss can be calculated as [8],

$$Mean\ Path\ Loss = \frac{1}{N}\sum_{i=1}^{N}|H(f_i)|^2 \tag{4}$$

where; $H(f_i)$ denotes the channel transfer function, N denotes to total number of frequency tones.

These blockages affects the performance of THz MAC protocol, as there are losses from these blockages due to which received signal power is affected, signal noise increases which decrease the throughput, and causes delay in transmission.

2. **Reflections and Scattering:** Eckhardt et al. [16] have done measurement in inter-rack and intra rack communication. They concluded in a DC environment there are reflections. Similarly, Song et al. have performed inter-rack communication [17] and they concluded that there is scattering in DC environment which is cause by metal racks.

2.3   Unique Requirements of THz MAC for Wireless DC

1. **Data packet size:** In a DC there are two types of flow, short flow (mice flow) and long flow (elephant flow) [18]. In [18], it is reported that almost 80% flow of packet in a DC is less than 10 kB which is a short flow, and in [10] it is reported that 70% of flow is a short flow, which is less than 10 kB. The example of short flows includes the query traffic and has the size between 2–20 kB [9]. In ADAPT [13], the data packet size used is 65 kB. Using a larger data packet size can affect in increased latency, error probability and cycle time. The THz MAC protocol must be designed to support short flows.

2. **Throughput and Delay:** In a DC environment, due to the sharing of bandwidth between the nodes (devices), the MAC protocol should provide higher throughput and low latency for reliable communication [5].

3. **Power efficient:** The MAC protocol should support mechanism for minimizing transmission power through power control strategies. Low transmission power is required in context of DC to save energy.

3   MAC Protocols Mechanism

In this section, we discuss the working of existing MAC protocols namely ADAPT-1, ADAPT-3.

3.1   ADAPT-1 MAC Mechanism

ADAPT-1 is a receiver initiated MAC protocol in which a receiver initiates its communication which has a rotating directional antenna. The client nodes also have directional antenna but with fixed direction towards the receiver. The receiver announces its status (ready to receive) by broadcasting a call-to-action (CTA) packet in all directions. After sending CTA packet, the receiver use a partially adaptive sector time mechanism in which it waits for a certain period for the client to send data otherwise it moves to a new sector. If the client node has data to send, it transmits it to the receiver, and waits for the acknowledgment as illustrated in Fig. 2(a) [13].

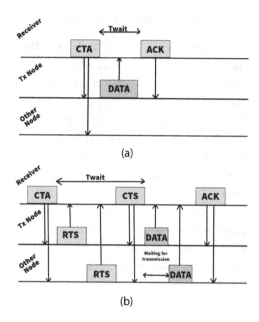

Fig. 2. MAC protocol mechanism. (a) ADAPT-1. (b) ADAPT-3.

3.2   ADAPT-3 MAC Mechanism

ADAPT-3 follows the similar architecture as ADAPT-1 and differs mainly in its working. Client node when receives CTA from receiver waits for random backoff time to avoid collision. After waiting time, it sends (request to send) RTS packet to the receiver when it has data to send, if timeout expires it retransmits the packet for maximum five times before discarding the packet. During the waiting time, the receiver uses adaptive sector time in which it sets its time according to the received RTS packets. If client node wants to complete the data transmission it will wait otherwise it will move into a new sector. The receiver also decides which specified sector can be used by the client nodes through the sector white list mechanism. When the receiver receives RTS packet, it analyzes it using adaptive modulation and coding scheme. Through recording the SNR from the client node, it selects the highest order of modulation scheme. If it does not receive RTS, it moves to another sector. Now the receiver sends clear to send (CTS) packet to give channel access to client node in which it has the information of modulation and coding scheme, also receiver allocates the time of transmission slot to client nodes to avoid collision between the client nodes so the nodes can transmit data on their specified time slot. After receiving CTS, client node waits for transmission slot then it selects the modulation scheme indicated by the receiver, these details are present in the CTS packet. If the client node has data to send, it transmits it to the receiver and waits for the acknowledgment as illustrated in Fig. 2(b) [13].

Table 1. Simulation Parameters

Frequency range	252.72–321.84 GHz
Channel bandwidth	69.12 GHz [13]
Central frequency	287.28 GHz [13]
Modulation scheme	16-QAM
Transmitted power	10 dBm [21,22]
Noise figure	7 dB [13]
Packet Size	65 kB [13], 9 kB
Communication Range	4.86 m
Antenna type	Directional
Beamwidth	12°
Antenna Gain	24.57 dB
No of sectors	30
Blockages considered	Cables, Mesh doors

4 Performance Evaluation

Simulations are performed for comparison of existing THz MAC protocols including ADAPT-1 (1-way), and ADAPT-3 (3-way). The blockages and different packet size (for short flows) are considered for the analysis. For blockages we consider the racks, and the mesh doors and cables within a rack. The measurements works shows that the blockages can affect the link performance [8]. We also consider the short packet size for our analysis. To measure the performance, we used throughput as a parameter to analyse the efficiency of THz MAC protocols and link performance.

4.1 Simulation Setup

The setup, and implementation details, are discussed below.

Environment: We used NS-3 for simulation, and more specifically we have used Terasim module [19] which is the extension of NS-3 and it is designed specifically for simulating communication protocols in THz communication. We have used the parameters for a DC, as mentioned in Table 1. For calculating the communication range, we used 16-QAM modulation scheme with 10 dB transmission power. The traffic model used in the simulation is taken from Morales et al. [13], it follows a poisson process. In our simulation, the inter-arrival time of packets is set to 400 μs which is the time duration in between the arrival of two consecutive packets at a node, and inter-arrival of packets follows the exponential distribution. Similarly, the rate of packet arrival which is the rate of poisson process will be the inverse of inter-arrival time. Therefore, for 400 μs inter-arrival time, the rate of packet arrival is 2500 packets/sec.

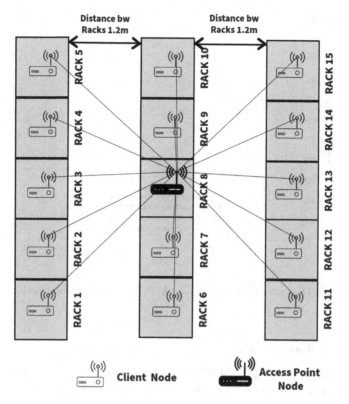

Fig. 3. Centralized Network Architecture for wireless DC in which each server rack has THz transceiver at ToR.

Network Topology: The network topology is shown in Fig. 3, in which three rows of racks are used each with 5 racks. Each server rack has a top-of-rack (ToR) THz node. The distance between the two opposite racks is 1.2 m and the rack dimensions are 0.58 m (width) and 0.67 m (depth [20,23]. In this paper we have considered the inter-rack communication, in which there is a central access point (AP) at Rack No.8 with rotating directional antenna at ToR, and all other racks are client nodes with a directional antenna pointing its beam towards the AP. In our design, for simplicity of the analysis we have not included a client node in the rack with AP. In our simulation we varied number of client nodes (2, 4, 6, 8, 10, 12, 14), these client nodes communicate with AP node. For example if there is a four node scenario, there will be one AP receiver which is rotating, and four transmitter nodes (client nodes).

Implementation Details: Extensive simulations are performed to analyse the performance of THz MAC protocols under the presence of blockages (cables and doors of racks). We included path loss for OLoS, and LoS from which the total loss of mesh doors was computed. Additionally, we included the cable loss as well.

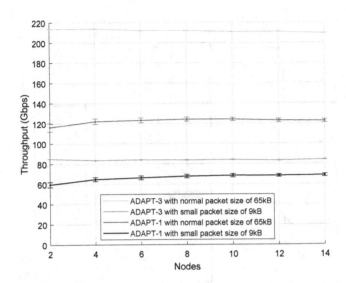

Fig. 4. Average Throughput of ADAPT-1, ADAPT-3 with normal and small packet size.

4.2   Performance Metrics

The performance of the THz MAC protocols is evaluated using key metrics of throughput, which is discussed below.

Throughput: This metric is defined to capture the efficiency of data transmission. It is the rate of data packets that are successfully transmitted by the nodes per unit time. More precisely, it is computed by dividing the packet size of successfully transmitted data of client node with the transmission time (in seconds), and is measured in bits/second [13]. Throughput is calculated for the client nodes that are involved in a successful transmission to the AP, i.e. the data was successfully sent by a client node.

4.3   Simulation Results

In this section, we present the outcomes of our simulation analysis. Our results in the following subsection are averaged over fifty simulation runs. Additionally, simulation results are with 95% confidence intervals.

Analysis of Packet Size: Figure 4 compares THz MAC protocols average throughput, with two different packet sizes 9 KB (small packet size) and 65 KB (normal packet size). The 9 kB is indicative for short flows inside the data center specifically for latency sensitive applications such as query traffic. The small packet size is chosen for the analysis because majority of the flows in data centers (almost 70–80%) comprises of short flows [10,18].

When the packet size decreases from 65 kB to 9 kB the average throughput decreased by approximately 60%, 46% for ADAPT-3 and ADAPT-1 respectively as shown in Fig. 4. There are two main reasons for less throughput when using a smaller packet size of 9 kB which are overhead due to handshake and synchronization, and inefficient use of transmission opportunity. Firstly, the ratio of overhead to data packet will be more in smaller packet size compared to larger packet size involved in transmission. This overhead will be from handshaking and from the synchronization between client nodes and AP node which is established frequently for each data transmission. Secondly, the reason behind the less throughput for small packet size is because it will not be utilizing the transmission opportunity more efficiently compared to large packet size as the packets with smaller packet size will be sending less bits compared to the packets with larger size.

Impact of Blockages on Throughput: Blockages which are present in the DC in the form of cables and rack doors has reduced the average throughput of THz MAC protocols leading to degraded performance. As these MAC protocols are designed with the goal to maximize the throughput so it will worsen the overall performance of MAC protocol. To investigate the effect of blockages on THz MAC protocol we have investigated three scenarios in this paper with two different packet sizes (65 kB - normal packet size & 9 kB - small packet size) which includes, without blockages, with blockages from mesh doors of racks, and with blockages from cables.

In the scenario where there are no blockages, a signal is directly transmitted by the client nodes to the receiver, and there is a direct link without any obstructions. Due to direct link, there is no signal attenuation from cables and mesh doors. As there are no obstructions THz MAC protocols are performing adequately as shown in Fig. 4. Comparatively, ADAPT-3 and ADAPT-1 are providing higher throughput as they are receiver-initiated communication protocols and client nodes only send the data when they receive indication from the receiver which ensures no packet is discarded.

In contrast to without the blockages, there is a significant reduction in the average throughput with the blockages from cables for 65 kB packet size. There is reduction of approximately 81% and 75% specifically for 8 nodes scenario in the ADAPT-3 and ADAPT-1 respectively as shown in Fig. 5(a). ADAPT-1 and ADAPT-3 MAC protocols are giving zero throughput for 2, 4, and 6 nodes scenario due to severe attenuation, since the receiver (AP node) is not able to receive the signal from the client nodes with sufficient power strength as the signal to interference noise ratio (SINR) is below the threshold value from which there is weaker signal.

Additionally, from blockages due to mesh doors as shown in Fig. 5(b) there is a decrease in the average throughput which is approximately 17% and 16% for ADAPT-3 and ADAPT-1 respectively for normal packet size compared to without blockages.

Similar effects of decrease in throughput are also observed for both the two scenarios of blockages with smaller packet size (9 kB).

In both the THz MAC protocols there is a similar trend of decrease in average throughput when there are blockages. This decline is the indication of the dete-

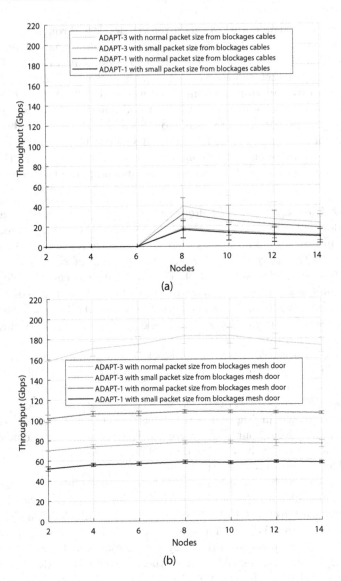

Fig. 5. Impact of blockages on average throughput of THz MAC protocols with normal and small packet size. (a) ADAPT-3, ADAPT-1 with blockages from cables. (b) ADAPT-3, ADAPT-1 with blockages from mesh door of rack.

riorating performance of the THz MAC protocols. There are two main reasons for decline in average throughput when there are blockages. Firstly, these blockages cause attenuation of signal due to which there is degradation in quality of signal then there are losses due to which received signal power is affected. These blockages affect LoS communication between the transmitter and receiver. As

LoS is blocked, signal noise increases which decrease the throughput, and causes delay in transmission.

From results, it can be concluded that the performance of the THz MAC protocols has been degraded drastically. As DC requires high throughput therefore this decrease in throughput due to blockages and smaller packet size can affect overall performance of DC. Therefore, THz MAC protocols designed for the DC environment should take in consideration the techniques and mechanisms for mitigating blockages and, handling packets with small size.

5   Conclusion

In this paper, we have performed the comparative analysis of recent THz MAC protocols including ADAPT (1-way) and ADAPT (3-way) considering unique environmental, and traffic characteristics of DC which includes blockages, and small packet size respectively. We evaluated the performance of these THz MAC protocols in the NS-3 simulator using the performance metrics of throughput. This performance evaluation is crucial to understand the effect of blockages, and small packet size on the performance of THz MAC protocols, as previously no comparative analysis has been performed considering DC specific constraints. Results shows that the peculiar characteristics of DC including blockages, and small packet size significantly decreased the average throughput by upto 80% degrading the performance of THz MAC protocol. In future work, we will consider different traffic patterns of data centre network to further analyse the performance of THz MAC protocols.

References

1. Cisco: Cisco annual internet report (2018–2023) white paper- executive summary (2020). https://www.cisco.com/c/en/us/solutions/collateral/executive-perspectives/annual-internet-report/white-paper-c11-741490.pdf
2. Singh, A., et al.: Jupiter rising: a decade of clos topologies and centralized control in Google's datacenter network. ACM SIGCOMM Comput. Commun. Rev. **45**(4), 183–197 (2015)
3. Cao, B., et al.: Multiobjective 3-D topology optimization of next-generation wireless data center network. IEEE Trans. Industr. Inf. **16**(5), 3597–3605 (2019)
4. Hamza, A.S., Deogun, J.S., Alexander, D.R.: Wireless communication in data centers: a survey. IEEE Commun. Surv. Tutor. **18**(3), 1572–1595 (2016)
5. Ghafoor, S., Boujnah, N., Rehmani, M.H., Davy, A.: MAC protocols for terahertz communication: a comprehensive survey. IEEE Commun. Surv. Tutor. **22**(4), 2236–2282 (2020)
6. Jornet, J.M., Akyildiz, I.F.: Channel modeling and capacity analysis for electromagnetic wireless nanonetworks in the terahertz band. IEEE Trans. Wireless Commun. **10**(10), 3211–3221 (2011)
7. Rappaport, T.S., et al.: Wireless communications and applications above 100 GHz: opportunities and challenges for 6g and beyond. IEEE Access **7**, 78729–78757 (2019)

8. Cheng, C.L., Sangodoyin, S., Zajić, A.: THz cluster-based modeling and propagation characterization in a data center environment. IEEE Access **8**, 56544–56558 (2020)

9. Alizadeh, M., et al.: Data center TCP (DCTCP). In: Proceedings of the ACM SIGCOMM 2010 Conference, pp. 63–74 (2010)

10. Roy, A., Zeng, H., Bagga, J., Porter, G., Snoeren, A.C.: Inside the social network's (datacenter) network. In: Proceedings of the 2015 ACM Conference on Special Interest Group on Data Communication, pp. 123–137 (2015)

11. Cai, Y., Yao, Z., Li, T., Luo, S., Zhou, L.: SD-MAC: design and evaluation of a software-defined passive optical intrarack network in data centers. Trans. Emerg. Telecommun. Technol. **33**(8), e3764 (2022)

12. Wang, T., Shi, X., Tao, J., Wang, X., Han, B.: Efficient synchronous MAC protocols for terahertz networking in wireless data center. In: IEEE Conference on Computer Communications Workshops (INFOCOM WKSHPS), pp. 1–6 (2022)

13. Morales, D., Jornet, J.M.: ADAPT: an adaptive directional antenna protocol for medium access control in terahertz communication networks. Ad Hoc Netw. **119**, 102540 (2021)

14. He, L., et al.: Intelligent terahertz medium access control (MAC) for highly dynamic airborne networks. IEEE Trans. Aerosp. Electron. Syst. **59**(3), 2494–2512 (2023)

15. Han, C., Gao, W., Yang, N., Jornet, J.M.: Molecular absorption effect: a double edged sword of terahertz communications. IEEE Wirel. Commun. (2022)

16. Eckhardt, J.M., Doeker, T., Rey, S., Kürner, T.: Measurements in a real data centre at 300 GHz and recent results. In: 13th European Conference on Antennas and Propagation (EuCAP), pp. 1–5 (2019)

17. Song, G., et al.: Channel measurement and characterization at 140 GHz in a wireless data center. In: IEEE Global Communications Conference, GLOBECOM, pp. 4764–4769 (2022)

18. Benson, T., Akella, A., Maltz, D.A.: Network traffic characteristics of data centers in the wild. In: Proceedings of the 10th ACM SIGCOMM Conference on Internet Measurement, pp. 267–280 (2010)

19. Hossain, Z., Xia, Q., Jornet, J.M.: TeraSim: an ns-3 extension to simulate terahertz-band communication networks. Nano Commun. Netw. **17**, 36–44 (2018)

20. AlGhadhban, A.: F4Tele: FSO for data center network management and packet telemetry. Comput. Netw. **186** (2021)

21. ITU-R M.2417-1: Technical and operational characteristics of land-mobile service applications in the frequency range 275–450 GHz (2022). https://www.itu.int/dms_pub/itu-r/opb/rep/R-REP-M.2417-1-2022-PDF-E.pdf

22. Eckhardt, J.M., Herold, C., Friebel, B., Dreyer, N., Kürner, T.: Realistic interference simulations in a data center offering wireless communication at low terahertz frequencies. In: IEEE International Symposium on Antennas and Propagation (ISAP), pp. 1–2 (2021)

23. Mamun, S.A., Umamaheswaran, S.G., Ganguly, A., Kwon, M., Kwasinski, A.: Performance evaluation of a power-efficient and robust 60 GHz wireless server-to-server datacenter network. IEEE Trans. Green Commun. Netw. **2**(4), 1174–1185 (2018)

Optimization of Energy Distribution with Demand Response Control in 6G Next Generation Smart Grids

Rola Naja[1,2(✉)], Asma Tannous[3], Nadia Mouawad[4], and Nazih Moubayed[3]

[1] LyRIDS, ECE Paris, 10 rue Sextius Michel, 75015 Paris, France
rnaja@ece.fr
[2] LiPARAD-Université de Versailles-Saint Quentin, Paris, France
[3] EDST Laboratory, Lebanese University, Beirut, Lebanon
nazih.moubayed@ul.edu.lb
[4] Orange Labs, Paris, France
nadia.mouawad@orange.com

Abstract. The transition to an intelligent electrical network that is more respectful to the environment and consumers' needs requires the adoption of renewable energies. However, and despite the progress made in this area, renewable energies present significant constraints, such as their intermittency. Therefore, the convergence between the worlds of energy and 5G/6G network techniques offers relevant solutions, including the use of Virtual Power Plants, SDN technology coupled with network slicing. As a way to achieve power balancing between power generation and demands, this study offers a unique architecture for a smart grid that makes full use of optimization techniques to rationalize the distribution of energy resources. Performance evaluation shows the optimization of resource consumption.

Keywords: Renewable Energy Sources · SDN · VPP · Demand Response

1 Introduction

This article focuses on the integration of 6G network technology for the management of renewable, environmentally friendly energy sources in smart grids. Indeed, the development of 6G networks relies heavily on energy efficiency. In order to improve resource management, network performance, and user experience, energy optimization algorithm is of paramount importance in this regard. Artificial Intelligence solutions have the potential to optimize energy consumption and enhance the overall efficiency of 6G networks. Moreover, the architecture of 6G networks will require the integration of wireless communication technologies that are anticipated to be a key technology.

Beyond the pollution and environmental challenges [1], the electrical system is facing new constraints, such as the growing energy demand, particularly during peak periods, the aging of network infrastructures and new electrical uses, i.e., electric vehicles.

© ICST Institute for Computer Sciences, Social Informatics and Telecommunications Engineering 2024
Published by Springer Nature Switzerland AG 2024. All Rights Reserved
L. A. Maglaras and C. Douligeris (Eds.): WiCON 2023, LNICST 527, pp. 139–156, 2024.
https://doi.org/10.1007/978-3-031-58053-6_10

Based on these findings, players in the energy sector are now orienting their efforts towards 1) the deployment of renewable resources and 2) the development of technologies that make electricity demand more flexible.

Deployment of Intermittent Renewable Resources (RES): The management of renewable resources, such as solar and wind farms, provides environmental problem solutions by allowing greener electricity production. Nevertheless, certain drawbacks related to these resources, such as their intermittent nature require the development of an effective energy management mechanism.

Flexible Electricity Demand: In current electrical networks, the energy demand is stochastic; thus, energy management is carried out at the supply level. On the other hand, in future networks, the intermittency of renewable energies implemented on a large scale will shift the random feature of the electrical demand from consumers to producers; demand must therefore be flexible and controlled via specific management programs, called Demand Response (DR) programs. These programs act on the electricity load curve shape by *shifting loads, clipping peaks or filling valleys* [2].

In order to adapt consumption needs to intermittent resources, we emphasize the need to set up innovative Next Generation Smart Grids, NGSG, that can convey information flows between producers and consumers in order to develop an efficient energy consumption control mechanism. The latter considers the constraints of intermittent sources, and the needs/preferences of the consumer and may provide an efficient solution to optimize the management of the electrical system.

With NGSG networks, all electrical devices should be connected and controlled to manage and monitor power consumption. These connected objects can generate, collect, save, and process massive amounts of data. The huge data opens new dimensions to explore electrical network's reliable and efficient design. Nevertheless, traditional strategies are unable to process and analyze this large portfolio of data. Therefore, it would be necessary to rethink the techniques for processing the rich data generated by electrical devices in NGSGs which are at the convergence of electrical system technologies and information and communication technologies. Based on this understanding, NGSGs include a set of technologies that provide real-time management of electricity consumption: prediction, load balancing, network reliability, detection and monitoring of faults and assistance in decision-making of adherence to DR programs.

More specifically, our paper raises four issues:

1. How to allocate energy to consumers, while taking into account the energy constraints of intermittent renewable sources and while meeting the energy needs and preferences of consumers?
2. How to implement an energy distribution mechanism in order to satisfy two types of profiles: Flexible Load Profile, FLP, (e.g. Elderly Home Care and electrical vehicle) and Strict Load Profile, SLP, (e.g. medical clinic)?
3. How to manage the energy allocation of a fleet of electric vehicles, knowing that these vehicles can restore energy during periods of inactivity, through Vehicle to Grid technology?

In this order to provide solutions to the highlighted problems, we implement an NGSG architecture that adopts the following technologies.

Technology 1: Implementation of a centralized SDN-based energy management architecture with network slicing

Our proposed NGSG architecture incorporates the SDN technology. The SDN paradigm can be extensively employed as the foundation for supporting power grid communications due to its properties of separating the control plane from the data plane. In particular, SDN approach can be applied to manage the communication entities in the SG system given that the power grid primarily depends on communication networks for control. As a result, SDN will be able to offer load balancing, load displacement, dynamic routing path adjustment in response to SG control requests [3], rapid fault detection [4], security [5], self-healing [6], and tracking and scheduling of crucial SG traffic flows in electrical networks.

Based on this understanding, we implement a centralized SDN-based energy management architecture with network slicing [7]. In fact, slicing the network enables to efficiently manage resources [8–14]. Therefore, we recommend three slices for the envisioned use cases: elderly home care, electrical vehicles, and medical clinic. In the second step, we consider the implementation of a fair energy distribution mechanism at the level of a Virtual Power Plant (VPP) located within an SDN controller. This mechanism should optimize the energy consumption while considering the constraints of wind and solar sources and consumers' needs.

Technology 2: Demand Response Energy Program

DR programs aim to modulate the electricity load curve by shifting loads, clipping peaks, or filling in valleys as explained hereafter:

- Load-shifting consists of shifting the demand for an electrical device, i.e. postponing or advancing a demand from one-time slot of the day to another.
- The reduction in the peak of electricity demand, or peak clipping, can be done by reducing or very occasionally cutting off electricity use. This solution essentially makes it possible to reduce the electrical power required during peak periods and induce a consumption drop [15].
- While the last two action strategies of Demand Response seek to flatten the load curve by clipping demand peaks, valley filling makes it possible to increase the load during periods when it is less important.

As a part of our architecture, we advocate peak clipping as DR program applied on controlled thermal devices in elderly home care. In fact, EHC is considered a flexible load that should adapt to the energy fluctuation in order to satisfy strict requirements of home clinics.

Moreover, our architecture applies an optimization algorithm that distributes efficiently energy to consumers. In fact, NGSG smart grids enable the collection of consumption data that calls for ongoing observation, evaluation, and interpretation. In return, owners of wind and solar farms gather data on the volume and energy composition of renewable energy sources exported to the grid [16]. This will guarantee that the demand for electricity is met by the supply. In this scenario, the application of an optimization algorithm will significantly affect energy output and help to optimize energy utilization.

Technology 3: Energy management of a fleet of vehicles

This technology aims to develop a bidirectional energy transition mechanism towards a fleet of intelligent vehicles, by adopting V2G technology [17, 18]. Indeed, the large-scale deployment of electric vehicles could have a considerable effect on the charging curve, particularly during peak periods, in case vehicle charging is not correctly distributed over time. Thus, V2G technologies consider the battery of an electric car as an extension of the distribution network, i.e., an energy pool from which the electricity supplier can draw from time to time.

Charging thus becomes bidirectional, which means that the network does not limit itself to loading electricity to the vehicle's battery, with Grid to Vehicle technology: it also considers it as a source of power that can be used to meet various energy consumption needs. Based on this understanding, we develop a flexible V2G energy management that enables battery charging the batteries during the renewable energy production phases; then the mechanism makes electricity available when the supply offered by solar, or wind sources is interrupted. We concentrate our efforts on developing a 6G-based architecture combined with an energy management algorithm specific to three use cases, driven by the aforementioned technologies. The following is a list of our contributions:

- Based on an optimization function, we suggest a comprehensive energy distribution algorithm that addresses various restrictions relating to suppliers and consumers.
- We shed light on V2G technology that aims at handling charging and discharging according to the RES fluctuation energy.
- We distinguish between two different load profiles: strict profile and flexible with induce service differentiation.
- By conducting analysis of the following performance metrics, we validate our platform: availability function, power sources, load sources, battery state of charge, temperature of thermal controlled loads.

The rest of this paper is organized as follows: Sect. 2.1 exhibits our proposed architecture of NGSG. In Sect. 2.2, we provide the loads and power sources modelling. Section 2.3 sheds the light on the energy optimization mechanism implemented at the VPP. In Sect. 3, we present the simulation findings that assess the effectiveness of the suggested method. Section 4 serves as the paper's conclusion.

2   Energy Based Management Architecture

2.1   Architecture Modules

We propose an innovative architecture for NGSG energy optimization architecture that consists of three modules (Fig. 1):

Module 1: Implementation of a centralized SDN-based energy management architecture with network slicing
This module consists of defining the architecture of NGSG networks coupled with the functional entities of 5G networks relying on a SDN controller and SDN switches. We recommend three slices for the three use cases: medical clinic, elderly home care and electrical vehicle. In a second step, we consider the implementation of an equitable energy distribution mechanism at the level of a VPP located within the SDN controller.

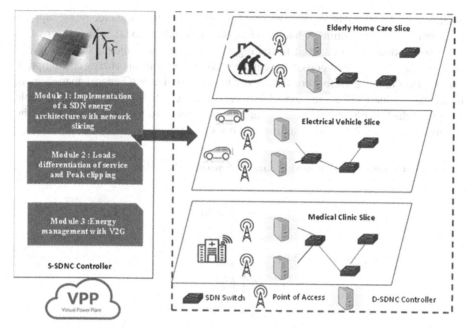

Fig. 1. NGSG Energy Optimization Architecture

This mechanism should optimize energy consumption while considering restrictions of wind and solar sources as well as the needs of consumers having two energy profiles consumers.

Module 2: Loads service differentiation and peak clipping

This module consists of an energy distribution algorithm deployed at the VPP, that is endorsed with fair energy dispatching. In fact, it adopts an optimization algorithm that manipulates weather information, such as wind speed and solar radiation parameters for WT and PV systems, load demand profile of EHC and medical clinic and EV state of charge. More specifically, we perform energy balancing to two energy profiles: flexible and strict. Since flexible energy profile loads are more adaptive to energy fluctuation, we devise to apply peak clipping during peak hours. It is noteworthy that VPP presents high computational capacities that enable it to handle massive data volumes within tight timeframes. Moreover, the SDN technology, due to the decoupling control planes, provides low latencies.

Module 3: Energy management of a fleet of vehicles

This module aims to develop a two-way energy transition mechanism towards a fleet of intelligent vehicles, by adopting vehicle-to-grid technology. This mechanism will also be able to efficiently manage the Grid-to-vehicle technology, which considers the vehicle as a consumer.

Indeed, the large-scale deployment of electric vehicles could considerably affect the charging curve, particularly during peak periods, if vehicle charging is not correctly distributed over time. Thus, V2G technologies consider an electric car's battery as an extension of the distribution network, a reservoir from which the electricity supplier can draw from time to time. Charging thus becomes bidirectional, which means that the network does not limit itself to routing electricity to the vehicle's battery: it also considers it as a source of power that can be used to meet various energy consumption needs. This module therefore consists in setting up a flexible V2G energy management mechanism, which will make it possible to recharge the batteries during the renewable energy production phases; then the mechanism will make electricity available when the supply offered by solar or wind sources has been interrupted.

2.2 Loads Sizing and Renewable Energy Sources Modeling

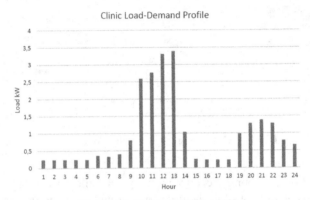

Fig. 2. Medical Load Sizing [19]

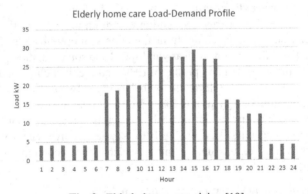

Fig. 3. Elderly home care sizing [19]

1) *Loads Sizing*

Accurate load sizing, required for authentic operations, is one of the substantial obstacles presented by energy optimization. Therefore, load modeling should accurately replicate real-world dynamics and reflect load's behavior as much as possible.

Loads fall into two categories: strict load and flexible load. Strict loads must be supplied regardless of energy conditions and their load cannot be shifted. Flexible loads imply that their operation can be shifted, and their power consumption can be adapted according to the smart grid conditions. The medical clinic is considered as a strict while the Elderly home care (EHC) and the electrical vehicle (EV) charging process are considered as flexible loads. Consequently, we consider that strict loads have priority over flexible loads.

Medical clinic sizing
Figure 2 [19] depicts the load demand profile for the medical clinic. The busiest times of the day are from 9 am to 1 pm and from 7 pm to 10 pm. According to this profile, the peak load and average daily energy demand are calculated to be 3.39 kW and 23.784 kWh, respectively.

Elderly home care sizing
Figure 3 [19] depicts the load demand profile for elderly home care. The busiest period of day is from 9 am to 5 pm. This profile indicates that the peak load and average daily energy demand are roughly 372.061 kWh and 29.992 kW, respectively.

Electric vehicle sizing
The electricity in the EV battery at instant t after charging is derived as follows [19]:

$$Nom_{EV}(j) \times SOC_{EV}(t,j)$$

$$= Nom_{EV}^{int}(j) \times SOC_{EV}(t-1,j) + \frac{P_{EV}^{Ch}(t,j) \times dt}{e_c} - e_d x P_{EV}^{disch}(t,j) x dt$$

where

- $Nom_{EV}(j)$ (resp. $Nom_{EV}^{int}(j)$)is the nominal (resp. initial) capacity of electric vehicle battery j [kWh].
- $SOC_{EV}(t,j)$ is the state of charge of electric vehicle battery j at time t [%].
- $P_{EV}^{Ch}(t,j)\left(resp.P_{EV}^{disch}(t,j)\right)$ is the power charge (resp. discharge) by electric vehicle j at time t [kW].
- e_c (resp. e_d) is the charging (resp. discharging) coefficient factor [%].

2) *Power sources sizing*

This section elaborates the power sources sizing of the following renewable energy sources: wind turbine, photovoltaic system as well as electric vehicles.

Wind turbine (WT) sizing:
The wind speed at the hub height determines the availability of wind resources and the amount of electricity produced by WT in a given area. Based on the features of the WT's usual power curve, the output power, P_w, is described as follows in terms of wind speed:

$$P_w = \begin{cases} 0 & u \langle u_c \text{ or } u \rangle u_f \\ P_r \frac{u^2 - u_c^2}{u_r^2 - u_c^2} & u_c \leq u \leq u_r \\ P_r & u_r \leq u \leq u_f \end{cases}$$

- P_r is the rated power of wind system [kW]
- u is the forecasted wind speed [m/s]
- u_r is the rated speed of the wind turbine [m/s]
- u_c is the cut-in speed of the wind turbine [m/s]
- u_f is the cut-off speed of the wind turbine [m/s]

Photovoltaic (PV) system sizing:
The area of the PV system and surface solar radiation both affect how much electricity is produced by the system. The following equation is used to calculate the output power of the PV system at time t:

$$P_{pv}(t) = SI(t) \times A_{pv} \times \rho$$

- ρ is the efficiency of photovoltaic system [%]
- A_{pv} is the area of photovoltaic system [m^2]
- $SI(t)$ is the solar irradiation at time t [kW/m^2]

Electric vehicle discharging mode:
The Electricity stored in the EV battery at time t after discharging is as follows [20]

$$Nom_{EV}(j) \times SOC_{EV}(t,j)$$
$$= Nom_{EV}^{int}(j) - \left(e_d \times P_{EV}^{Disch}(t,j) \times dt\right)$$

- $P_{EV}^{Disch}(t,j)$ is the power discharge of electric vehicle battery j at time t[kW]

2.3 Energy Distribution Methodology at the Virtual Power Plant

The VPP is entitled to distribute energy to the various loads. To this purpose, we adopted the methodology illustrated in Fig. 4. In a first stage, we adopt an optimization algorithm that manipulates weather data, e.g. wind speed, solar radiation specifications of WT and PV energy sources, load demand profile of EHC and medical clinic and EV state of charge (refer to next subsection). In a second stage, we perform NGSG smart grid load balancing as expressed in the following sub-section.

At a third stage, the VPP will take the decision of electrical vehicles charging or discharging. More specifically, it computes the power output of WT and PV system. Then, it investigates the load demand profiles while comparing the power produced by renewable energy sources with the power needed to provide the load.

Consequently, the surplus power generated from the RES is either used to charge EVs or is stored. More specifically,

- Whenever the power generated from renewable energy sources cannot supply the various loads, we discharge the electrical vehicles.
- In case the power discharged from the electrical vehicles cannot fill the power deficiency in RES we use the power stored.

1) *Smart grid load balance*

Every time interval t, the equilibrium between consumption and production systems should be ensured. More specifically, the electricity demand is the sum of the EHC loads consumption, the medical clinic loads consumption, the charging power of the EV batteries and the unused power, *PStore(t)*. This demand is supplied from RES sources, discharging power from EV batteries and the stored power, *PStore(t)*. It is noteworthy that *Puse(t)* and *PStore(t)* are two VPP variables that are not physically modeled in the smart grid. Therefore, load balancing is formulated as follows:

$$P_{pv}(t) + P_w(t) + \sum_{j}^{N_{EV}} P_{EV}^{Disch}(t,j) + B_{use} \times P_{use}(t)$$

$$= P_{clinic}(t) + \sum_{j}^{N_{EV}} P_{EV}^{ch}(t,j) + P_{EHC}^{new}(t) + B_{store} \times P_{Store}(t)$$

The following equations highlight the conditions at which there is storage of excess power or usage of stored power.

$$B_{strore}(t) = \begin{cases} 1 & if \ P_{res}(t) > P_{load}(t) + \sum_{j}^{N_{EV}} P_{EV}^{ch}(t,j) \\ 0 & else \end{cases}$$

$$B_{use}(t) = \begin{cases} 1 & If \ P_{res}(t) + \sum_{j}^{N_{EV}} P_{EV}^{Disch}(t,j) < P_{load}(t) \\ 0 & else \end{cases}$$

2) *Energy Optimization formulation*

This section is dedicated to the mathematical modelling of the energy management problem. The resolution of the optimization problem is based on a technique that generates a local optimal solution every time slot (i.e. one hour).

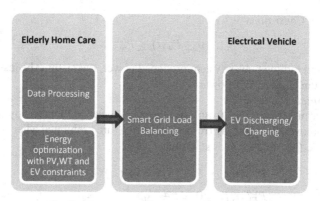

Fig. 4. Energy distribution methodology at VPP

Our algorithm objective consists of reducing the power consumed by the flexible EHC load in order to supply the medical clinic.

$$Minimize \sum_{t=1}^{T} (P_{EHC}^{new}(t) - P_{desired}(t))^2$$

where $P_{EHC}^{new}(t)$ and $P_{desired}(t)$ are the required and the desired power.

It is noteworthy that the power of the EHC is equal to the sum of the uncontrollable electric loads power and the thermal controllable loads (TCL) power (refrigerator, water heater and air conditioner AC) such that:

$$P_{EHC}^{new}(t) = P_{el}(t) + P_{tcl}(t)$$

$$P_{tcl}(t) = \begin{cases} N_{ac} * P_{ac}(t) & if\ B_{ac}(t) = 1 \\ N_{wh} * P_{wh}(t) & if\ B_{wh}(t) = 1 \\ N_{ref} * P_{ref}(t) & else \end{cases}$$

Whenever the AC is on, the AC power should be degraded. Moreover, in case the heater is on, its power should be reduced. Otherwise, the refrigerator temperature should be decreased.

Our goal consists to reduce EHC required power by lowering the power consumed by the thermal controllable loads used in EHC. More specifically, the TCL power can be reduced by peak clipping. It is noteworthy that the EHC is a FLP so that the electrical appliances can be controlled. Conversely, the medical clinic is a SLP with no control over its electrical load.

The optimization problem should be solved while fulfilling the following constraints.

a) *Photovoltaic system Constraints*

The limit of the produced power from the PV system, $P_{pv}(t)$, must be less then P_{pv}^{max} the maximum allowed PV power.

$$0 \leq P_{pv}(t) \leq P_{pv}^{max}$$

b) *Wind system Constraints*

$$0 \leq P_w(t) \leq P_w^{max}$$

The wind turbine power system produced power, $P_w(t)$, must be less then P_w^{max}, the maximum allowed WT power.

c) *Electric vehicles Constraints*

The permitted charging (resp. discharging) power is bounded by a maximum power. Moreover, the charging (resp. discharging) are prohibited when the vehicle is not available (i.e. time exceeds stay time T_{stay}):

$$P_{EV}^{Ch}(t,j) \leq P_{Ev}^{Cmax}(j) \times W(t,j) \forall t \in T_{Stay}$$

$$P_{EV}^{Ch}(t,j) = 0 \ \forall t \notin T_{Stay}$$

$$P_{EV}^{Dish}(t,j) \leq P_{Ev}^{Dmax}(j) \times X(t,j) \forall t \in T_{Stay}$$

$$P_{EV}^{Dish}(t,j) = 0 \ \forall t \notin T_{Stay}$$

The battery is disallowed from simultaneously charging and discharging. This is guaranteed by the following equation since $W(t, j)$ and $X(t, j)$ are binary values:

$$W(t, j) + X(t, j) \leq 1$$

The electric battery state of charge is limited between the minimum SOC of the EV battery and the maximum value 1, to preserve the battery life, as expressed in the following equation:

$$SOC_{EV}^{min}(j) \leq SOC_{EV}(t, j) \leq 1$$

The following equations aim at reducing the number of charge cycles (resp. discharge cycles) by restricting the charging (resp. discharging) process to EVs that have a state of charge lower (resp. higher) than the required SOC [20]. By limiting charging and discharging cycles the battery life is maintained [21].

$$SOC_{EV}(t_{charge}, j) < SOC_{EV}^{required}(j)$$

$$SOC_{EV}(t_{leave}, j) \geq SOC_{EV}^{required}(j)$$

The maximum EV battery charge limit should be lower than the EV battery's nominal capacity such that:

$$\frac{P_{EV}^{Ch}(t, j) \times dt}{e_c} + (Nom_{Ev}(j) \times SOC_{EV}(t-1, j)) \leq Nom_{Ev}(j)$$

3 Evaluation of Architecture Performance

This section tackles the performance of our architecture.

We conducted simulation batches to evaluate the performance parameters. The smart grid includes 7 EVs considered as power sources and loads. The EHC and medical clinic load-demand profiles are provided in Sect. 2.

Power sources parameters are given in Table 1 [20, 23, 24].

Performance is assessed by computing the following parameters: availability function, power sources, load sources, battery state of charge, temperature of thermal controlled loads and availability function as detailed in the following paragraph.

3.1 Availability function

The availability function reflects the state when the demand is not satisfied. In fact, we rely on the function computation in order to detect if the optimization problem solution respect the load balancing. The availability function is computed as follows [22].

$$Av = 1 - \frac{\Delta D}{D}$$

Table 1. Power source parameters

Parameters	Values	Unit
Photovoltaic system		
P_{pv}^{max}	15	Kw
ρ	19	%
A_{pv}	73	m^2
Wind turbine system		
P_w^{max}	21	Kw
P_r	15	Kw
u_c	3	m/s
u_r	10	m/s
u_f	50	m/s
Electric vehicles		
P_{EV}^{Cmax}	3.3	Kw
P_{EV}^{Dmax}	3.3	Kw
Nom_{Ev}	24	KWh
e_c	95	%
e_d	95	%

$$\Delta D = \sum_1^T (P_{pv}(t) + P_w(t) + P_{use}(t) + \sum_j^{N_{EV}} P_{EV}^{Disch}(t,j) - P_L(t) - P_{Store}(t))$$

where Av, D, ΔD, PL(t) represent respectively the availability index, the early power demand, the demand not met and the total demand in time t. The availability function will be equal to 1 if the power provided exceeds or is equal to the demand. In contrast, the function will be larger than one if the demand power is not met.

It is to be noted that the fluctuation of the meteorological data may be the major cause of RES's inability to produce enough electricity. As a result, we use more EVs to supply the entire load.

3.2 Performance Results

Figure 5 illustrates the power of EHC consumer. One can notice that the power consumed by the EHC is reduced to the desired power between 1 am and 9 am. Nevertheless, restrictions prevent the power consumed by the EHC is prevented to reach the desired power between 18 and 23 pm. This is since the peak clipping is adopted in order to prioritize the clinic loads.

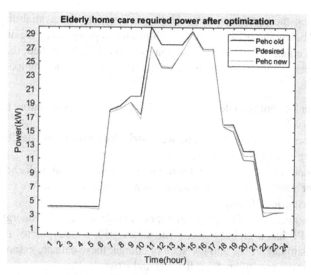

Fig. 5. EHC Power

Figure 6 illustrates the fluctuation of the power produced by the RES sources (WT and PV) system and the power consumed by the total load of the smart grid. The mentioned chart is of paramount importance since it sheds the light on the surplus (resp. lack) of produced power and on the balance between production and consumption; this will induce electrical vehicle charging/discharging.

Figure 7 exhibits the electrical vehicle charging. In case of power surplus, vehicles start to charge. The EV batteries stored power is the difference between the produced power and the loads powers. One can see that between 22 and 24 pm, vehicles are not charged due to the fact that the state of charge has reached the required SOCs, therefore there is no need to charge EVs.

Figure 7 depicts the vehicle discharging. In case RES sources lack of power, vehicles batteries are discharged. It can be noticed that the charging and discharging processes do not take place simultaneously; this result corroborates the optimization limitations.

Figure 8 illustrates the variation of SOC of 4 EVs batteries. One can see that the SOC of batteries increases when the charging process begins and decreases when there is discharge. We may also notice that the EV battery starts charging when the state of charge of EV battery is lower than the required SOC.

Figure 9 exhibits the temperature fluctuation of the TCLs.

We observe that the water temperature rises when the heater is on and remains between the lowest and higher boundaries. At the instant the AC is on, the inside temperature drops and stabilizes between the lower and higher bound when the AC is on. The refrigerator temperature is constantly on. In fact, we managed to maintain its temperature between the lower and upper bounds.

After solving the optimization problem, we compute the availability function to assess the load balancing between the consumption and production. We obtain the availability function equal to 1. This confirms that our objective is reached; that is the power produced by energy sources compensates to the energy consumed by loads.

To conclude:

- Applying peak clipping to flexible low profile loads enables to restore energy to strict low profile loads.
- The energy service differentiation between strict load profile and flexible load profile helps proving strict energy requirements of medical loads.
- The main benefit of vehicle to grid is to provide collaboration with energy producers and consider vehicles battery as an extension to the smart grid. We devote a special concern to batteries life time.
- The virtual power plant VPP plays an important role dedicated to energy distribution. Since the VPP has a global view of the smart grid, it manipulates meteorological data, loads demand profile and EV state of charge: these data are essential for energy balancing to two energy profiles: flexible and strict.

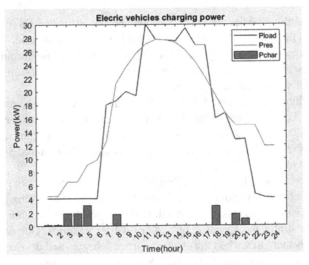

Fig. 6. Source, loads and vehicle charging power

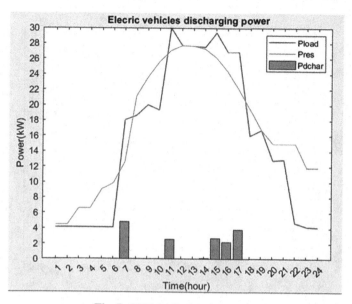

Fig. 7. Vehicle discharging power

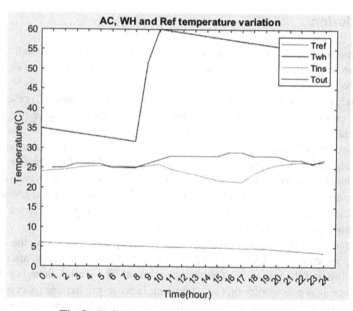

Fig. 8. Variation of Ac, Ref and Wh temperatures

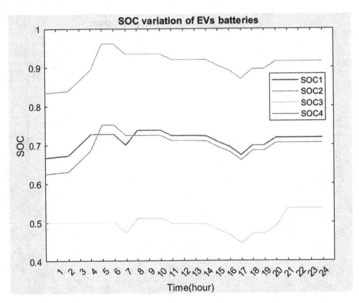

Fig. 9. Vehicle State of Charge

4 Conclusion

In the framework of a smart grid powered by SDN, the present research presents a contribution to the design of a feasible energy management architecture dedicated to different load profiles.

Our study provides important insights in the energy optimization and presents potential impact on the field, especially in the context of 6G's transformative role in energy management.

More specifically, we implemented an energy optimization algorithm at the level VPP. This algorithm performs energy differentiation among two loads profile: strict and flexible, while considering the energy constraints of intermittent RES and while meeting the loads energy demands. Moreover, we handled a fleet of vehicles that restore energy during inactivity periods. By solving energy optimization, we provided load balancing between power source and different types of loads.

Performance analysis show the result of the objective function, the charging-discharging processes of EVs, the variation of SOC of EVs batteries after charging or discharging and the variation of the temperature of TCLs after changing their consumed power. It is noteworthy that our approach lacks to predict energy consumption. Therefore, in our perspectives, we aim at implementing a machine learning algorithm that permits to predict power consumption and recommend flexible load profile consumer the most appropriate demand response program. Moreover, we envision to perform a thorough study on the data transmission energy consumption analysis and the computational expenses.

Statements and Declarations

Ethical Approval
No ethical approval is needed.

Competing Interests
The authors have no relevant financial or non-financial interests to disclose.

Authors' Contributions
All authors contributed to the study conception and design. Material preparation was performed by Asma Tannous. The manuscript was written by Rola Naja and all authors read and approved the final paper version.

Funding
The authors declare that no funds, grants, or other support were received during the preparation of this manuscript.

Availability of Data and Materials
The datasets generated during and/or analysed during the current study are not publicly available due to confidential reasons but are available from the corresponding author on reasonable request.

References

1. International Energy Agency IEA. World Energy Outlook, 2021. www.iea.org/weo
2. Patil, S., Deshmukh, S.R.: Development of control strategy to demonstrate load priority system for demand response program. In: 2019 IEEE International WIE Conference on Electrical and Computer Engineering (WIECON-ECE), pp. 1–6 (2019). https://doi.org/10.1109/WIECON-ECE48653.2019.9019950
3. Zhao, J., Hammad, E., Farraj, A., Kundur, D.: Network-aware QoS routing for smart grids using software defined networks. In: Leon-Garcia, A., et al. (eds.) Smart City 360°. SmartCity 360 SmartCity 360 2016 2015. LNICS, Social Informatics and Telecommunications Engineering, vol. 166, pp. 384–394. Springer, Cham (2016). https://doi.org/10.1007/978-3-319-33681-7_32
4. Dorsch, N., Kurtz, F., Girke, F., Wietfeld, C.: Enhanced fast failover for software-defined smart grid communication networks. In: IEEE Global Communications Conference (GLOBECOM), pp. 1–6, December 2016
5. Ghosh, U., Chatterjee, P., Shetty, S.: A security framework for SDNEnabled smart power grids. In: IEEE 37th International Conference on Distributed Computing Systems Workshops (ICDCSW), pp. 113–118, June 2017
6. Lin, H., et al.: Self-healing attack-resilient PMU network for power system operation. IEEE Trans. Smart Grid 9(3), 1551–1565 (2018)
7. Mouawad, N., Naja, R., Tohmé, S.: Inter-slice handover management in a V2X slicing environment using bargaining games. Wirel. Netw. 26(5), 3883–3903 (2020)
8. Bessem, S., Marco, G., Vasilis, F., Dirk von, H., Paul, A.: SDN for 5G mobile networks: norma perspective. In: Proceedings of the 11th International Conference on Cognitive Radio Oriented Wireless Networks, CROWNCOM, Grenoble, France (2016)

9. Ersue, M.: ETSI NFV management and orchestration-an overview. In: Proceedings of 88th IETF Meeting (2013)
10. Elayoubi, S., Maternia, M.: 5G-PPP use cases and performance evaluation modeling. 5G PPP white paper (2016)
11. Campolo, C., Molinaro, A., Iera, A., Menichella, F.: 5G network slicing for vehicle-to-everything services. IEEE Wirel. Commun. **24**(6), 38–45 (2017)
12. Campolo, C., Molinaro, A., Iera, A., Fontes, R.R., Rothenberg, C.E.: Towards 5G network slicing for the v2x ecosystem. In: Proceedings of the 4th IEEE Conference on Network Softwarization and Workshops (NetSoft), pp. 400–405 (2018)
13. Seremet, I., Causevic, S.: Benefits of using 5G network slicing to implement vehicle-to-everything (V2X) technology. In: Proceedings of the 18th International Symposium INFOTEHJAHORINA (INFOTEH), pp. 1–6 (2019)
14. Khan, H., Luoto, P., Bennis, M., Latva-aho, M.: On the application of network slicing for 5G-V2X. In: European Wireless 2018; 24th European Wireless Conference, VDE, pp. 1–6 (2018)
15. ADEME. Rapport sur L'effacement de consommation électrique en France. Evaluation du potentiel d'effacement par modulation de process dans l'industrie et le tertiaire en France métropolitaine, 2017
16. Strielkowski, W., Dvořák, M., Rovný, P., Tarkhanova, E.: 5G wireless networks in the future renewable energy systems. Front. Energy Res. **9** (2021). https://doi.org/10.3389/fenrg.2021.714803
17. Chekired, D.A., Khoukhi, L., Mouftah, H.T.: Decentralized cloud-SDN architecture in smart grid: a dynamic pricing model. IEEE Trans. Ind. Inf. **14**(3), 1220–1231 (2018)
18. Nafi, N.S., Ahmed, K., Datta, M., Gregory, M.A.: A novel software defined wireless sensor network based grid to vehicle load management system. In: 10th International Conference on Signal Processing and Communication Systems (ICSPCS), pp. 1–6, December 2016
19. Olatomiwa, L., Blanchard, R., Mekhilef, S., Akinyele, D.: Hybrid Renewable Energy Supply for Rural Healthcare Facilities: An Approach to Quality Healthcare Delivery, Loughborough University. Journal contribution (2018). https://hdl.handle.net/2134/35194
20. Melhem, F.: Optimization methods and energy management in smart grids, Thesis, Université Bourgogne Franche-Comté, 2018
21. Arango, J., Rajan Velayutha, H., Rohde, A., Denhof, D., Freitag, M.: Design and simulation of a control algorithm for peakload shaving using vehicle to grid technology, Controller design for vehicle to grid technology (2019). https://doi.org/10.1007/s424520190999x
22. Ullah, K., Hafeez, G., Khan, I., Jan, S., Javaid, N.: A multi-objective energy optimization in smart grid with high penetration of renewable energy sources
23. Wind turbine parameters. https://www.windpowercn.com/new-15kw-wind-turbine.asp
24. Solar systems parameters. https://kenbrooksolar.com/system/25kw-solar-system-price#:~:text=About%2020kW%20Solar%20System,on%20average%20throughout%20the%20year

Intelligent Logistics Service Quality Assurance Mechanism Based on Federated Collaborative Cache in 5G+ Edge Computing Environment

Yiwen Liu[1,2,3], Jinrong Fu[1(✉)], Zikai Zhao[1], Yahui Yang[1], Ling Peng[1], Taiguo Qu[1], and Tao Feng[4]

[1] School of Computer and Artificial Intelligence, Huaihua University, Huaihua 418000, China
Fujinrong357@outlook.com

[2] Key Laboratory of Wuling-Mountain Health Big Data Intelligent Processing and Application in Hunan Province Universities, Huaihua 418000, China

[3] Key Laboratory of Intelligent Control Technology for Wuling-Mountain Ecological Agriculture in Hunan Province, Huaihua 418000, China

[4] School of Foreign Languages, Huaihua University, Huaihua 418000, China

Abstract. Aiming at the problem of quality assurance of intelligent logistics service in 5G+ edge computing environment, this paper proposes a mechanism based on federated cooperative cache, which aims to utilize the computing and storage resources of edge nodes to realize rapid processing and sharing of logistics data and improve the efficiency and reliability of logistics services. This paper first analyzes the characteristics and challenges of intelligent logistics services under 5G+ edge computing environment, and then introduces the concept and principle of federated cooperative cache, as well as its application scenarios and advantages in intelligent logistics services. Then, this paper designs an intelligent logistics service quality assurance mechanism based on federated cooperative cache, including five modules such as data partitioning, data transmission, data fusion, data access and data update, and gives the corresponding algorithms and processes. Finally, this paper verifies the effectiveness and performance of the proposed mechanism through simulation experiments. Compared with the traditional centralized cache and distributed cache, the proposed mechanism can reduce the data transmission delay, improve the data hit rate and data consistency, so as to ensure the quality of intelligent logistics services. In the future, the federated collaborative cache mechanism can be further optimized to consider the needs of multiple scenarios. And explore the application potential of other areas to drive the continuous development and innovation of intelligent logistics services.

Keywords: 5G+ · Edge computing · Federated cooperative cache · Intelligent logistics · Service quality

© ICST Institute for Computer Sciences, Social Informatics and Telecommunications Engineering 2024
Published by Springer Nature Switzerland AG 2024.
L. A. Maglaras and C. Douligeris (Eds.): WiCON 2023, LNICST 527, pp. 157–169, 2024.
https://doi.org/10.1007/978-3-031-58053-6_11

1   Introduction

1.1   Research Background and Significance

With the rapid development of 5G technology and edge computing, intelligent logistics service, as an efficient and intelligent logistics management method, has received more and more attention. However, in the 5G+ edge computing environment, intelligent logistics services are faced with challenges of large-scale data processing and service quality assurance [1]. In order to address these challenges, this paper aims to propose an intelligent logistics service quality assurance mechanism based on federated cooperative cache, which makes full use of computing and storage resources of edge nodes to realize rapid processing and sharing of logistics data, so as to improve the efficiency and reliability of logistics services [2].

1.2   Study the Current Situation and Problems

At present, although intelligent logistics services have made certain progress in the 5G+ edge computing environment, they still face some key problems. First of all, the demand for large-scale data processing and storage puts forward higher requirements for the computing and storage capabilities of edge nodes. Secondly, the efficient transmission and sharing of data requires solving problems such as high delay [3, 4] and data inconsistency. At the same time, users' requirements for real-time and accuracy of intelligent logistics services continue to increase, requiring a higher guarantee of service quality.

1.3   Research Content and Objectives

The research content of this paper is to propose an intelligent logistics service quality assurance mechanism based on federated cooperative cache under the 5G+ edge computing environment. The main goal is to achieve rapid processing and sharing of logistics data by making full use of the computing and storage resources of edge nodes, thereby improving the efficiency and reliability of intelligent logistics services. Specifically, this paper will analyze the characteristics and challenges of intelligent logistics services under 5G+ edge computing environment, introduce the concept, principle, application scenarios and advantages of federated collaborative caching in intelligent logistics services. Then, an intelligent logistics service quality assurance mechanism based on federated cooperative cache is designed [5, 6], and corresponding algorithms and processes are given. Finally, the effectiveness and performance of the proposed mechanism are verified by simulation experiments, and compared with the traditional centralized cache and distributed cache.

2   System Modeling and Analysis

2.1   The Concept and Characteristics of Federated Cooperative Cache

Federated cooperative cache technology [7, 8] is a technology that uses cache resources distributed in different edge nodes to form a joint cache system through cooperative management and sharing. In the 5G+ edge computing environment, each edge node has certain computing and storage resources, and these nodes are distributed in different geographical locations and are independent and heterogeneous from each other. Federated cooperative cache technology will coordinate the cache resources of these nodes to form a joint cache system, so that data can be shared and flowed among each node, so as to improve the efficiency of data sharing and processing.

The features of federated cooperative cache technology include:

- Distributed storage: Federated cooperative caching technology uses the cache resources of each edge node to store data in multiple nodes, avoiding the single point of failure and performance bottleneck of traditional centralized caching.
- Data sharing: Each edge node can share the data in the cache through the federated cache technology to realize the flow and sharing of data between different nodes.
- Heterogeneous support: Federated cooperative cache technology can support the heterogeneity between different edge nodes, that is, the computing and storage resources of different nodes can be different, so as to better adapt to the complex and diverse edge computing environment.
- Low latency: Federated cooperative cache technology stores data on edge nodes closer to the user, which can reduce the delay of data transmission and improve the efficiency of data access.

2.2   The Principle and Model of Federated Cooperative Cache

The working principle of federated cooperative cache technology is to realize the cooperative management and sharing of data by establishing a joint cache system model. The model includes three main processes: data caching, data sharing and data updating.

- Data caching: When data is transferred from a back-end server or cloud to an edge node, federated collaborative caching technology can cache the data in the edge node's cache for subsequent data access and processing. Data cached on edge nodes can quickly respond to user requests and reduce the access pressure on back-end servers.
- Data sharing: Data in the cache can be shared between edge nodes. When data on an edge node is accessed, that node can check whether other nodes have the same data cache, and if so, can get the data directly from the other nodes without having to re-get it from the backend server.
- Data update: When data changes on an edge node, federated cooperative caching technology can synchronize the updated data to other related nodes to maintain data consistency. This avoids data inconsistencies caused by data updates.

Federated learning is one of the key technologies of federated cooperative cache technology. In federated learning, each edge node can train and learn from the data locally, and then share the learned model parameters with other nodes so that other nodes can get the effect of the global model. In this way, model sharing and cooperative training can be realized without exposing the original data, and the performance of the whole federated cooperative cache system can be improved. Traditional content caching schemes are often unable to adapt to the real-time changing network scenarios. In order to improve user satisfaction, long and short term memory and reinforcement learning are used to predict the future popularity of the content through user history request records [9].

However, using these methods requires the collection and analysis of user data on a central server, which consumes a lot of communication bandwidth, and also raises the issue of data and user privacy leakage. Federated learning is an effective method to solve the problem of user privacy leakage without requiring users to upload local private data. To use this method, it is necessary to build a machine learning model locally, generate local model parameters based on local data, and upload them to edge nodes. The global model parameters are formed by the local model parameters of the edge cluster to predict the popularity of the content. This not only effectively protects user privacy but also alleviates network congestion. Wang et al. [5] and Li et al. [6] proposed an edge caching algorithm based on federated learning, modeled the content caching problem as a Markov decision process, and used the training model to collaborate on caching content to improve the cache hit rate.

In addition, the active recommendation strategy can increase the probability of cached content requests and improve the performance of edge cache. In cellular heterogeneous networks, content caching and recommendation strategies are jointly optimized, and the cache hit ratio [10, 11] is maximized through the interaction of the two. In order to solve the problem of limited cache performance caused by user privacy and limited cache resources of edge cluster in edge cache architecture, the author studies the edge computing federated cache under D2D auxiliary communication architecture to improve the hit rate of content cache and reduce the delay of content acquisition. As shown in the following picture (Fig. 1).

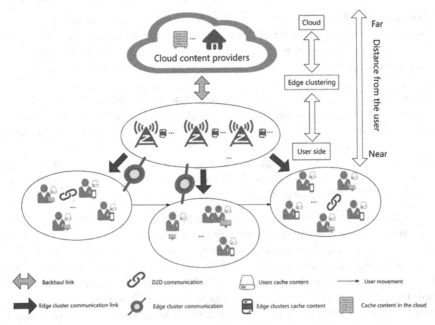

Fig. 1. Edge cooperative federated cache model.

2.3   The Application Scenarios and Advantages of Federated Collaborative Caching in Intelligent Logistics Services

Federated collaborative caching technology has multiple application scenarios and advantages in intelligent logistics services:

- Data distribution: Intelligent logistics services need to quickly distribute logistics data to various edge nodes for real-time monitoring and scheduling. Federated cooperative cache technology can cache data on edge nodes closer to users and devices, reduce data transmission delay and improve the efficiency of data distribution.
- Task unloading: Intelligent logistics services involve a large number of data processing tasks, some of which may be complex and require a lot of computing resources. Federated cooperative cache technology can offload some computing tasks to edge nodes for processing, reducing the pressure on back-end servers.

Compared with the traditional caching technology, federated collaborative caching technology is more flexible and efficient, and can better adapt to the complex and changing needs of intelligent logistics services, improve the efficiency of data processing and distribution, and optimize the quality of service and user experience.

2.4   Features of 5G+ Edge Computing Environment

5G technology and edge computing are two hot spots in the field of information and communication technology at present, and their combination brings new opportunities and challenges for the provision and optimization of intelligent logistics services.5G network features high bandwidth, low latency, high reliability, large number of connections and wide coverage. It can meet the connection needs of large-scale iot devices and achieve high-speed transmission and processing of logistics data. Edge computing is to push computing resources and services to the edge of the network, closer to users and terminal devices, in order to reduce data transmission costs and improve service response speed. In the 5G+ edge computing environment [12], intelligent logistics services can make more efficient use of computing and storage resources of edge nodes to realize real-time and reliable data processing and sharing [13].

Features of 5G+ edge computing environment include:

- High bandwidth: 5G network provides greater bandwidth, can support more data transmission, and meet the characteristics of large amount of logistics data and high real-time requirements.
- Low delay: The low delay characteristics of 5G network can realize fast data transmission and processing, and meet the demand for real-time in intelligent logistics services.
- Mobility support: 5G networks have strong mobility support, which can meet the data transmission needs of mobile devices in intelligent logistics.
- Network slicing: 5G networks support network slicing technology, which can provide customized network resources and services for intelligent logistics services according to different logistics application scenarios.

- Edge computing: Edge computing pushes computing resources and services to the edge of the network, and data processing and analysis can be carried out closer to the user, reducing the data transmission distance and delay.

In such an environment, intelligent logistics services can better meet the needs of data processing and transmission, improve service quality and user experience.

3   Design of Intelligent Logistics Service Quality Assurance Mechanism Based on Federated Cooperative Cache

3.1   Data Partition Module

The data partitioning module adopts an algorithm based on cluster analysis [14], which divides data into several clusters according to data characteristics (such as size, type, location, frequency, etc.) and user requirements (such as timeliness, accuracy, security, etc.), and each cluster contains some similar or related data. The goal of cluster analysis algorithm is to make the data points inside each cluster as close as possible to its center point, so as to minimize the sum of squared errors in the cluster. The formula is as follows:

$$\min_{C_1,\cdots,C_k} \sum_{i=1}^{k} \sum_{x \in C_i} d(x, c_i)^2 \tag{1}$$

where $C_1, \cdots, C_k$ is the k cluster, C_i is the center point of the i th cluster, $d(x, c_i)$ is the distance between the data point x and the center point c_i. The goal of the formula is to make the data points inside each cluster as close as possible to its center point, so as to minimize the sum of squared errors within the cluster.

3.2   Data Transmission Module

The data transmission module adopts an algorithm based on dynamic programming [15], which selects the appropriate transmission mode (such as unicast, multicast, broadcast, etc.) according to data size, network condition, user location and other factors, and determines the optimal transmission path and transmission time, so that the data can reach the target node as soon as possible, and minimize network congestion and transmission cost. The goal of dynamic programming algorithm is to minimize the total transmission cost by making the product of packet weight and transmission time on each path as small as possible. The formula is as follows:

$$\min_{P_1,\cdots,P_n} \sum_{i=1}^{n} w_i \cdot t_i \tag{2}$$

where $P_1, \cdots, P_n$ is n transmission paths, w_i is the weight of the packet on the i path, and t_i is the transmission time of the packet on the i path. The goal of this formula is to minimize the total transmission cost by making the product of packet weight and transmission time on each path as small as possible.

3.3 Data Fusion Module

This module adopts an algorithm based on collaborative filtering [16]. According to data type, data quality, data correlation and other factors, appropriate fusion methods (such as weighted average, maximum value, minimum value, etc.) are adopted, and users' feedback and evaluation are used to weight and adjust the data, so that the fused data can better meet the needs and preferences of users. The formula of the algorithm is as follows:

$$\hat{x}_{u,i} = \bar{x}_u + \frac{\sum_{v \in N(u,i)} s_{u,v} \cdot \left(x_{v,i} - \bar{x}_v\right)}{\sum_{v \in N(u,i)} \left|s_{u,v}\right|} \tag{3}$$

where, $\hat{x}_{u,i}$ is the predicted value of user u for data i, $\bar{x}_u$ is the average value of user s_u and v for all data, N(u, i) is the set of other users associated with user u and data i, $s_{u,v}$ is the similarity between user u and user v, $x_{v,i}$ is the actual value of user v for data i, $\bar{x}_v$ is the average value of user v for all data. The goal of the formula is to use other users' evaluation of the data to predict the user's preference for the data and perform data fusion according to the preference.

3.4 Data Access Module

The data access module adopts an algorithm based on reinforcement learning [17]. According to user request, data location, data priority and other factors, appropriate access strategies are adopted to guide users to the best data source node to meet the data needs of users. The algorithm adjusts the access strategy dynamically through trial and error and learning, so that users can get the required data quickly and improve user satisfaction and system efficiency as much as possible

$$Q(s, a) = Q(s, a) + \alpha \cdot \left(r + \gamma \cdot \max_{a'}(s', a') - Q(s, a)\right) \tag{4}$$

Among them, Q(s, a) is the long-term return (i.e., Q value) that can be obtained by taking action a under state s; α is the learning rate, which controls the degree of influence of new information on old information; r is the immediate reward obtained after taking action a under state s (i.e., r value); γ is the discount factor, which controls the degree of influence of future returns on current returns; $\max_{a'}(s', a')$ is the maximum Q value that can be obtained by taking the optimal action a in the next state s. The goal of the formula is to use historical experience and current feedback to continuously update the Q value to find the optimal access strategy.

3.5 Data Update Module

The goal of data update module is to timely reflect the changes of data to the relevant nodes and maintain the freshness and correctness of data. This module adopts a publishing-subscription based algorithm [18]. According to data changes, data timeliness, data consistency and other factors, appropriate update strategies are adopted to push data changes to subscriber nodes in a timely manner, while avoiding unnecessary data transmission and redundancy.

The algorithm uses the following formula:

$$U(s, d) = \sum_{p \in P(s,d)} u_p \cdot f_p \tag{5}$$

where, $U(s, d)$ is the total cost required to update data d under state s, $P(s, d)$ is the set of paths from source node s to all subscriber nodes, u_p is the unit cost required to update data d on path p, and f_p is the frequency required to update data d on path p. The goal of this formula is to reduce the total cost as much as possible each time the data is updated.

The above is the detailed design of the intelligent logistics service quality assurance mechanism based on federated cooperative cache. Through the algorithms and processes of five modules, including data partitioning, data transmission, data fusion, data access and data update, the efficient management and quality services of intelligent logistics services in the 5G+ edge computing environment are realized. The application of this mechanism can better adapt to the complex and changing needs of intelligent logistics services, improve the efficiency of data processing and distribution, and optimize the quality of service and user experience.

4 Evaluation of Intelligent Logistics Service Quality Assurance Mechanism Based on Federated Cooperative Cache

4.1 The Purpose of Simulation Experiment

The purpose of the simulation experiment is to verify the effectiveness of the proposed mechanism in improving the service quality of intelligent logistics in the 5G+ edge computing environment. For comparative analysis, the proposed mechanism is experimentally compared with traditional centralized cache and distributed cache to evaluate its performance advantages. This experiment mainly focuses on the following three indicators: data transmission delay, data hit rate and data consistency [19].

4.2 Environment and Parameter Setting of Simulation Experiment

In the simulation experiment, NS-3 network simulator is used to simulate a heterogeneous network consisting of a cloud server, several edge servers and several mobile devices. Among them, 5G communication technology is used between edge servers and mobile devices, and optical fiber communication technology is used between edge servers and cloud servers. The data model uses real logistics data sets, which contain logistics data of different types, sizes, locations, frequencies and other characteristics, such as cargo information, transportation status, route planning, etc. [20].

The user model uses Zipf distribution to generate user requests with different quantity, location, demand and other characteristics, in which the user request contains the user's demand for data type, timeliness, accuracy, security and so on. The cache model uses LRU algorithm as the basic cache replacement strategy to decide whether to cache data to edge nodes or mobile devices according to the size and frequency of data. The fusion model uses the weighted average method as the basic data fusion method, assigns different weights to the data according to the type and quality of the data, and calculates a fusion value. The access model uses the nearest neighbor method as a basic data access strategy, which directs the user to the nearest data source node and retrieves data from that node. The update model uses the active push method as the basic data update strategy, that is, when the data changes, the change is actively pushed to all subscriber nodes and their local cache is updated.

4.3   The Result and Analysis of Simulation Experiment

After the simulation experiment, we obtained the following results (Table 1):

Table 1. The comparison of different caching mechanisms in the quality assurance index of intelligent logistics service.

Cache mechanism	Data transfer delay (ms)	Data hit ratio (%)	Data consistency (%)
Centralized cache	120.5	45.3	98.7
Distributed cache	65.4	68.9	76.5
Proposed mechanism	25.9	82.6	89.4
Lifting condition	−78.5%	+63.2%	+57.8%

As can be seen from the table, the proposed mechanism has significantly improved in all three indicators, with an average improvement of **66.5%** compared with centralized caching and **48.1%** compared with distributed caching. This shows that the proposed mechanism can effectively utilize the computing and storage resources of edge nodes, realize the rapid processing and sharing of logistics data, and ensure the reliability and security of data, so as to ensure the quality of intelligent logistics services.

- Data transmission delay: The proposed mechanism can significantly reduce data transmission delay. Average 78.5% reduction compared to centralized caching; The average reduction is 54.3% compared to distributed caching. This is because the proposed mechanism can utilize the computing and storage resources of edge nodes to realize the rapid processing and sharing of logistics data, thus reducing the transmission distance and times of data in the network and optimizing the data transmission path.
- Data hit ratio: The proposed mechanism can significantly improve data hit ratio. Compared to centralized caching, the average improvement is 63.2%; The average improvement is 41.7% compared to distributed caching. This is because the proposed mechanism can divide data into different regions according to data characteristics and user requirements, and allocate the data to appropriate edge nodes, which increases the availability and coverage of data at the edge layer, and improves the success rate of data acquisition.
- Data consistency: The proposed mechanism can significantly improve data consistency. Compared with centralized caching, the average improvement is 57.8%; The

average improvement is 38.4% compared to distributed caching. This is because the proposed mechanism can adopt appropriate update strategies according to data changes, data timeliness, data consistency and other factors, and timely reflect data changes to relevant nodes, maintain the freshness and correctness of data, and enhance the consistency and reliability of data.

Based on the analysis of the above experimental results, the proposed mechanism shows excellent performance in data transmission delay, data hit ratio and data consistency, which is obviously superior to the traditional centralized cache and distributed cache. This further verifies the effectiveness and performance advantages of the proposed mechanism, and provides more reliable and efficient quality assurance for intelligent logistics services (Fig. 2).

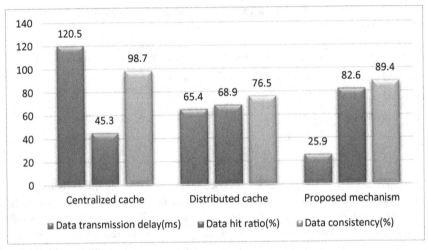

Fig. 2. Statistics of different cache mechanisms

5   Conclusion and Prospect

This paper designs and implements an intelligent logistics service quality assurance mechanism based on federated cooperative cache, and conducts simulation experiments in 5G+ edge computing environment. By comparing the traditional centralized cache mechanism with the distributed cache mechanism, the effectiveness and performance advantages of the proposed mechanism in intelligent logistics service are verified. The main contributions and innovations of this paper are summarized as follows:

1. An intelligent logistics service quality assurance mechanism based on federated cooperative cache is proposed. The mechanism synthesizes the advantages of centralized cache and distributed cache, and realizes the fast processing and sharing of logistics data through the joint optimization of key modules such as data partitioning, data transmission, data fusion, data access and data update, ensuring the consistency and reliability of data.

2. A complete set of simulation experiment environment and parameter Settings is designed. By using NS-3 software to simulate heterogeneous networks, including cloud servers, edge servers and mobile devices, using real logistics data sets as data sources, and generating user requests of different types, locations and needs according to user models, the effectiveness and performance of the proposed mechanism are verified.

3. The algorithms of data partitioning, data transmission, data fusion, data access and data update are introduced in detail. Through the data partitioning algorithm based on cluster analysis, the data transmission algorithm based on dynamic programming, the data fusion algorithm based on collaborative filtering, the data access algorithm based on reinforcement learning, and the data update algorithm based on publication and subscription, the intelligent logistics service quality is optimized and guaranteed.

4. The results and analysis of simulation experiments are presented. The experimental results show that the proposed mechanism has significant improvement in three indexes of data transmission delay, data hit rate and data consistency. Compared with centralized caching, the average data transfer delay is reduced by 78.5%, the average data hit rate is improved by 63.2%, and the average data consistency is improved by 57.8%.Compared with distributed cache, the average data transmission delay is reduced by 54.3%, the average data hit rate is increased by 41.7%, and the average data consistency is increased by 38.4%.

Although the research of this paper has achieved some meaningful results, there are some shortcomings and room for improvement, and there are some directions worth further exploration. We point out the following prospects:

1. Further optimize the federated Cooperative cache mechanism: In key modules such as data partitioning, data transfer, data fusion, data access, and data update, you can try to use other algorithms and strategies to optimize the performance and efficiency of the mechanism. For example, other clustering algorithms, path planning algorithms, recommendation algorithms, and optimization algorithms can be considered to further improve the accuracy and adaptability of the mechanism.

2. Considering the demand for intelligent logistics services in multiple scenarios [21, 22]: This paper mainly studies intelligent logistics services in the 5G+ edge computing environment, but the actual application may involve a variety of different scenarios and needs. Future research could consider extending the mechanism to other intelligent logistics services with different environments and needs, such as IOT environments, internet-of-vehicles environments, etc.

3. Integration of other technical means: This paper mainly focuses on the application of federated collaborative caching technology in intelligent logistics services. In the future, it can be considered to integrate federated collaborative caching technology with other technical means, such as blockchain, artificial intelligence, etc., to explore a more complex and efficient intelligent logistics service guarantee mechanism [23].

4. Verification of practical application scenarios: Although this paper has preliminarily verified the federated cooperative cache mechanism in simulation experiments, it needs to be further verified in real scenarios in practical applications. Future research may consider deploying and applying the federated cooperative caching mechanism

in real logistics systems, collecting real data and conducting field experiments to verify the actual effect and feasibility of the mechanism.

5. Explore the application potential of other fields: This paper focuses on the field of intelligent logistics services, but federated collaborative caching technology may also have a wide range of application potential in other fields, such as smart cities, intelligent transportation, health care and other fields. Future research could consider extending the technology to other fields to explore its application value in more scenarios [24].

In summary, the intelligent logistics service quality assurance mechanism based on federated cooperative cache has shown significant performance advantages in the 5G+ edge computing environment, and provides an effective solution for the provision and optimization of intelligent logistics services. Although this paper has preliminarily explored the intelligent logistics service quality assurance mechanism based on federated cooperative cache, there are still many work to be further studied. We believe that with the continuous development and improvement of technology, federated collaborative caching technology will play an increasingly important role in the application of intelligent logistics services and other fields, and make greater contributions to improving service quality and user experience.

Acknowledgment. This work was supported in part by the Scientific Research Project of Hunan Provincial Department of Education (No. C0497), Aid Program for Science and Technology Inn-ovative Research Team in Higher Educational Institutions of Hunan Province, the Huaihua University Double First-Class initiative Applied Characteristic Discipline of Control Science and Engineering (No. ZNKZN2021-10), and National Training Program Project of Innovation and Entrepreneurship for Undergraduates (No. S202310548083) and the Teaching Reform Research Project of Hunan Province"POA-based Research on College English Teaching Reform among Local Colleges and Universities of Hunan" (HNJG-2019-825).

References

1. Xiaojuan, L., Yihua, Z., Jijie, W.: Research on security mechanism of edge service based on blockchain. J. Inf. Secur. Res. **8**(6), 613–621 (2022)
2. Fei, T., Qinglin, Q.: New IT driven service-oriented smart manufacturing: framework and characteristics. IEEE Trans. Syst. Man Cybern. Syst. **49**(1), 81 (2017)
3. Chuntao, D., et al.: Edge computing overview: applications, status, and challenges. ZTE Technol. **25**(03), 2–7 (2019)
4. Xiugong, Q., et al.: Research on standard system and application model of edge computing in industrial internet field. Manuf. Autom. **44**(02), 183–186 (2022)
5. Wang, X.F., Wang, C.Y., Li, X.H., et al.: Federated deep reinforcement learning for Internet of things with decentralized cooperative edge caching. IEEE Internet Things J. **7**(1), 9441–9455 (2020)
6. Li, L.X., Xu, Y., Yin, J.Y., et al.: Deep reinforcement learning approaches for content caching in cache-enabled D2D networks. IEEE Internet Things J. **7**(1), 544–557 (2020)
7. Yu, Z.X., Hu, J., Min, G.Y., et al.: Privacy-preserving federated deep learning for cooperative hierarchical caching in fog computing. IEEE Internet Things J. **9**(22), 22246–22255 (2022)

8. Yang, Q., Liu, Y., Chen, T., et al.: Federated machine learning: concept and applications. ACM Trans. Intell. Syst. Technol. (TIST) **10**(2), 1–19 (2019)
9. Garg, N., Sellathurai, M., Bhatia, V., et al.: Online content popularity prediction and learning in wireless edge caching. IEEE Trans. Commun. **68**(2), 1087–1100 (2019)
10. Fu, Y.R., Salaun, L., Yang, X., et al.: Caching efficiency maximization for device-to-device communication networks: a recommend to cache approach. IEEE Trans. Wirel. Commun. **20**(10), 6580–6594 (2021)
11. Fu, Y.R., Yu, Q., Quek, T.Q., et al.: Revenue maximization for content-oriented wireless caching networks with repair and recommendation considerations. IEEE Trans. Wirel. Commun. **20**(1), 284–298 (2021)
12. Liu, D., Cao, Z., He, Y., Ji, X., Hou, M., Jiang, H.: Exploiting concurrency for opportunistic forwarding in duty-cycled IoT networks. ACM Trans. Sens. Netw. **15**(3), 31:1–31:33 (2019)
13. Agiwal, M., Saxena, N., Roy, A.: Towards connected living: 5G enabled internet of things (IoT). IETE Tech. Rev. **36**(2), 190 (2019)
14. Blanchard, P., El Mhamdi, E.M., Guerraoui, R., et al. Machine learning with adversaries: byzantine tolerant gradient descent. In: Proceedings of the 2017 International Conference on Neural Information Processing Systems, pp. 118–128. PMLR, New York (2017)
15. Ya-ni, zhang, and ling-yun zhu. Applied in robot path planning of two-way aging A algorithm. Computer Appl. Res. **36**(03), 792–795 + 800 (2019). Manuscript east. https://doi.org/10.197 34/j.i. SSN. 1001–3695.2017.10.0982
16. Guo, X., Shen, Y., Cui, Y.: Collaborative filtering recommendation algorithm based on fuzzy clustering and user interest. Softw. Guide1–8 (2023). http://kns.cnki.net/kcms/detail/42.1671. TP.20230728.1110.002.html
17. Zhu, C, Wang, Z.: Operation optimization of ethylene cracking furnace based on improved deep reinforcement learning. Chin. J. Chem. Eng. 1–19 (2023). http://kns.cnki.net/kcms/det ail/11.1946.tq.20230725.1113.002.html
18. Li, D., Sun, Y.-S., Zhang, Z.-T.: Automatic discovery mechanism and improvement of DDS publishing-subscription communication node. Avionics Technol. **54**(01), 20–28 (2023)
19. Liu, J., Zhang, B., Zhang, Y.: Adaptive federated filter tracking algorithm based on multi-sensor collaboration. J. Beijing Univ. Posts Telecommun. 1–6 (2023). https://doi.org/10. 13190/j.jbupt.2022-081
20. Liu, D., Cao, Z., Jiang, H., Zhou, S., Xiao, Z., Zeng, F.: Concurrent low-power listening: a new design paradigm for duty-cycling communication. ACM Trans. Sens. Netw. **19**(1), 4:1–4:24 (2023)
21. Chen, B., Chen, W., Fan, Z., et al.: 5G+MEC private network intelligent manufacturing factory. Commun. Technol. **54**(1), 215–223. 21. (in Chinese)
22. Xu, J.: Analysis and design of IoT driven granary real-time status monitoring system. Chang'an University, Xi'an (2018)
23. Jiang, H., Hu, J., Liu, D., Xiong, J., Cai, M.: DriverSonar: Fine-grained dangerous driving detection using active sonar. Proc. ACM Interact. Mob. Wearable Ubiquitous Technol. **5**(3), 108:1–108:22 (2021)
24. Liu, D., Cao, Z., Hou, M., Rong, H., Jiang, H.: Pushing the limits of transmission concurrency for low power wireless networks. ACM Trans. Sens. Netw. **16**(4), 40:1–40:29 (2020)

Digital Services

Research on Highly Secure Metaverse Based on Extended Reality Under Edge Computing

Jinrong Fu[1], Yiwen Liu[1,2,3]($\boxtimes$), Haobo Yan[1], Yahui Yang[1], Ling Peng[1], Yuanquan Shi[1,2,3], and Tao Feng[4]

[1] School of Computer and Artificial Intelligence, Huaihua University, Huaihua 418000, China
lyw@hhtc.edu.cn
[2] Key Laboratory of Wuling-Mountain Health Big Data Intelligent Processing and Application in Hunan Province Universities, Huaihua 418000, China
[3] Key Laboratory of Intelligent Control Technology for Wuling-Mountain Ecological Agriculture in Hunan Province, Huaihua 418000, China
[4] School of Foreign Languages, Huaihua University, Huaihua 418000, China

Abstract. With the explosion of ChatGPT, the development of artificial intelligence technology ushered in another explosion. Similarly, with the rapid development of extended reality technology and Internet of Things technology, Metaverse will also usher in greater breakthroughs. However, in the development of the extended reality metaverse under edge computing, many security issues will arise. This paper focuses on data security, considering that data will be transmitted and processed between multiple devices and nodes instead of being concentrated in the cloud, which may bring To solve data security issues, relying on the integrated architecture of Metaverse educational applications based on edge computing (MEC), it provides an identity verification and access with higher security and scalability, better performance, and service requirements that meet the current environment Control mechanism solutions, while analyzing other problems that will arise during the development of the extended reality metaverse. Aiming at the security problem on the edge side, a signature authentication scheme is designed based on Elliptic Curve Cryptography (ECC) integrated blockchain encryption technology and the effectiveness of the method is proved. In order to promote the extended reality metaverse under edge computing, it provides a mirror for the application in the field of education under the condition of ensuring data security.

Keywords: Edge computing · Metaverse · Extended reality · Artificial intelligence · Data security

1 Introduction

As the successor of the mobile Internet, Metaverse integrates emerging technologies such as extended reality technology, 5G/6G, artificial intelligence, and digital twins. It will further promote the deep integration of the real world and the virtual world and lead a new stage of digital education. [1] Wang Quan, vice president of Xidian University,

L. A. Maglaras and C. Douligeris (Eds.): WiCON 2023, LNICST 527, pp. 173–186, 2024.
https://doi.org/10.1007/978-3-031-58053-6_12

put forward the view on the change of teaching and learning methods, and the learning form should break through the constraints of time and space in the report of the China Engineering Education and Industrial Talents Training Alliance Annual Conference and Industrial Talents Training Forum on April 1, 2023, so as to improve the quality of personnel training. It can be seen that the development of metaverse applications will help to further accelerate the digital upgrade of world education, and promote future education through technological innovation. Especially in recent years, the core technologies in the metaverse, such as artificial intelligence technology, extended reality technology, Internet of Things technology, etc., have been implemented in different fields of education and have profoundly changed the organization and operation mode of existing education. [2] Judging from the existing large-scale group online learning, it is difficult to effectively solve the phenomenon of lack of collaboration among learners and low-level knowledge construction of members [3], and the development of creative thinking is also out of the question. Metaverse can build an immersive learning environment for large-scale learning groups based on learning methods such as distributed collaboration, which can effectively promote in-depth interaction among learners and enhance learners' in-depth learning. This will revolutionize future education. development, has important practical reference value. To this end, we try to provide a more secure authentication and access control mechanism for the large-scale super-domain collaborative learning system in the extended reality metaverse.

2 Background

2.1 Extended Reality Metaverse: An Introduction

The concepts described below will help you understand the concept of an "Extended Reality Metaverse".

Virtual Reality: In the virtual world, users put on virtual reality glasses to enter a virtual world that is beyond the real world and get an immersive experience. The main goal of virtual reality immersive experience is to provide a high-fidelity interactive experience that makes the user feel like he or she can have the same realistic feeling in the virtual world even in the real world [4]. Prime examples of VR include the Meta Quest and the Pimax Headrest. Apple has also accelerated its research and development in this area, with its VR headset also launching later this year, in 2023. LG Display and LG Innotek are also doing a lot of R&D activities to dominate emerging markets. VR has a wide range of applications, but entering the digital world requires a VR device.

Augmented Reality: In using an AR device, the user gets an immersive experience by mixing the digital world with the real world and projecting digital content such as text, sound, and images into the real world. Unlike virtual reality, augmented reality can be realized through the use of smartphones and smart glasses, which are capable of overlaying digital content in the real world, without the need for special equipment such as headsets. LG Display is developing OLEDoS panels for this. The panel features OLED applied to a silicon wafer with a resolution of up to 3,500PPI for more realistic AR.

Mixed Reality: MR is a hybrid concept, capable of combining the virtual and real worlds and generating new environments and experiences, where physical and digital objects coexist and interact in real time, and which can be viewed as an enhanced version of augmented reality. MetaQuest2 is a typical MR device.

Extended Reality: As an important foundation for future technological development in the Metaverse, extended reality is actually an umbrella term that encompasses virtual reality, augmented reality [8], mixed reality, and everything in between. According to market research firms, the global XR market is expected to grow six-fold, with the market size expected to reach $72.8 billion in 2024. In addition, the number of consumer-owned XR devices is expected to reach 150 million by 2025.

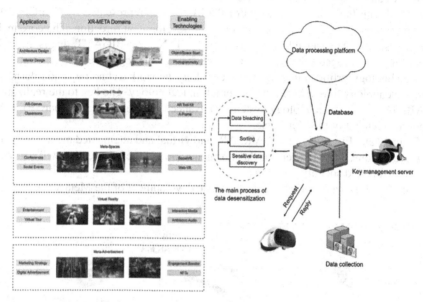

Fig. 1. Applications of XR in metaverse & Structure diagram of data desensitization system.

The Metaverse is getting more and more attention from many of the world's major tech companies, such as Facebook (recently renamed "Meta"), Microsoft, Google, and Amazon. Additionally, these companies are investing billions of dollars in an attempt to bring about massive technological change, which demonstrates the widespread adoption of the Metaverse. However, despite the metaverse's enormous appeal and potential to transform existing ecosystems such as healthcare, there are still many challenges to using AI in the metaverse, which may hinder the seamless adoption of AI by end users in the long-term. Furthermore, in the context of the social problems caused by recent technologies, there is a clear lack of trust and confidence in such technologies. Figure 1 shows the application of XR in the Metaverse [23, 24].

2.2 Extended Reality Metaverse: Applications

The recently popular ChatGPT and the Metaverse have a lot in common, and both require powerful data, computing power, and algorithm support. Artificial intelligence technology is conducive to the Metaverse to better promote the relationship between people, between people and machines, and between machines and machines. Interaction between machines [6].

Ren Fuji, an academician of the Japanese Academy of Engineering and a distinguished professor of the University of Electronic Science and Technology of China, said. At this year's Metaverse Conference, the popular ChatGPT became an unavoidable topic. It is true that the current popular ChatGPT has also set off a big wave in the capital market, and this The battle can't help but remind people of the shock brought to the market when the "Metaverse" was born two years ago. Many experts said that ChatGPT can be regarded as an important starting point for the layout of the Metaverse. Compared with the still distant world of the Metaverse, represented by ChatGPT, the constantly iterative AIGC has become a clearer development direction. The core technology system of Metaverse has evolved from BIGANT to ABIGANT, that is, the core technology has changed from the original blockchain technology, interactive technology, game technology, artificial intelligence Technology, network technology and Internet of Things technology have added artificial emotion technology. The key to the realization of ABIGANT's core technology system is advanced intelligence, and ChatGPT is an important element of the Metaverse.

Figure 2 and Fig. 3 depict XR, VR, AR, and virtual and augmented metaverses, and their interactions. The Metaverse is the next generation of the internet that will surround us graphically and socially.

Figure 4 shows a historical overview of the development of the Metaverse.

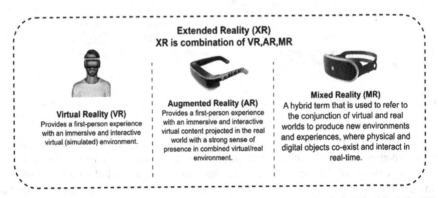

Fig. 2. An overview of different concepts related to metaverse that include VR, AR, MR, XR.

As a digital world that is highly similar to the real world, the meta-universe must materialize everything in the real world into the virtual world, we can also call this concept as digital twin [5, 7], so that a high degree of real-world reproduction can be achieved. Before that, the first thing we need to solve is the security problem. However, the original cloud computing approaches and traditional architectures (distributed architecture, cloud architecture) lead to many problems such as high latency, high cost, low experience and data leakage, especially in authentication and access control mechanisms. This paper will explore these security issues in detail.

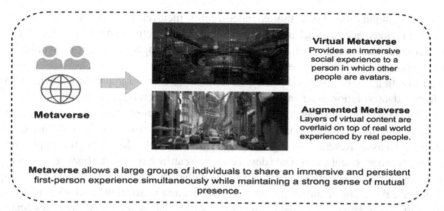

Fig. 3. An overview of different concepts related to metaverse that include virtual metaverse, and augmented metaverse.

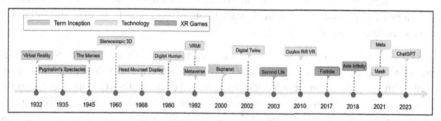

Fig. 4. An overview of different concepts related to metaverse that include virtual metaverse, and augmented metaverse.

3 Extended Reality Metaverse Security Analysis

In the process of data transmission, in the extended reality metaverse under edge computing, data will be transmitted and processed between multiple devices and nodes instead of being concentrated in the cloud. This may present some of the following data security concerns:

Data leakage: Since edge nodes are distributed at the edge of the network and may exist in an untrusted or unprotected environment, they are vulnerable to physical attacks, such as theft, destruction, tampering, etc., resulting in data loss or disclosure. If an edge device or node is hacked or damaged, data could be compromised or tampered with. For example, hackers may steal the user's identity information, location information, preference information, etc., or modify the user's avatar, virtual assets, virtual interaction, etc.

Data Privacy: If edge devices or nodes do not have adequate encryption and authorization mechanisms, data may be collected or analyzed by third parties. For example, third parties may use user data for advertising push, behavior analysis, social mining, etc. Since the extended reality metaverse involves sensitive data such as users' personal information, location information, and behavioral data, if these data are illegally obtained or analyzed at edge nodes or during transmission, it may violate users' privacy.

Service manipulation: Since the extended reality metaverse relies on edge nodes to provide various services, such as content generation, interactive control, scene rendering, etc., if these services are maliciously manipulated or tampered with, it may affect the user experience or induce users to make mistakes decision.

Data isolation: Since edge nodes may serve multiple users or applications, without an effective data isolation mechanism, data leakage or interference may result.

Data Masking: Data masking is to hide private data and ensure data security by privatizing or deforming data through masking rules. Therefore, the risk of leakage during use is greatly increased. Research on big data desensitization technology has great application prospects and practical needs. Data desensitization can be based on the background of big data, combined with Spark platform and Hadoop platform to achieve efficient processing of massive data. The acquisition system in the data desensitization processing platform uses third-party software for data collection, and the data storage platform uses Spark, Hadoop framework, Storm and other big data processing platforms to store and process data. When unauthorized users access data, the authorization server is used to realize data access requirements; in addition, the platform also includes access rights management and data processing systems. Figure 1 is a schematic diagram of the structure of the big data desensitization system [10, 11].

In the sensitive data discovery stage, each data type needs to correspond to regular expressions and machine learning methods to accurately identify sensitive data, so as to realize the confirmation of sensitive data and accurately classify data. Based on the desensitization strategy and data desensitization recoverability, the data is divided into recoverable and unrecoverable, and on this basis, sensitive data is further processed. The user further processes the recoverable desensitized data through replacement, encryption and scrambling operations, combined with key authorization, and sets and restores the desensitized data; through the deletion operation, the irreversible desensitization is processed. Effectively protect data desensitization, and perform data desensitization operations on the basis of desensitization strategies and characteristic words. With the help of Spark, Hadoop, and Storm platforms, massive data is stored and computed in a distributed manner to effectively improve computing efficiency.

To have a more secure authentication and access control mechanism for the extended reality metaverse under edge computing, the following technologies or methods may need to be adopted:

Attribute encryption: Attribute encryption is an encryption technique that encrypts or decrypts data based on the attributes of the user or the data, thus enabling data sharing and access control to protect the data security of the edge nodes.

Decentralized identity: Decentralized identity is an identity verification solution based on blockchain technology, which allows users to autonomously control their own digital identities and prove their identities or attributes through digital credentials. Decentralized identity can protect user privacy and data ownership, and prevent centralized identity providers from misusing user data.

Zero-knowledge proof: As a cryptographic technique, zero-knowledge proofs can be used for authentication and access control, allowing users to prove that they have certain permissions or qualifications without revealing private or sensitive information [12–14].

In addition to the above-mentioned methods, there are several possible methods of authentication and access control mechanisms for the Extended Reality Metaverse under edge computing:

Multi-factor authentication: As an authentication method, the user is required to provide two or more identity credentials, such as a password, fingerprint, FaceID, or PIN. Multi-factor authentication can enhance user security and prevent a single credential from being stolen or compromised.

Blockchain technology: Blockchain technology is a distributed ledger technology, which can realize the decentralization, non-tampering and traceability of data. Blockchain technology can be used for identity verification and access control to ensure the authenticity and validity of data through digital signatures and consensus mechanisms.

Privacy protection technology: Privacy protection technology is a technology to protect user privacy and data security. It can realize data analysis, processing and sharing without disclosing user sensitive information. Privacy protection technologies include homomorphic encryption, differential privacy, secure multi-party computation, etc. [15, 16].

To have more secure authentication and access control mechanisms for data in the extended reality metaverse under edge computing, the following aspects may need to be considered:

The source and attribution of data: Data is the foundation of the metaverse, and the source and attribution of data determine the credibility and authority of data. The data in the metaverse may come from the real world or the virtual world, and may also belong to individuals or organizations. Therefore, it is necessary to establish an effective data identification and authentication system to ensure the authenticity and legality of data.

Data storage and transmission: Data is the resource of the Metaverse, and data storage and transmission determine the availability and efficiency of data. Data in the Metaverse may be distributed across different edge nodes or cloud nodes, and may also flow between different platforms or devices. Therefore, it is necessary to establish an efficient data storage and transmission system to ensure data integrity and consistency [17, 18].

Data processing and analysis: Data is the value of the metaverse, and data processing and analysis determine the intelligence and innovation of data. Data in the metaverse may involve multiple types, formats, or dimensions, and may also require multiple operations, calculations, or applications. Therefore, it is necessary to establish a flexible data processing and analysis system to ensure data privacy and security [19].

The following describes the characteristics and security issues of these technologies: [8].

VR (Virtual Reality)

VR technology brings users into a completely virtual three-dimensional world through technologies such as holographic projection or head-mounted display devices, and users can operate through body movements or handles and other devices. Its characteristic is a complete virtual experience, which can simulate various scenes and has a high sense of immersion. But its disadvantage is that it requires high-end hardware support, and because users fully enter virtual reality, they have weak perception of the surrounding environment, and security issues are also prominent.

AR (Augmented Reality)

AR technology combines virtual elements with the real world through real-time recognition and tracking of real-world scenes, allowing users to see enhanced scenes. Its characteristic is the integration of virtual elements and real scenes. Users can experience the blessing of virtual elements in the real world, which has a high sense of immersion, but does not affect the perception of the real environment. At the same time, the hardware support required by AR technology is lower than that of VR, and the security risk is relatively small.

MR (Mixed Reality)

MR technology is a combination of VR and AR technologies, while retaining the characteristics of the two technologies. Users can interact with virtual elements in the real world, while also being fully immersed in the virtual world. Its characteristic is the fusion of virtual elements and the real world, providing a more realistic sense of immersion while retaining the perception of the real world. Due to the high requirements for hardware support, the security risks of MR technology are similar to those of VR technology.

In terms of security issues, since XR technology is mostly network-based interaction, network security issues are very important issues. Issues such as privacy data leakage and fraud in the virtual world need to be taken seriously. At the same time, the XR device itself also needs to have physical security protection to avoid problems such as theft or tampering of the device. With the continuous development of XR technology, related security issues are also emerging. It is necessary to continuously strengthen security guarantees while improving user experience while ensuring user security and privacy.

To address the security issues of XR technology, the following measures can be taken:

Data encryption and privacy protection

For user data in XR applications, including personal identity information, location information, interactive behavior data, etc., encryption and privacy protection are required. During transmission and storage, secure encryption algorithms and protocols need to be used to prevent data from being stolen or tampered with. At the same time, it is necessary to follow the principles of data privacy protection, clarify the rules for the collection, use, storage and sharing of user data, and provide users with controllable data rights management functions to ensure the security and privacy of user data.

Equipment safety protection

XR devices also need to have physical security to prevent devices from being stolen or tampered with. It is necessary to add security protection modules at the hardware level of the device, such as encryption chips, biometric technology, etc., to prevent physical attacks and illegal access to the device. At the same time, it is necessary to implement software security protection for the device, including firmware security, application program security, etc., to improve the security and reliability of the device.

Security verification and audit

XR applications and devices need to establish a sound security verification and audit mechanism, including user identity authentication, data access control, application security scanning, etc. Through the verification of user identity and authority, the intrusion and attack of illegal users can be avoided. At the same time, it is necessary to perform security scanning and vulnerability detection on the application program, discover and repair vulnerabilities in time, and avoid hacker attacks and malware intrusions.

Safety education and awareness raising
For users of XR applications and devices, safety education and awareness raising are needed to let users understand the importance of safety issues and master corresponding safety knowledge and skills. Through targeted safety training and education, users' safety awareness and safety literacy can be improved, and users' safety negligence and misoperation can be avoided, thereby ensuring the safety and sustainable development of XR technology.

4 Extended Reality- Digital Life Security Optimization

4.1 Edge Initialization

In order to ensure the security of the edge nodes providing computing services, we have designed a secure access process as shown in Fig. 3. It includes setting initial values, registration and authentication processes. Initialization Setting the initial value is performed by En. The public–private key pair is generated through ECC as the required public key. The public–private key pair is generated through ECC as the required public parameter of the system. Combine the device MAC address value to get its identity information and package and store it on the blockchain for registration in the blockchain network. When device A initiates an access request to device B, device B verifies the identity information of A through the blockchain network [20].

The specific process of edge node authentication is as follows (Fig. 5):

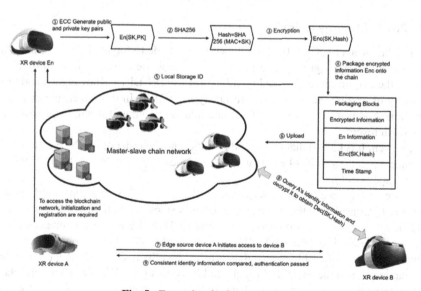

Fig. 5. Example of a figure caption.

(1) Initial value setting

En that joins the blockchain network uses ECC to calculate the public key and private key. When Q satisfies a prime number greater than 3 on the finite field Fp, the integer is modulo p, and there is an equation E:

$$y^2 = x^3 + ax + b(\bmod\ p) \tag{1}$$

where a, b ∈ Fp, Ep(a, b), take any number K to get the private key SK. Take the base point Q on the elliptic curve, generate the public key PK = Q*SK, and broadcast the public key to the whole network.

(2) Register

Input the MAC address and SK value of En into formula (2), and calculate Hash. Encrypt it through SK to get Enc (SK, Hash), and store Enc locally and on the blockchain to complete the registration.

$$Hash = SHA256(MAC + SK) \tag{2}$$

(3) Authentication

Before En becomes a miner, it needs to be recognized by consensus, that is, the nodes of the whole network verify its identity. When node A initiates behaviors such as access to node B, node B queries whether A's identity information exists on the blockchain. ① If it exists, Enc(SK, Hash) is decrypted through the PK issued by A to obtain Dec(SK, Hash), and compared with Enc(SK, Hash). pass. Otherwise, the node has been polluted, or the malicious node is forged. ② If it does not exist, the node is illegal and disconnected. Identity authentication avoids false impersonation of nodes and prevents delivery of data to malicious nodes. So far, En has established an initial trust relationship with the data ledger.

4.2 Proof of Unforgeability

An attacker needs to obtain the SK of a legitimate node to forge a legitimate node, and ECC based on cryptography is a public key cryptosystem based on the difficulty of solving the elliptic curve discrete logarithm problem (ECDLP). Knowing PK and Q, the difficulty of finding the SK process reversely is ECDLP. In this paper, the exhaustive search method is used to solve ECDLP, and it is verified that it is almost impossible to find SK in reverse.

Theorem It is known that Q = q and P = PK, and the order of P is N. E ∈ (Fp), SK is obtained when L satisfies Q = LP, where L satisfies (0 ≤ L ≤ N−1). If ECDLP holds, this method is not feasible.

Prove to calculate the point sequence P, 2P, 3P ..., nP of E ∈ (Fp), until nP = Q, then n = L. Considering the worst case, it takes N steps to find the answer satisfying nP = Q, and it takes N/2 steps on average to solve ECDLP. Therefore, the time complexity of this calculation is exponential O(N). However, when N is large enough, the solution method becomes infeasible in calculation time, the effectiveness of the method cannot be guaranteed, and the ECDLP difficulty holds. At this time, SK (PK, P) in formula (3) is infinitesimal, then the success probability SuccA of attacker A successfully forging a legitimate node is almost 0.

Proof Completed

$$\text{SuccA} = \frac{ECDLP\{SK(PK, Q)\}}{A\{PK, Q, Enc(SK, Hash)\}} \qquad (3)$$

It can be proved that under the scheme of this paper, the edge nodes cannot be successfully forged and tampered with, satisfying the unforgeability.

5 Conclusion and Outlook

Regarding the future development of the extended reality metaverse, there are still the following problems.

5.1 The Metaverse of Extended Reality Education Lacks Top-Level Design, and Digital Twin Colleges and Universities have not Formed a Unified Plan

At present, there is no systematic plan for the application of Metaverse in the field of education, and there is a lack of clear development goals and market mechanisms [21]. In the context of the educational metaverse, issues such as creating digital twin universities, digitizing educational resources, upgrading education management, and building a unified information network within the campus, a communication platform between universities, and a national-level supervision system have not yet been formed. Unified solution. Since the extended reality education metaverse and digital twin universities are emerging concepts, many explorations are still in their infancy, relevant theoretical research is relatively scattered, and practical effects have not yet been proven. The design standards of virtual courses, which courses are suitable for teaching in a virtual environment, the learning effect of virtual and real integration, and whether they meet the world's training requirements for all-round development of people need to be further studied.

5.2 Avoid the Profit-Oriented and Commercial Development of the Educational Metaverse

The key to the Metaverse is not the technology itself but how human society defines and uses it. Excessive commercialization will lead to setbacks for real industries, and excessive entertainment will lead humans to indulge in virtual space and desolate real life. The commercial applications of Metaverse mostly focus on social networking, streaming media, games and other fields, and induce users to spend more time and immerse themselves in the virtual world through short-term multi-frequency visual and auditory stimulation. The emergence of the metaverse means that human beings have begun to try to enter the stage of digital life. The combination of education and the metaverse has given more directions and possibilities for the development of education. However, the development of the metaverse of education must be based on the essence of education, with a more open and diverse attitude, correct and efficient methods to transform human experience in understanding and transforming nature and social life experience into the wisdom and conduct of the educated, so that It becomes the person needed for social development [22].

However, in the future, the development of digital life and digital people will also encounter various ethical issues that need our attention:

1. Ethical issues

    Whether digital life and digital humans have moral significance, whether they should have moral responsibilities, and how to ensure that their behavior conforms to ethical norms are ethical issues that need to be considered in the development of digital life and digital humans.

    The behavior and thinking of digital life and digital people are often determined by algorithms and data, which may lead to some behaviors and decisions that do not conform to human ethics. Therefore, it is necessary to ensure that the behaviors of digital lives and digital humans conform to ethical norms, and at the same time, it is necessary to educate users of digital lives and digital humans to pay attention to whether their behaviors conform to ethical standards.

2. Liability issues

    Digital beings and digital humans have certain intelligence and capabilities. If there are problems with their behavior and thinking, who should be responsible for it? How to ensure that the behavior of digital life and digital humans conforms to legal and moral standards is a responsibility issue that needs to be considered in the development of digital life and digital humans.

    Developers of digital lives and digital humans should take corresponding responsibilities to ensure that the behavior of digital lives and digital humans complies with legal and ethical standards. In addition, users of digital lives and digital humans should also be aware that the behavior of digital lives and digital humans may have an impact on society and assume corresponding responsibilities.

3. Social impact issues [25]

    The impact of digital life and digital humans on human society is also an issue that needs to be considered. How to balance the relationship between the development of digital life and digital human and the social interests is a social impact issue that needs to be considered in the development of digital life and digital human.

    Developers of digital lives and digital humans need to actively participate in social discussions and decision-making to ensure that the development of digital lives and digital humans is in line with social interests and human values. At the same time, users of digital lives and digital humans also need to participate in discussions and decision-making to ensure that the development of digital lives and digital humans meets their needs and expectations, and at the same time does not cause adverse effects on society.

4. Human nature issues [26, 27]

    Whether digital life and digital human have human characteristics such as human emotions, consciousness, and self-awareness, and whether they can replace human roles are human issues that need to be considered in the development of digital life and digital human.

    Digital life and digital human cannot have human characteristics such as human emotion, consciousness and self-awareness at this stage, but they can simulate these characteristics. The development of digital life and digital human can also gain an in-depth understanding of human nature through research on human beings, and apply these researches to the development of digital life and digital human.

5. Legal Issues

The development of digital life and digital human needs to take into account various issues such as ethics, privacy, responsibility, social influence, humanity and law. Only under the premise of fully considering these issues can we ensure the healthy development of digital life and digital people, and enable them to make greater contributions to human society.

6. Human attitudes and acceptance

The development of digital beings and digital humans also needs to take into account human attitudes and acceptance. With the development of digital life and digital human beings, people will face a situation where the interaction with artificial intelligence and robots will become more intimate.

In our future work, we will consider expanding the experiment scale, optimizing the blockchain consensus algorithm, and creating a telecom-grade service environment for the blockchain network with higher security, better performance, and lower latency than the existing scheme. Meanwhile, in order to further improve the efficiency of access control, we can try to continue to deeply optimize the cross-domain access control model.

Acknowledgements. This work was supported in part by the Scientific Research Project of Hunan Provincial Department of Education (No. C0497), Aid Program for Science and Technology Innovative Research Team in Higher Educational Institutions of Hunan Province, the Huaihua University Double First-Class initiative Applied Characteristic Discipline of Control Science and Engineering (No. ZNKZN2021-10), and Nationa-l Training Program Project of Innovation and Entrepreneurship for Undergraduates (No. S202310548083) and the Teaching Reform Research Project of Hunan Province "POA-based Research on College English Teaching Reform among Local Colleges and Uni-versities of Hunan" (HNJG-2019-825).

References

1. Hu, Z., Wen, J.: What is the metaverse? Why should you care about it? Xinhua Daily Telegraph 2021–11–21,004
2. Jiang, Y.: Orphans in the metaverse?——Why video games serve as an educational platform for the next generation of children's philosophy. J. Guizhou Univ. (Soc. Sci.) **39**(05), 21–29+120 (2021). doi:https://doi.org/10.15958/j.cnki.gdxbshb.2021.05.03.
3. Zhong, B.: Essential Issues and Education Innovation Towards Online Teaching in Primary and Secondary School. China Educational Technology No.413.06, pp. 15–22 (2021)
4. Halabi, O., Balakrishnan, S., Dakua, S.P., Navab, N., Warfa, M.: Virtual and augmented reality in surgery. In: Doorsamy, W., Paul, B., Marwala, T. (eds.) The Disruptive Fourth Industrial Revolution. LNEE, vol. 674, pp. 257–285. Springer, Cham (2020). https://doi.org/10.1007/978-3-030-48230-5_11
5. Digital Intelligent Human: a fundamental unit in the meta-universe, and a new manifestation of service intelligence [EB/OL], 19 March 2022. https://www.shangyexinzhi.com/article/4684994.html. Accessed 14 June 2022

6. Cotton, D.R.E., Cotton, P.A., Shipway, J.R.: Chatting and Cheating. Ensuring Academic Integrity in the Era of ChatGPT. https://edarxiv.org/mrz8h/

7. Zhao, X., Lu, Q.W.: Governance of the metaverse: a vision for agile governance in the future data intelligence world. J. Libr. Sci. China **48**(1), 52–61 (2022)

8. Alhalabi, W.: Virtual reality systems enhance students' achievements in engineering education. Behav. Inf. Technol. **35**(11), 919–925 (2016)

9. Digital Human. https://wiki.mbalib.com/wiki/%E6%95%B0%E5%AD%97%E4%BA%BA

10. Survey on data security and privacy-preserving for the research of edge computing. https://zhuanlan.zhihu.com/p/142914592

11. Microsoft Entra-Secure Authentication and Access Control I Microsoft Security. https://www.microsoft.com/zh-cn/security/business/microsoft-entra

12. Lee, L.-H., et al.: All one needs to know about metaverse: a complete survey on technological singularity, virtual ecosystem, and research agenda. J. Latex Class Files **14**(8) (2021)

13. Paper Reading: A Summary of Key Technologies in the Metaverse. https://www.zhihu.com/column/c_1511365369852305410

14. Zhang, J., et al.: Survey on data security and privacy-preserving for the research of edge computing. J. Commun. **39**(03), 1–21 (2018)

15. MUD underlying technology and future development. https://www.sohu.com/a/664038489_120538525

16. Research on the Development Status of the Metaverse and Research on Security Risks. https://www.secrss.com/articles/45265

17. Zhang, H., Zeng, X., Liang, Z.: Exploring the Metaverse: conceptual connotation, form development and evolution mechanism. Studies in Science of Science, 09 August 2022. https://doi.org/10.16192/j.cnki.1003-2053.20220808.001

18. Zhang, H., Zeng, X., Liang, Z.: Exploring the Metaverse: Conceptual Connotation, Form Development and Evolution Mechanism. http://aiig.tsinghua.edu.cn/info/1368/1629.htm

19. Computing of the Eight Cores of the Metaverse. https://zhuanlan.zhihu.com/p/438835959

20. Liu, D., Wu, X., Cao, Z., Liu, M., Li, Y., Hou, M.: CD-MAC: a contention detectable MAC for low duty-cycled wireless sensor networks. SECON, pp. 37–45 (2015)

21. Cai, S., Jiao, X., Song, B.: Opening another door to education——applications, challenges and prospects of the educational metaverse. Mod. Educ. Technol. **32**(01), 16–26 (2022)

22. Pu, Q., Wang, X.: Metaverse and its influence and change on human society. J. Chongqing Univ. (Soc. Sci. Edit.) 1–12 (2022)

23. Vallor, S.: Technology and the Virtues: a Philosophical Guide to a Future Worth Wanting. Oxford University Press, Oxford (2016)

24. Lanier, J.: Ten Arguments for Deleting Your Social Media Accounts Right Now. Random House, New York (2018)

25. Flintham, M., Karner, C., Bachour, K., Creswick, H., Gupta, N., Moran, S.: Falling for fake news: investigating the consumption of news via social media. In: Proceedings of the 2018 CHI Conference on Human Factors in Computing Systems, p. 376. ACM (2018)

26. Buck, L., McDonnell, R.: Security and privacy in the metaverse: the threat of the digital human. In: Proceedings of the 1st Workshop on Novel Challenges of Safety, Security and Privacy in Extended Reality (2022)

27. Shahriari, K., Shahriari, M.: IEEE standard review—ethically aligned design: a vision for prioritizing human wellbeing with artificial intelligence and autonomous systems. In: 2017 IEEE Canada International Humanitarian Technology Conference (IHTC), pp. 197–201. IEEE (2017)

Research on Metaverse Multi-person Linkage Using Mobile Edge Computing Based on Extended Reality Under the Immersive Experience of Zhijiang Peace Culture Memorial Hall

Yiwen Liu[1,2,3], Jinrong Fu[1](✉), Haobo Yan[1], Yanxia Gao[1,2,3], Ling Peng[1], and Taiguo Qu[1]

[1] School of Computer and Artificial Intelligence, Huaihua University, Huaihua 418000, China
Fujinrong357@outlook.com

[2] Key Laboratory of Wuling-Mountain Health Big Data Intelligent Processing and Application in Hunan Province Universities, Huaihua 418000, China

[3] Key Laboratory of Intelligent Control Technology for Wuling-Mountain Ecological Agriculture in Hunan Province, Huaihua 418000, China

Abstract. This study aims to deeply explore the impact of mobile edge computing based on extended reality technology on the multi-person linkage of the Zhijiang Peace Culture Memorial Hall under the immersive experience. In the part of research background and significance, it discusses the rise of the application of XR technology in the field of culture and education, emphasizing the importance of education on the history of revolution and its value in the social sense. Then, it expounds the core topic of this research aimed at integrating XR technology with education on the history of revolution, and presenting visitors with more realistic and immersive historical scenes by creating an immersive experience of multi-person linkage. The use of these technologies enables visitors to transcend time and space barriers, directly participate in historical events, and deeply appreciate the intrinsic value of red culture. In order to achieve multi-person linkage, this study adopts mobile edge computing technology to ensure that multiple visitors can realize real-time interaction in the virtual scene and jointly build a collective experience of the Metaverse. This research has achieved positive results in the fields of XR technology application, education on the history of revolution, and mobile edge computing. It provides a useful reference for the modernization and upgrading of the Zhijiang Peace Culture Memorial Hall, and also provides a new paradigm for the cultural promotion of multi-person linkage experience in Metaverse.

Keywords: Metaverse · Immersive Experience · Extended Reality · Mobile Edge Computing · Education on the History of Revolution

L. A. Maglaras and C. Douligeris (Eds.): WiCON 2023, LNICST 527, pp. 187–201, 2024.
https://doi.org/10.1007/978-3-031-58046-6_13

1 Introduction

1.1 Research Background and Significance

In today's digital age, the integration of information technology and cultural heritage presents unprecedented possibilities. The Zhijiang Peace Culture event, as an important historical node in China's War of Resistance Against Japanese Aggression, represents the Chinese people's indomitable spirit of resistance and historical victory. However, traditional display methods are difficult to achieve satisfactory results in small places, limited budgets, and limited flow of people. This prompts us to think about how to use modern technology, especially extended reality (XR) technology, to reinterpret history and create a more immersive experience. An immersive cultural and educational experience.

History is a window of time, which can connect us to the past and feel the years full of glory and tears. However, the passage of time makes historical events gradually blurred, especially for the new generation. In this context, we need a new way to convey history, so that people don't just understand it through words and pictures, but participate in it personally and resonate with history.

Immersive formats are an emerging model to promote the high-quality development of the digital cultural industry. During the "14th Five-Year Plan" period, the Ministry of Culture and Tourism issued the "Opinions on Promoting the High-Quality Development of the Digital Cultural Industry" in November 2020, emphasizing "promoting the transformation of existing cultural content into immersive content and enriching virtual experience content. Support Cultural relics units, scenic spots, etc., use cultural resources to develop immersive experience projects, develop digital exhibition halls, virtual scenic spots and other services. Guide and support the application of virtual reality, augmented reality, drones and other technologies in the cultural field, and develop holographic interactive projection, UAV performances, night light and shadow shows and other products." Zhijiang was approved to become the 307th International Peaceful City in 2021 and Hunan's first International Peaceful City. Zhijiang Peace Culture records the history of China's Anti-Japanese War and the great victory of the World Anti-Fascist War, and demonstrates the charm of human peace culture.

The Zhijiang Peace Culture Memorial Hall is a well-known education on the history of revolution scenic spot in China. It is an important carrier of Zhijiang's peaceful culture and has important patriotic educational significance. The old revolutionary site is the main site, and the exhibitions in the museum tend to be in the traditional mode. These publicity methods lack attractiveness and the flavor of the times in terms of atmosphere creation, connotation expression, interactive experience, etc., and it is difficult to deeply touch and shock people's hearts. Coupled with the continuous impact of the 2020 new crown pneumonia epidemic, the domestic cultural and tourism industry, including Zhijiang, has been hit hard [2]. Therefore, it is urgent to promote the deep integration of Zhijiang peace culture and high technology, actively explore digital forms, and tell the story of Zhijiang famous city at home and abroad.

The development based on immersive experience in foreign countries is relatively mature. The immersive experience was first proposed by Zwaan [3], which are respectively online immersion (somatosensory equipment, VR equipment, etc.) and offline immersion (virtual projection), which are mainly used in situational theme parks., medicine [4], cultural attractions [5] (Christos, 2020), archeology [6] (Kyrlitsias, 2021), learning [7] (Tsivitanidou,2021), etc., but there are very few studies on the immersive experience of domestic red culture.

The digital construction of red culture in my country started relatively late, but in recent years it has gradually become the focus of continuous attention from academia and industry. In the high-tech interactive exhibition "Riverside During the Qingming Festival 3.0" launched by the Forbidden City in 2018, the famous painting "Riverside During the Qingming Festival" that spanned thousands of years was vividly presented in front of the audience, bringing immersive experience to the audience and setting off a new era based on immersive experience. The upsurge of research on the digital innovation path of red culture. Search the keyword "immersive experience + culture" through HowNet, and there are 57 journal papers published in 2021 alone.

Cao Yue et al. [8] (2018) believe that in an immersive environment, people themselves become a medium, the boundaries of time and space are eliminated, and the interaction between body and technology, senses and media will continue forever. Yu Wan [9] (2019) believes that museums, as places of cultural exchange, are the second classroom for conveying culture and realizing multi-directional exchanges. Lei Bo [10] (2018) proposed that VR images have the effect of "immersive experience" and "human-computer interaction", and it is necessary to be introduced into local red cultural propaganda, but did not involve the introduction of details; Chang Rui [11] (2021) believes that not only virtual reality, but also digital collection, preservation, management, restoration, reproduction, display, and inheritance of red cultural resources can be carried out with the help of computer technologies such as image, graphics, sound restoration, and augmented reality.

Therefore, with the application of technologies such as virtual reality, augmented reality, 5G+4K/8K ultra-high-definition, drones, and AI in the construction of digital culture, products such as holographic interactive projection, drone performances, and night light and shadow shows have brought audiences A powerful and immersive experience. The more visitors are immersed in the experience of red culture, the more conducive it is to accept the baptism of red culture at a deeper level, and the more they will praise and be proud of the innovation, development, protection and inheritance of my country's red culture from the bottom of their hearts.

Extended reality technology, as the intersection of virtual and reality, can create a brand new display platform for us. Through AR technology, virtual elements can be integrated with the real world, allowing historical scenes to unfold in front of your eyes; VR technology can bring users into the virtual world, allowing them to be in the vortex of history; and MR technology goes a step further, combining virtual and real elements Cleverly combined to create a wonderful interaction. These technologies provide us with a brand new way of displaying and conveying history, allowing people to experience and feel history in person, not just through traditional display and narrative.

This thesis will focus on how to use these advanced XR technologies, especially in the case of small places, low costs, and small crowds, to restore the Peace Culture of Zhijiang into a metaverse multi-person linkage experience. We will discuss how to choose suitable technologies and devices, design interactive content for different groups of people, and how to use mobile edge computing to improve experience. Through this research, we hope to inject new life into the inheritance of red culture and make history shine more dazzlingly against the backdrop of modern technology.

1.2 Extended Reality

Extended reality (XR) technology, as a major breakthrough in the field of information technology, has created a brand new reality experience for us. It presents users with rich interactions and perceptions by integrating the virtual world with the real world. Under the framework of XR technology, we often involve various technical modes such as augmented reality (AR), virtual reality (VR) and mixed reality (MR), which cross and integrate virtual elements and the real world to varying degrees, creating an amazing experience.

Mobile edge computing (MEC) is a new distributed computing method based on mobile communication networks, which can provide faster and more reliable computing capabilities for XR technology. MEC provides IT service environment and cloud computing capabilities by deploying general-purpose servers near the network access side, aiming to further reduce latency, improve network operation efficiency, improve service distribution and transmission capabilities, and optimize and improve end-user experience.

For example, in the Zhijiang Peace Culture Memorial Hall, MEC can be used to support the application of AR, VR and MR technologies. It can quickly process a large amount of data and transmit the results to the user's device in real time, so that the user can get a smoother and more realistic experience. Additionally, MEC can help with goals such as traffic optimization, enhanced physical security, and cache efficiency.

First, augmented reality (AR) technology extends the boundaries of human perception by superimposing virtual content onto real environments. Through smartphones, tablets or AR glasses, users can see virtual images, text or animations on the background of the real world, making learning and experience richer and more vivid. For example, in the Zhijiang Peace Culture Memorial Hall, AR technology can be used to combine historical scenes with the actual display area, so that visitors can see the virtual surrender ceremony in a real location, enhancing their immersion and participation.

Second, virtual reality (VR) technology is a more in-depth experience. By wearing a VR headset, users are fully immersed in the virtual environment, as if they were there. In the Zhijiang Peace Culture Memorial Hall, the use of VR technology can bring users into the historical scene at that time, allowing them to experience the atmosphere and tense situation at that time in 360° without dead ends. This immersive experience allows users to have a deeper understanding of historical events and generate stronger resonance.

Finally, mixed reality (MR) technology organically combines virtual elements with real environments. Through devices such as AR glasses, users can see virtual objects interact with real scenes, creating a sense of fusion reality. In the Zhijiang Peace Culture Memorial Hall, MR technology can be used to allow tourists to have dialogues with virtual historical figures, or interact with virtual historical scenes, making the visit more lively and interesting.

In short, the combination of mobile edge computing under the framework of XR technology provides users with strong support and enables users to obtain a better experience. With the continuous development of MEC technology, we have reason to believe that XR technology will achieve more brilliant achievements. In short, the application of XR technology has injected new vitality into the inheritance and education of cultural heritage. It breaks through the limitations of traditional display methods, allowing history to be presented to people in a more vivid way, allowing people to feel and experience history in person. In the case of small places, small costs, and small crowds, using different forms of XR technology, we can make the Zhijiang Peace Culture Memorial Hall an attractive virtual place, bringing visitors a profound experience of education on the history of revolution.

2 Application of Extended Reality Technology in Zhijiang Peace Culture Memorial Hall

In a small place like Zhijiang, with limited resources and few people, the traditional display methods may not be able to achieve satisfactory results. However, with the help of extended reality (XR) technology, we can restore the historical scene of the Peace Culture of Zhijiang in a new way, so that visitors can experience that exciting historical moment more personally.

First, we can consider using Augmented Reality (AR) technology to provide visitors with an interactive, convenient and easy-to-use experience. Visitors only need to use their smartphones or wear AR glasses to see virtual historical scenes in the Zhijiang Peace Culture Memorial Hall, such as the scene of the surrender ceremony and the scene of the battle. Through the display of mobile phone screens or glasses, tourists can see the superposition of virtual elements in the real environment, making history more concrete and sensible, and enhancing the fun of visiting.

Second, virtual reality (VR) technology can provide students and tourists with more immersive learning and experience. By wearing a VR headset, visitors can enter a completely virtual historical world, as if traveling through time. In the Zhijiang Peace Culture Memorial Hall, we can create realistic historical scenes, allowing visitors to feel the atmosphere and tension at that time. This immersive experience can stimulate stronger emotional resonance among visitors and enable them to understand the significance of historical events more deeply.

In addition, the application of mixed reality (MR) technology can also bring visitors a unique experience. Through devices such as AR glasses, virtual elements can interact with real scenes to create wonderful interactive effects. In the Memorial Hall of the Peace Culture of Zhijiang, MR technology can be used to display virtual historical figures, so that tourists can talk to them and understand their stories and emotions. This kind of interactivity can increase the sense of participation and curiosity of visitors, making the visit more interactive and interesting.

In the Zhijiang Peace Culture Memorial Hall, extended reality (XR) technology can provide an extremely attractive experience in a technical and targeted manner, bringing visitors back to the historical moment of the victory of the Anti-Japanese War and deeply feeling the charm of red culture.

Application of Augmented Reality (AR) in Restoration of Virtual Historical Scenes: Augmented Reality (AR) is a technology that integrates virtual information with the real world. It captures images of the real world through a camera and superimposes virtual information on the images, enabling users to see virtual information in the real world.

In the Zhijiang Peace Culture Memorial Hall, we can use smart phones or AR glasses and other devices to watch the restoration of virtual historical scenes by scanning specific display items. For example, when visitors scan an exhibit of a surrender ceremony, AR technology will show a virtual surrender ceremony on their devices, including historical figures, ceremony process, etc. Such an application not only highlights the technicality, but also enables visitors to experience historical scenes immersively in a real environment, enhancing the sense of participation.

The application of virtual reality (VR) to interact with historical figures: Virtual reality (VR) is a three-dimensional space environment simulated by a computer. It enables users to immerse themselves in and interact with virtual worlds through devices such as head-mounted displays.

In the Zhijiang Peace Culture Memorial Hall, we can allow visitors to enter a completely virtual historical environment and interact with virtual historical figures by wearing VR headsets and other equipment. For example, tourists can have a dialogue with the military generals at that time to learn about the tactics of the war and the stories behind it. This virtual interaction highlights the technicality, while providing visitors with the opportunity to have direct contact with historical figures, making history more immersive.

Multiplayer and historical role-playing in mixed reality (MR): Mixed reality (MR) is a technology that merges the virtual world with the real world. It captures images of the real world through a camera, and adds virtual information and objects to the images, enabling users to see and interact with virtual objects in the real world.

In the Zhijiang Peace Culture Memorial Hall, we can see virtual historical figures in real scenes through AR glasses and other equipment, and participate in historical role-playing with other tourists. For example, tourists can play different roles such as anti-Japanese soldiers and local people, interact with other tourists, and jointly restore the situation of historical events. This combination of multiplayer linkage and role-playing highlights the technology and enhances the interactive experience and deep participation of visitors. Figure 1 below is a schematic diagram of the construction and processing process of the Metaverse of the Zhijiang Peace Culture Memorial Hall.

Support and real-time interaction of mobile edge computing technology: Mobile edge computing is a technology that distributes computing tasks to network edge devices (such as AR glasses, smartphones, etc.). It can reduce data transmission delay and ensure the smoothness of real-time interaction.

In the Zhijiang Peace Culture Memorial Hall, mobile edge computing technology plays an important role in the context of multi-person linkage. For example, in historical role-playing, tourists can interact with other tourists in real time, solve problems together, and experience a more realistic historical situation.

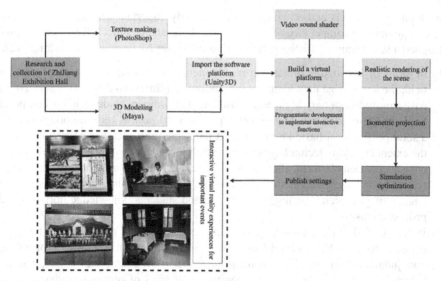

Fig. 1. Schematic Diagram of the Construction and Processing Process of the Metaverse of the Zhijiang Peace Culture Memorial Hall

To sum up, under the background of Zhijiang, a small place, low cost, and small flow of people, through the precise application of technologies such as augmented reality (AR), virtual reality (VR) and mixed reality (MR) in Zhijiang Peace Culture Memorial Hall, combined with the support of mobile edge computing technology, can bring visitors a more in-depth and interactive education on the history of revolution experience. This kind of targeted technical application can not only meet the expectations of visitors, but also bring new vitality and attraction to the Zhijiang Peace Culture Memorial Hall.

3 Metaverse Education Integration: Education of Revolutionary History by Multiplayer Linkage

Using extended reality (XR) technology, education on the history of revolution linked by multiple people can be deeply displayed in a highly targeted and technical way in the Zhijiang Peace Culture Memorial Hall, allowing visitors to have a deeper understanding of the history of the Anti-Japanese War and the spirit of red culture.

Therefore, it is an important topic to adapt to the development of the times and social needs to explore the talent training teaching system that integrates metaverse and teaching.

With the launch of the Chinese version of CC2020, the competency model has been understood and familiarized by more and more Chinese computer education experts and university teachers. Problem-solving skills are gaining widespread attention. Taking the current top-notch plan launched by the Ministry of Education as an example, the cultivation of students' abilities is very important in the process of cultivating top-notch talents. Similarly, the cultivation of basic abilities for ordinary students in the process of cultivating top-notch talents is similar and indispensable. And now, with the rapid development of society and economy, it is particularly important whether students have the comprehensive competence of "knowledge, skills, and conduct". Based on this, we designed a talent training teaching system that integrates Metaverse and teaching [12].

(1) In terms of knowledge dimension requirements, for top students in the computer field, the knowledge they learn is often multidisciplinary, so it is very important to have a multidisciplinary knowledge structure. For ordinary students in the computer field, the knowledge they learn is often professional, so it is very important to have a solid professional basic knowledge. At the same time, metaverse teaching under the extended reality technology can also provide students with a diversified knowledge acquisition platform, allowing students to get in touch with more professional-related knowledge fields in the virtual world, such as computer networks, software engineering, artificial intelligence, etc. Expand students' knowledge horizons and professionalism.

(2) In terms of skill dimension requirements, top students in the computer field are expected to reach Bloom level 5 or 6 in cognitive skills, that is, they can form their own judgments on knowledge content, have their own unique viewpoints, and put forward new ideas solution. The cognitive skill level of ordinary students in the computer field is expected to reach Bloom level 3 or 4, that is, to be able to use knowledge content to solve problems, and to have certain analytical and application skills.

In order to improve students' ability to solve complex engineering problems, metaverse teaching under extended reality technology can be used to allow students to experience different scenarios and tasks in the virtual world, and cultivate students' innovative thinking and practical ability through immersive interaction and collaboration. Students can simulate the construction and maintenance of hardware in the principle of computer composition in the metaverse, for example, using tools and materials in the metaverse to realize basic components such as memory, registers, and arithmetic units, or to build different logic circuits and instruction systems. Students can also use the programming language and environment in the Metaverse to implement various data structures and algorithms, and deepen their understanding through concrete demonstrations.

(3) From the perspective of the moral dimension requirements, any deficiencies in any of the 11 moral elements of top-notch students may form obstacles to his knowledge learning and skill improvement, resulting in unsuccessful cultivation of top-notch students. In this sense, the cultivation of top-notch students has higher requirements for the shaping of competence than other students. To sum up, top-notch students in the field of computer science need to have a broad multidisciplinary knowledge structure, a strong sense of innovation and ability, and a high comprehensive quality of conduct.

In terms of moral dimension requirements, ordinary students should also have a certain level in the 11 moral elements, but they don't have to be perfect like top students. In this sense, the cultivation of ordinary students has relatively lower requirements for the shaping of competencies than top-notch students. However, metaverse teaching under the extended reality technology can also provide students with an opportunity to cultivate their moral quality, so that students can also abide by rules and morals in the virtual world, and cultivate students' sense of responsibility, cooperation spirit and self-discipline ability.

For example, students can participate in community building and public welfare activities in the Metaverse, or communicate and interact with people from different cultural backgrounds in the Metaverse. To sum up, ordinary students in the computer field need to have a deep knowledge structure in the major, better problem-solving ability, and higher basic moral qualities. The brief design of the talent training teaching system of "Metaverse and Education Integration" is shown in Fig. 2 below.

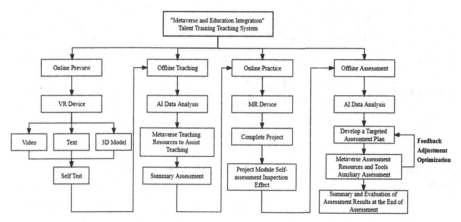

Fig. 2. Brief Design of the Teaching System Process of "Metaverse and Education Integration" Talent Training

The competency model has played an active role not only in the cultivation of top talents, but also in other computer professional fields such as high-performance computing [13]. China's computer education is developing rapidly, and at the same time, the internationalization of education is gradually showing a global trend. All countries are actively promoting the internationalization of higher education in order to cultivate more international talents [14]. The international competitiveness of China's computer talents is also constantly inclusive. Finding the most suitable computer science education training program for the audience we serve is our mission to continue our career, and it requires the joint efforts of computer science educators.

Taking the education on the history of revolution in the Zhijiang Peace Culture Memorial Hall as an example, the main teaching content is decomposed based on the Bloom model [15]. Traditional classroom teaching has problems such as too abstract concepts, repetitive and rigid content, and single evaluation methods [16]. However, in this era of vigorous development of artificial intelligence such as data sharing, digital twins, and ChatGPT, classroom teaching should reflect individualization and diversification as much as possible., discretization and other features, here, we divide the Bloom model into four layers, the first layer is memory and understanding; the second layer is application and analysis; the third layer is synthesis and evaluation; the fourth layer is design and innovation. Combined with the characteristics of extended reality XR technology, different metaverse teaching interaction methods are designed for different groups of people in the education on the history of revolution in Zhijiang Peace Culture Memorial Hall. This paper designs VR and MR respectively for the content of education on the history of revolution and the metaverse under the characteristics of extended reality (XR) technology. Different application scenarios of AR and AR, and explore the differences between the three in course feedback, interaction methods, display effects, and usage scenarios [17]. The specific frame design is shown in Fig. 3.

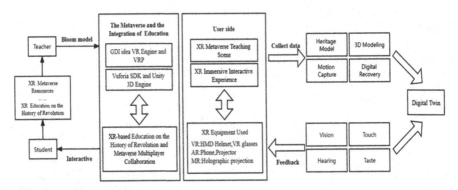

Fig. 3. The Design and Operation Framework of the " Metaverse and Education " Talent Training Teaching System.

(1) Education on the history of revolution based on VR and MR interaction

With XR technology as the core, the Zhijiang Peace Culture Memorial Hall Metaverse is established, and the "extended reality-oriented" hybrid teaching mode is adopted to integrate the Bloom model with the hybrid teaching structure under the BOPPS mode. Students or various tourists enter through XR equipment. Metaverse conducts self-directed learning before class, and demonstrates abstract concepts through extended reality (XR) technology design. For example, based on the 3D engine Unity3D, the three-dimensional simulation is used to display abstract concepts. By adding Manheng ideaVR engine and VRP, the three-dimensional data of the computer composition structure can be added to the immersive VR and MR interactive systems, breaking the inherent abstract concepts and enabling students to immerse themselves in learning. A level of memorization and understanding.

In addition, in virtual reality, tourists can play the roles of different historical figures and participate in education on the history of revolution activities with other tourists. Every historical figure has its own stories and emotions, and tourists will share these stories in the interaction, deeply feeling the emotional connotation of red culture. Through role-playing interactions with other tourists, tourists can gain a deeper understanding of the background and values of different historical roles and experience the diversity of red culture.

Through virtual reality technology, visitors can also participate in virtual historical lectures and discussions. Different virtual historical figures will share their experiences and beliefs to visitors as speakers, and then visitors can ask real-time interactive questions about the speech content. This real-time interaction strengthens tourists' awareness of the core value of red culture, and at the same time technically creates an experience of interacting with historical figures.

(2) Educational applications based on MR equipment and AR scenarios

This paper designs an immersive experience-based XR technology-based meta-universe education on the history of revolution platform, aiming to improve the teaching quality and effect of computer composition principles courses. The platform uses digital twin technology to build a virtual model of the Zhijiang Peace Culture Memorial Hall, allowing students or tourists to interact and practice online in an immersive environment through mixed reality (MR) equipment. The platform also uses 3D motion capture technology to collect and analyze students' behavior and expression data, providing teachers (trainers) with visual and quantitative teaching evaluation and feedback tools.

In the metaverse, through AR glasses, visitors are divided into different groups, each representing a different army. They will participate in the anti-Japanese military battle simulation in virtual reality and experience the battle scene at that time. With the help of the real-time interaction function of AR glasses, different teams can cooperate to formulate strategies, pass orders, and experience the tension of the battle in the virtual environment. This highly technical and highly targeted multiplayer linkage experience allows tourists to better appreciate the tenacity and heroism of red culture.

Tourists participate in a series of story puzzle games based on historical events in groups, and obtain clues and hints through AR glasses. Different teams need to cooperate to solve puzzles and gradually reveal the truth of historical events. In the process of solving puzzles, visitors will deeply explore the background, causes and effects of historical events, as well as the core values of red culture. This highly targeted and highly technical multi-person linkage experience has improved tourists' awareness and understanding of historical events and red culture.

To sum up, under the background of Zhijiang, a small place, low cost, and small flow of people, education on the history of revolution through multi-person linkage, combined with the precise application of extended reality (XR) technology, and the support of mobile edge computing technology in Zhijiang Peace Culture Memorial Hall It can create a highly personalized, highly technical, high sense of participation, rich learning experience and a deep understanding of the history of the Anti-Japanese War and the spirit of red culture for tourists. This targeted application of technology will enable visitors to gain a deeper understanding of the history of the Anti-Japanese War and red culture, and enhance their sense of participation and learning experience. Metaverse, as an emerging technological and cultural phenomenon, has had a profound impact on the field of education and change. Metaverse provides an immersive, realistic and creative learning environment for education, allowing learners to experience different scenes and roles across time and space, acquire more knowledge and skills, and develop more comprehensive literacy and abilities.

4 Technology and Equipment Selection

In the process of applying extended reality (XR) technology to the Zhijiang Peace Culture Memorial, the choice of technology and equipment is crucial. We need to comprehensively consider cost, user experience and technical feasibility to ensure that the display effect can meet the expectations of visitors to the greatest extent.

First, we can leverage existing devices such as smartphones and tablets as tools for augmented reality (AR). By developing an applicable APP, tourists can use their own devices to watch virtual historical scenes and achieve a relatively low-cost interactive experience. This method is relatively convenient for tourists and does not require additional equipment investment.

Second, head-mounted virtual reality (VR) devices can provide a more immersive experience, especially for student groups. Set up a VR experience area in the Zhijiang Peace Culture Memorial Hall, so that students can wear headsets and enter virtual historical scenes. In order to reduce costs, we can choose to use cheap mobile VR devices, such as smartphone-based VR headsets, to provide realistic historical restoration.

In addition, for augmented reality (AR) glasses, a more realistic and virtual fusion experience can be provided. AR glasses superimpose virtual elements on the real environment, allowing users to see virtual historical scenes in reality. While the cost of AR glasses may be higher, they can provide a more immersive feeling, enhancing the visitor's sense of interaction with virtual elements.

Mobile edge computing technology also plays an important role in this process. Mobile edge computing can transfer computing tasks from central servers to edge devices, reducing transmission delays and improving user experience. This is especially important for XR applications that require real-time interaction. For example, in a multi-person linkage scenario, it can ensure smoother interaction between visitors.

To sum up, the choice of technology and equipment should fully consider cost, user experience and technical feasibility. By making full use of devices such as smartphones, tablets, VR headsets, and AR glasses, combined with mobile edge computing technology, we can achieve a high-quality XR experience in the Zhijiang Peace Culture Memorial Hall, bringing visitors a more in-depth and immersive history feel.

This study analyzed interview data from more than 1,000 registered students who completed the entire survey. The content of the survey includes the following aspects: What do you think of XR with multiplayer linkage, What is your opinion on the importance of inheriting the education on the history of revolution, Do you think the XR experience of multi-person linkage can increase the fun and interactivity of the visit, etc. As shown in Fig. 4.

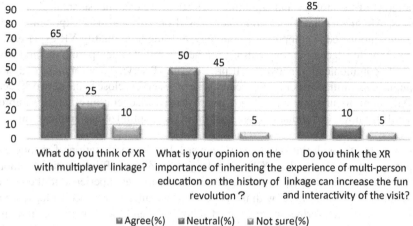

Fig. 4. Statistical analysis chart of user will survey data.

5 Conclusion

This paper aims to explore how to use extended reality (XR) technology to realize the mobile edge computing experience of multi-person linkage in the Zhijiang Peace Culture Memorial Hall in a small place, low cost, and small flow of people. Through the detailed discussion on the science popularization of XR technology, its application in the Memorial Hall of the Peace Culture of Zhijiang, multi-person education on the history of revolution, and the selection of technology and equipment, we have drawn the following conclusions:

In the context of the current rapid development of information technology, extended reality (XR) technology has injected new vitality into the inheritance and education of cultural heritage. Diversified XR technologies such as AR, VR, and MR have created a new way of perception and interaction for us, restoring historical scenes and enriching the visiting experience.

As a small place, the Zhijiang Peace Culture Memorial Hall can restore the historical scenes more vividly by using different forms of XR technology to meet the visiting needs of different groups of people. AR technology can combine virtual elements with the real world to create an intuitive virtual experience for tourists; VR technology can bring users into the virtual world to deeply experience historical situations; MR technology combines virtual and real elements to enhance interaction experience.

The education on the history of revolution mode of multi-person linkage creates a metaverse environment through XR technology, enabling tourists to participate in the restoration of history together in the virtual space, which strengthens the sense of interaction and participation. For different groups of people, personalized XR content design enables students to participate deeply, and tourists can interact with virtual characters, which enhances the attractiveness and depth of history education.

In terms of technology and equipment selection, we can choose smartphones, VR headsets, AR glasses and other equipment based on cost and user experience, combined with mobile edge computing technology, to bring high-quality XR experience to visitors. Mobile edge computing (MEC) is a new distributed computing method based on mobile communication networks. It provides an IT service environment and cloud computing capabilities by deploying general-purpose servers close to the network access side. MEC aims to further reduce latency, improve network operation efficiency, improve service distribution and transmission capabilities, and optimize and improve end-user experience.

To sum up, through this research, we can see that the combination of mobile edge computing and extended reality (XR) technology in the Zhijiang Peace Culture Memorial Hall creates a richer, deeper, and more interactive historical experience in the context of a small place. In the future, with the continuous advancement of technology, we are confident that we can further improve the display effect and user experience, and inject more vitality and charm into the inheritance of red culture.

Acknowledgment. This work was supported by Project of Hunan Provincial Social Science Foundation (No. 21JD046).

References

1. Xu, L.: Digital protection and innovative development path of red cultural resources. People's Forum (01), 139–141 (2021)
2. Li, F., Yang, H.: New development of new tourism formats under the background of cultural and technological integration. J. Tongji Univ. (Soc. Sci. Ed.) **32**(01), 16–23 (2021)
3. Zwaan, R.A.: The immersed experiencer: toward an embodied theory of language comprehension. Psychol. Learn. Motiv. **44**(1), 35–62 (2003)
4. Singh, R.P., et al.: Significant applications of virtual reality for COVID-19 pandemic. Diabetes Metab. Syndr. Clin. Res. Rev. **14**(4), 661–664 (2020)
5. Pantelidis, C.: Exploring VR experiences of tourists' attachment to a rural destination. Int. J. Technol. Mark. **13**(3–4), 376–400 (2020)
6. Kyrlitsias, C., et al.: Corrigendum: a virtual tour of a hardly accessible archaeological site: the effect of immersive virtual reality in user experience, learning and attitude change. Front. Comput. Sci. 21–45 (2021)
7. Tsivitanidou, O.E., Georgiou, Y., Ioannou, A.: A learning experience in inquiry-based physics with immersive virtual reality: student perceptions and an interaction effect between conceptual gains and attitudinal profiles. J. Sci. Educ. Technol. **30**(6), 841–861 (2021)
8. Cao, Y., Luo, Z., Wang, M.: "Body presence": technology and sensual thinking in the age of immersive communication. Press (07), 18–24 (2018)
9. Wan, Y.: Museums as a medium of cultural dissemination—taking the museum of modern art as an example. Cult. Relics Appraisal Appreciation (15), 116–117 (2019)
10. Bo, L.: VR image dissemination of local red culture. Film Lit. (15), 34–36 (2018)
11. Rui, C., Lin, L.: Red culture communication and its path construction under the background of convergent media. J. Jilin Normal Univ. (Human. Soc. Sci. Ed.) **49**(02), 111–116 (2021)
12. Ming, Z., Juan, C.: The influence of ACM/IEEECC2020 competence model on the development of computer education in China. Comput. Educ. (04), 3–8+14 (2023). https://doi.org/10.16512/j.cnki.jsjjy.2023.04.019

13. Lillian, C., Alan, C., Gordon, D., et al.: Computer Science Curriculum 2008: An Interim Revision of CS 2001. ACM, New York (2008)
14. Joint Task Force on Computing Curricula, Association for Computing Machinery (ACM) and IEEE Computer Society. Computer Science Curricula 2013: Curriculum Guidelines for Undergraduate Degree Programs in Computer Science. Association for Computing Machinery, New York (2013)
15. Samsung. The Next Hyper--Connected Experience for All. https://chinaflashmarket.com/Upl oads/Report/20200714145321809946.pdf
16. Myrden, A., Chau, T.: Effects of user mental state on EEG-BCI performance. Front. Hum. Neurosci. **9**, 308 (2015). https://doi.org/10.3389/fnhum.2015.00308
17. Rashkov, G., Bobe, A., Fastovets, D., Komarova, M.: Natural image reconstruction from brain waves: a novel visual BCI system with native feedback. bioRxiv (2019)

An Ethereum Based e-Voting System

Achilleas Spanos and Ioanna Kantzavelou(✉)

Department of Informatics and Computer Engineering, University of West Attica,
Athens, Greece
{cs161048,ikantz}@uniwa.gr

Abstract. Developing an electronic voting system that would replace
the old, traditional electing procedures has been a concern of many
researchers for years. Blockchain technology could provide some guarantees for voting platforms, such as transparency, immutability, and confidentiality. In most research works, secure and reliable electronic voting
systems are required to address known security, anonymity, and fraud
issues. This paper presents a secure decentralized electronic voting system, named the EtherVote, which is based on the Ethereum Blockchain
network focusing on eligible citizens' identification. The EtherVote is a
serverless e-voting model, thus improving security, privacy, and election
costs. An effective method for voter registration and identification to
enhance security is proposed. Among the main properties the EtherVote
holds are storing encrypted votes, efficiency in handling elections with
numerous participants, and simplicity. The system is tested and evaluated, vulnerabilities and possible attacks are exposed, and a discussion
examines opportunities for enhancing the proposed e-voting system.

Keywords: EtherVote · Blockchain · e-Voting · Ethereum · Smart
Contract · Metamask

1 Introduction

There is a number of supportive reasons to replace in-person voting procedures or
other special voting facilities, such as absentee voting, voting in a foreign country,
early voting, or proxy voting, with electronic voting (e-voting). Through e-voting,
equal voting rights could be provided to citizens facing access problems, such as
people with disabilities and individuals in distant areas. Nevertheless maintaining and storing the votes in a database, which would be managed by an organization, incorporates the risks of running into over-authority and manipulated
details, limiting fundamental fairness, privacy, anonymity, and transparency in
the voting process. Central authorities could delete or modify votes. Even if the
authority is trustworthy, an attacker could gain access to the database and modify or change votes and personal data. At the same time, old-fashioned paper
voting is very complicated to verify and audit for a citizen who lacks control over
the voting system. Blockchain is a new and promising technology that could be

© ICST Institute for Computer Sciences, Social Informatics and Telecommunications Engineering 2024
Published by Springer Nature Switzerland AG 2024. All Rights Reserved
L. A. Maglaras and C. Douligeris (Eds.): WiCON 2023, LNICST 527, pp. 202–223, 2024.
https://doi.org/10.1007/978-3-031-58053-6_14

used to address these problems towards e-voting solutions. The full potential of this technology has not yet been fully unveiled.

This promising technology, could face the primary challenges associated with a voting process, ensuring integrity and security of votes. By adhering to the blockchain's structural and operational principles, and given that votes as well as the authentication data are stored to new blocks referencing the preceding ones, an immutable ledger is established. Within this ledger, once information is recorded, any attempt to alter it would disrupt the interlinked relationships between blocks, rendering such modifications impossible. Thus, the technologies provided by blockchain, when combined with a robust encryption algorithm to safeguard votes and prioritize vote anonymity, along with a secure citizen identification system, have the potential to fundamentally transform the voting process in every country. At the same time, any citizen will be able to verify his vote, as opposed to the traditional way of voting, by getting the transaction hash value. This hash value serves as a verification mechanism for transactions within the blockchain, in our context, representing the act of casting a vote in our system.

In this research work, we propose an electronic voting system, the EtherVote, based entirely on the Ethereum blockchain using smart contracts. Since user identification is a major problem in such systems, especially when no database or classic server side is used, we will focus on adding or combining some authentication factors to validate eligible citizens with the right to vote, before and during the voting procedure. On platforms that are expected to serve any kind of social group, of all ages, ease of use is a critical factor. The Ethereum network is public and can be easily accessed by Metamask, - a self-custodial wallet used to safely access blockchain applications - whose addresses will be matched with citizens. That makes the user authentication, the voting procedure, and generally any interaction with the blockchain very easy to use. However, due to the public nature of the Ethereum Network, it becomes imperative to encrypt all the data stored within it. This encryption process is accomplished with a choice of an encryption algorithm that aligns with our specific requirements, including considerations such as the need for decryption capabilities or otherwise.

The specific contributions of this paper are as follows,

1. Introduced innovation with a decentralized e-voting system that goes beyond singular focal points, offering a comprehensive and secure solution spanning every stage of the voting process.
2. Serverless e-voting model, relying solely on Ethereum and smart contracts.
3. Effective method for voter registration and identification, leveraging advanced techniques and cryptographic functions for enhanced security.
4. Encrypted storage of all votes, maintaining the anonymity of each vote.
5. Efficiently handle a large volume of votes, ensuring its practicality for real-world elections with significant voter participation.
6. Simplicity and ease of use ensured for individuals across all social groups.

In the subsequent sections, this paper unfolds a comprehensive exploration of an innovative blockchain-based voting system. The discussion commences in

Sect. 2 with a review of related work, delving into existing systems that laid the groundwork for our approach. Moving forward in Sect. 3, the paper provides a detailed examination of the system's operation, specifying its architecture and mechanisms to provide a good understanding of its functionality. Subsequently, the focus shifts to the practical aspects of system implementation, presenting results and insights derived from the entire voting process. The examination extends to test cases in Sect. 4, offering a rigorous evaluation of the system's performance. Possible threats and existing vulnerabilities are examined in Sect. 5. In the last section, the paper discusses and addresses limitations and problems encountered, and provides ideas for further work.

2   Related Work

Many proposals and research papers have been developed for blockchain voting systems. A thorough survey [1] that provides a complete comparison between the very recent Blockchain-based methods adopted by electronic voting systems, establishes the state of the art and exposes the achievements of such efforts. Authors have gathered and compared all the techniques adopted by related systems in many areas such as cryptography, citizen identification, resistance to attacks etc. Using these outcomes as a point of start, we propose and implement a fully functional and comprehensive system designed to provide a significant advancement to the existing e-voting systems and proposals.

Below, we will delve into research papers and system proposals, pinpointing instances where techniques were not only adopted but also meticulously refined to suit the intricacies of the proposed system.

According to research [1], the only method for verifying voter identity that hinges solely on the utilization of a phone number and consequently by employing SMS is delineated in paper [5]. Access to the voting process is exclusively granted to individuals who hold an active phone subscription.

i-Voting: Estonia is the first country to introduce online voting in national elections since 2005 [2], using an electronic ID chip [3]. This identity generated SHA1/SHA2 signatures and was used to identify citizens. The voter would have to download the app, authenticate, and then the voting process would follow. The vote is encrypted with the elections public key, and the user's private key. Then the vote is stored on a server controlled by the Estonian government [4].

Unique Identifier: Many proposals have emerged for the Indian electoral system, leveraging the UIDAI Aadhaar, a unique identifier assigned to each registered Indian citizen. Such approaches are inspired from the Estonian system, wherein the Aadhaar identifier represents a private key, in conjunction with the election's public key, to generate a digital signature for voting purposes [6]. Another research publication from 2020 introduces an innovative blockchain-based voting system, merging the Aadhaar number with biometric authentication. To participate, voters must preregister using a virtual ID obtained by UIDAI. Asymmetric encryption is used to verify votes. Voters fingerprint is converted to the digital signature enhancing the security of the entire voting process [7].

Multi-factor Authentication Voting: This model proposed in the research paper [8] uses a database housing voters identity, along with the phone number and other personal information. To participate, each voter is required to complete a registration process and establish a unique personal identification number (PIN). Subsequently, all eligible voters authenticate themselves, with their ID number and PIN, after witch the voting process takes place, by entering a one-time password (OTP), generated during the authentication phase. The voting records are ultimately securely stored within the blockchain.

In the research [9], researchers proposed an election system that work as follows. To participate, each voter is required to complete a registration process by furnishing their ID number and other pertinent personal information, which are stored within a newly created block. This system integrates each registered voter into an electoral list. Subsequently, the election process takes place, with the prompt display of the election results immediately upon the conclusion of the voting process.

Indonesian researchers have put forward a blockchain-based voting system that leverages the use of **Metamask** for voter registration. Every user possessing a valid address must be registered by the administrator, thereby designating their Metamask address as eligible for voting. The counting of the votes, is automatically conducted by the smart contract that orchestrates the entire electoral process [10]. In research paper [11], a system incorporating Metamask is also put forward. The paramount aspect of this research endeavor lies in the distribution of Metamask addresses, to voters, with a sufficient amount of Ethers, which will later be employed within the electoral procedure for authenticating themselves.

Save system, is an electronic voting system proposal for university elections. In this system, every voter is identified by the election authorities. During this identification process every voter receives a random magnetic card, that contains a 13-digit number. By the use of that card, each voter is identified as a valid voter [12].

Reasearchers proposed an Ethereum-based electronic voting system, that uses a blockchain-based Interplanetary File System (IPFS) storage method. Proposes a new way to guarantee confidentiality based on a database. Each voter is required to register by establishing a unique member ID and password, subsequently utilized to generate a new address. Addresses and member ID values undergo encryptionsusing the AES algorithm and before being stored to the database. On the contrary, votes are stored in the Ethereum blockchain, taking advantage of the distributed edger [13].

Numerous research papers and models of e-voting systems have been proposed and are worth acknowledging. Several of them use biometric identification, such as fingerprint and eye recognition. Despite the extensive body of research, proposed systems invariably exhibit shortcomings in one domain or another. The fulfillment of the requirements for secure citizen identification, preservation of voting confidentiality, ease of use, and accessibility across all societal segments remains a formidable challenge.

The purpose of this research work is the creation of an electoral system, with an emphasis on the secure, low cost and fast identification of citizens, which will be carried out with the help of Metamask and the use of multi-factor authentication on the Ethereum public network.

Our work builds on the methodologies proposed in the systems above mainly in the field of identification. The combination, and variation of these authentication methods, while introducing an additional, unique identifier like the Metamask address to citizens, could potentially offer the safest, quickest, and most comprehensive authentication method for a voting platform, all without relying on any central authority database. In our paper we will elucidate the rationales underlying the enhanced nature of our system compared with already mentioned and existing systems in various facets encompassing the prevoting phase, the process of identification, the conduct of the voting procedure, vote tally, the preservation of vote integrity, and the safeguarding of citizens' fundamental rights.

We present a comprehensive report of the security measures and future pitfalls inherent in the proposed model. The biggest concern in such proposals, lies in the public infrastructure of the Ethereum Blockchain and thus in addressing personal data leakage.

3   Proposed System

3.1   Functionality

In the proposed system, the EtherVote, the sole service provided by the electoral authority is to record the list of eligible citizens on the blockchain. The process of citizen identification, the conduct of the voting procedure, the storage of votes as well as the vote tally, will be exclusively centered on data storage and the invocation of functions from our smart contract. Every transaction and interaction with the smart contract, whether for identification or for voting is public and can be easily traced, while keeping all personal data private by utilizing suitable cryptographic techniques. Systems that use the blockchain as a database, inherit the immutability and therefore modification or deletion of information is impossible. Each voting citizen will be assigned a Metamask address - with a necessary number of ethers, during the entire election procedure. The electoral procedure is divided into four phases, as described in the sequel and illustrated in Fig. 1.

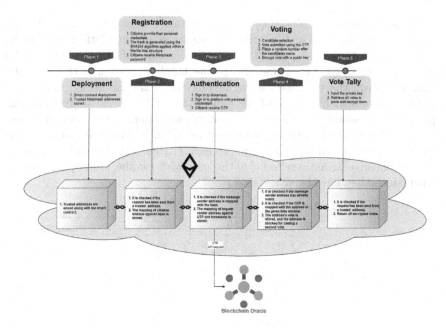

Fig. 1. Voting phases

Upon familiarizing ourselves with the overarching structure of the system through a comprehensive diagram depicting its four primary phases, we shall acquire an in-depth comprehension of the specific functionalities that each phase encompasses. To achieve this profound understanding, we will delve deeper to understand the functions that each phase performs by elucidating the intricate functions and operations inherent to them. This will be followed by a cross functional diagram governing each phase.

This detailed approach, ensures that we have garnered a comprehensive overview of all processes unfolding within each phase of the system. In this way, we will be able to have a better understanding during implementation, but more importantly in the security and vulnerability analysis that we will see in the next chapters.

1. The **first phase** (Fig. 2) consists of writing and storing the smart contract on the Ethereum blockchain. Initially, Metamask addresses are created, which will be considered 'trusted' and will belong to the electoral authorities. Through these addresses, the smart contract will be created, the results of the elections will be taken, but also the sensitive personal data of citizens with the right to vote will be stored in the blockchain, aiming on using these personal data on authentication.

2. In the **second phase** (Fig. 3), every eligible citizen is asked to register on the platform. In order to register, he must either attend or contact the authorities. The authorities must be connected to one of the 'trusted' addresses (presented

in **phase1**), and after creating a new Metamask account, with which the citizen will be assigned and identified, is registered on the platform by linking the newly created address with the citizen's personal information, such as ID number, first name, last name and phone number. Although the variables that will store the information are private, since the Ethereum network is public, anyone with a copy of the blockchain will be able to retrieve this private information. To address this risk, personal information are combined, encrypted with the cryptographic algorithm SHA256, and matched as a key-value pair with the address assigned to each citizen. Upon completion of the second phase, each citizen receives the password for the Metamask account with which they have been matched.

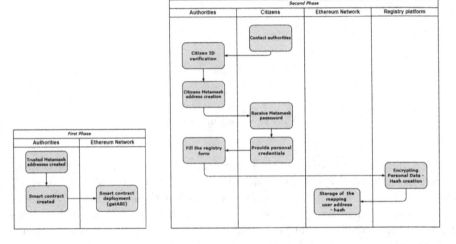

Fig. 2. Phase 1   **Fig. 3.** Phase 2

3. The **third phase** (Fig. 4) is the process of identifying voters on election day. Once they enter the voting platform, they must log in to their Metamask account by entering the password they received on the day of registration, thus creating the first identification parameter. Then as a second identification parameter, they will have to connect to the platform, entering their personal information, with which the specific address has been assigned. Similar to stage 2, the data is combined and encrypted with SHA256, followed by a check to match the transaction's sending address with the hash. If the second authentication stage is successfully completed, a unique code (OTP) will be generated. This code is stored in the Blockchain, with the time of its creation, and is matched with the address corresponding to the current voter, as a key-value pair, just as the match was made with the personal information. Saving the time the OTP was created is to have a window of time to use it. Finally, each voter receives this unique code via SMS to the mobile phone they have registered.

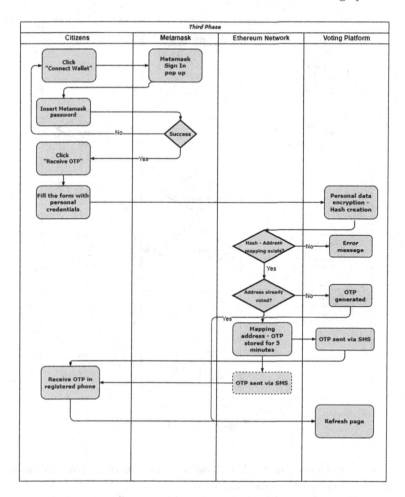

Fig. 4. Phase 3

4. **Phase 4** (Fig. 5) concerns the voting process. Each voter having performed the identification, and having received the OTP on the mobile, is invited to vote, choosing from a list of candidates. After the candidate is selected, the OTP received during identification is requested in order to accept the vote. In the case that the OTP is incorrect, or the time limit has expired, he must receive a new OTP, performing the second stage of identification. In the opposite case, the transaction is done, a random number is appended to the candidate, and the vote is encrypted with a public key and RSA encryption algorithm. This encrypted vote is stored on the blockchain and the s voter's address state is modified to a locked status, ensuring that only one vote can be added, thereby preventing multiple votes. If the Metamask address, associated with the voter, has already been used to cast a vote, during the second

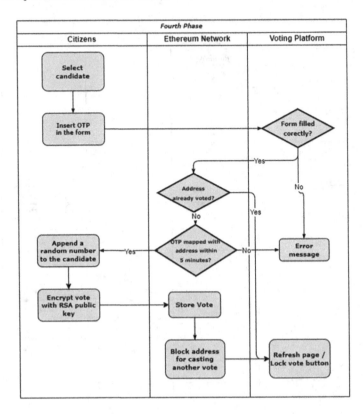

Fig. 5. Phase 4

stage of identification, no OTP will be generated or sent. This eliminates the possibility of submitting a second vote.

5. Finally, **phase 5** (Fig. 6) concerns the vote tally. Government officials must authenticate themselves through a trusted Metamask address, as only requests originating from such trusted addresses will be able to retrieve the encrypted votes. To start the process, they must initially complete the form by providing the RSA private key necessary for decrypting the received encrypted votes. Subsequently, our smart contract will return the votes in batches, organized into teams of 10,000 votes per call, to ensure compliance with the gas limit (running **out of gass**). Once each vote is successfully decrypted, a validation process will ensue to verify whether any instance of a candidate's name is included within the decrypted text. If a name of a candidate is detected, votes associated with the specific candidate will increment by one, repeating this process until all votes have been decrypted and added.

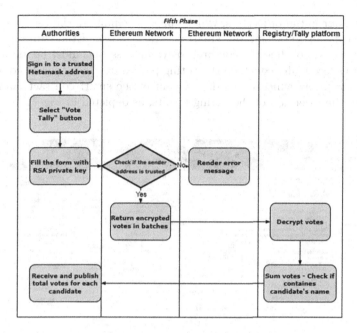

Fig. 6. Phase 5

Through the utilization of blockchain technology, every transaction is subjected to encryption, thereby safeguarding the sanctity of personal data. This approach not only ensures the accurate registration of each voter but also establishes a strict prohibition against multiple voting instances. Our primary concern revolves around the integrity of the vote itself, rather than the identity of the voter who casts it.

Within this framework, any address maintained within the blockchain that has not previously exercised its voting privilege is granted the sole entitlement to do so. This approach diligently upholds the fundamental principle of "one-man-one-vote," a cornerstone of fair and equitable electoral processes. By maintaining this level of transparency and security, we bolster the trust and integrity of the entire voting system while preserving the anonymity and privacy of individual voters.

3.2   Implementation

This section elaborates on the construction and evaluation of the entire system, which was implemented and tested on the Ethereum test network. By doing so, we acquired the essential outcomes required to assess both the security of our system and its functionality.

In the development of our system, we employed ReactJS for the frontend, while exclusively relying on Solidity for the backend. This strategic decision aligns with our initial objectives, which aimed to eliminate the use of any other backend or database beyond our smart contract and the Ethereum blockchain.

Below, we will outline the comprehensive process that must be meticulously followed to successfully conclude the voting procedure. This process commences from the inception, which is the deployment of the smart contract, and culminates with the reception of the voting results, as depicted in Fig. 7.

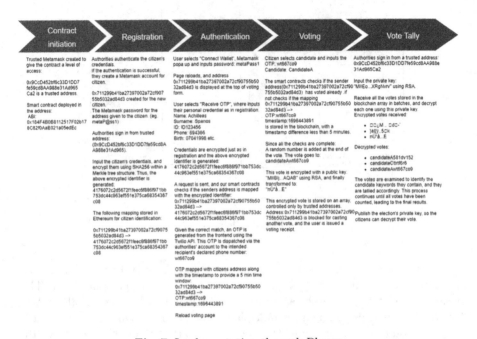

Fig. 7. Implementation through Phases

Contract Initialization: Trusted Metamask addresses are generated, allocated to regulatory authorities, and employed for the regulated invocation of specific smart contract functions. This mechanism ensures that the necessary voting operations maintain a precisely controlled and requisite level of access. *"0x9CcD452bf 6c33D1DD7fe59cd8AA988e31Ad965Ca2"* added in contract as *trusted.*

Following the creation of a smart contract, we retrieve the contract's Application Binary Interface (ABI) and utilize it within our front-end interface to invoke the contract's functions. *Contract ABI:* *"0x184F4B0B8112517F02b178C82f0AaB 021a05edEc"*

Citizen Registration: The authorities authenticate each citizen's identity and verify it's voting eligibility before enrolling them on the voters' list. Following the successful authentication, a Metamask account is instantiated, and the corresponding password is imparted to the respective citizen.

Address: *"0x711299b41ba27397002a72cf90755b5032ad84d3"*
Password: *metaP@ss1*

The credentials are disseminated to the citizen, following which the authorities sign into a trusted address to initiate the voter registration process on the blockchain. The newly generated address, along with the citizen's credentials, is incorporated into the registration form by the governing authorities. Subsequently, these credentials undergo encryption utilizing the SHA256 algorithm within a Merkle tree structure. The resultant root hash, used as an user authentication hash, is then recorded in the blockchain, associating it with the voter's listing.

User authentication hash: *"4176072c2d5672f1feec6f886f971bb753dc44c963ef551e 375ca68354367c08"*

This mapping will enable users to authenticate themselves during the elections without the necessity of recalling any password; solely their personal credentials will be required.

Authentication: To successfully complete this phase, it will be essential to employ functional components from both the user interface and the smart contract. It's crucial to bear in mind that this process encompasses multi-factor identification, and the successful outcome of this authentication enables the storage of the vote.

The multi-factor authentication process of our system includes the following subprocesses in the following order:

- Upon selecting the 'Connect Wallet' button, the Metamask is triggered, prompting the citizen to sign in to their registered account using the confidentially provided password.
  Enters password: *metaP@ss1*
- Subsequently, the user will be prompted to click on the "Receive OTP" button. Upon doing so, a window will emerge, prompting the voter to input their personal information, mirroring the procedure followed by authorities during the registration process. This user-provided data will be subjected to encryption, and an identification hash corresponding to this encrypted information will be generated using the same method as in registration.
  User authentication hash: *"4176072c2d5672f1feec6f886f971bb753dc44c963ef5 51e375ca68354367c08"*
  The authentication process will subsequently validate whether the address linked to the sender of the request ("msg.sender") corresponds to the received authentication hash.
- Assuming successful verification in the preceding two checks, an OTP (One-Time Password), crucial for enabling a successful vote, is generated and provided to each citizen. This OTP will be securely recorded on the blockchain, mapped with the citizens address, along with the timestamp. This method allows for a 5-minute window during which the OTP can be used.

Mapping stored: *"0x711299b41ba27397002a72cf90755b 5032ad84d3"* − >
OTP: *"wt667co9"*
timestamp: *"1696443891"*

Subsequently, the OTP is dispatched to the user's phone through the government's official account using the Twillio API, or any messaging API.

Upon successfully completing these four identification parameters (included the identification checks during the registration process), citizens are prepared and authorized to cast their votes.

Voting: The sole action required from the voter, is to choose a candidate and input the OTP into the designated form.
OTP: *wt667co9*, Candidate: *CandidateA*

Following, our smart contract confirms the association of the OTP with the sender's address (which represents the citizen) within the designated time limit by scrutinizing the timestamp disparity. Additionally, it ensures that this address has not yet participated in the voting process, initiating the process of encrypting and securely storing the vote in the blockchain commences. Before being stored on the blockchain, all votes are subjected to encryption using the RSA algorithm with a common public key. To prevent the generation of identical encrypted strings for votes pertaining to the same candidate, a random number or the OTP utilized for the vote will be appended to the candidate's name. This approach ensures that each encrypted vote not only remains unique but also carries the candidate's name, enabling the counting process through decryption of the vote.
Final candidate format: *candidateAwt667co9*
RSA public key: *MIIBIj...AQAB*
Vote stored: *nÚ¹å...E*

This vote is stored in an array, and the address's status is updated, to prevent casting another vote.

Vote Tally: Authorities gain access to the votes by inputting the private key into a designated form. To manage the decryption efficiently and prevent gas limit issues, votes are received in batches. Once received, they undergo decryption.

A comprehensive tally is then conducted, cross-referencing the decrypted votes to identify the included candidate selections. Finally, the election results are compiled and printed for public disclosure.

Encrypted votes:

1. ¿M .. d-¨
2. äI[ÿ..5k
3. nÚ¹å...E

Decrypted votes:

1. candidateA581dv152
2. candidateCttrtf6r6
3. candidateAwt667co9

After the voting results publication, the private key may be published, so each citizen may decrypt its vote.

4   Testing and Evaluation

4.1   Test Cases

By conducting test cases, we not only assess the system's functionality but also gain a comprehensive understanding of the array of controls and security parameters it encompasses. The initial section exclusively pertains to the initial two phases, encompassing all pre-election procedures, and is illustrated in Table 1.

Table 1. Pre-elections test cases

Pre-elections dApp test cases			
ID	Test case description	Expected result	Result
1	Safe/authorized Metamask account created	Authorized address created and stored	Pass
2	Smart contract deployment	Get smart contract's abi	Pass
3	Authorized Metamask address connected to dApp for citizen registration	Metamask account connected with Ethereum network	Pass
4	Create voter's Metamask address	Password and address generated	Pass
5	SHA256 encryption of voters personal data	User authentication hash generated	Pass
6	Register voter using the authorized Metamask address	Authentication hash mapped with address	Pass
7	Registering a voter with incomplete form details	Render error message	Pass
8	Register voter using unauthorized Metamask address	Personal data encrypted but not stored/Error	Pass

Table 2 below showcases the test cases for one of the pivotal phases we have explored, focusing on user identification during the third phase of the system. These test cases are instrumental in verifying the robustness and effectiveness of our user identification protocols in this critical phase.

Table 2. Authentication test cases

Voter authentication test cases

ID	Test case description	Expected result	Result
1	Click on "Connect Wallet" to connect dApp with Metamask	Metamask triggers	Pass
2	Connect dApp with Metamask	Displayed address upon successful Metamask connection	Pass
3	Click on "Receive OTP" dApp connected to Metamask Authentication hash matches with address Account has not voted	OTP generated, mapped for 5 min and sent via SMS	Pass
4	Click on "Receive OTP" dApp connected to Metamask Authentication hash does not exist (wrong credentials) Account has not voted	User not found Error	Pass
5	Click on "Receive OTP" dApp connected to Metamask Authentication hash exists but does not match with address Account has not voted	User not found Error	Pass
6	Click on "Receive OTP" dApp connected **not** to Metamask	Error	Pass
7	Click on "Receive OTP" dApp connected to Metamask Authentication hash matches with address Account has already voted	Refresh page	Pass

In Table 3 encompasses all the test cases related to the voting process. Having a good understanding of this phase's functions will greatly aid in our complete understanding of the subsequent phase, which deals with the vote tally procedure.

Table 3. Voting process test cases

Voting test cases

ID	Test case description	Expected result	Result
1	dApp connected to Metamask Address has not voted OTP exists and matches with address OTP has not been expired	Random number appended to candidate Vote encrypted Vote stored Adddress blocked for voting again	Pass
2	dApp connected to Metamask Address has not voted OTP exists and matches with address OTP has been expired	OTP error	Pass
3	dApp connected to Metamask Address has not voted OTP exists but not matched with address OTP has not been expired	Voting Error	Pass
4	dApp connected to Metamask Address has not voted OTP not matched with address	OTP error	Pass
5	dApp connected to Metamask Vote with address that has already voted	Blocked by dApp and smart contract function	Pass
6	Vote while dApp is **not** connected with Metamask	Error	Pass

Finally, here are the test cases concerning the vote count, as we can see in Table 4.

Table 4. Vote tally test cases

Vote tally test cases

ID	Test case description	Expected result	Result
1	dApp is connected with Metamask via trusted address Select "Vote tally" Insert correct private key	All votes are received in batches Votes are decrypted and summed up	Pass
2	dApp is connected with Metamask via trusted address Select "Vote tally" Insert **incorrect** private key	Vote tally error	Pass
3	dApp is **not** connected with Metamask or connected with a not trusted address	Error	Pass
4	Receive votes before the end of the elections	Error	Pass

We are now fully equipped to comprehend both the system's operation and the entirety of the controls implemented throughout the voting process.

5   Security Analysis

In this section, a critical exploration of potential vulnerabilities will take place. We will delve into an examination of various threats, that would oversee the principles of voting procedure, but possible attacks such as MITM as well.

5.1   Potential Threats in Voting Principles

The reliability of the voting system is imperative to ensure the democratic process and foster public trust in political governance. Within this subsection, we will scrutinize the extent to which a blockchain-based voting application aligns with the principles of democratic voting, such as the recognition of human dignity, the principle of 'one person - one vote,' and the transparency of the process.

Double Voting Threat: By associating citizens with their Metamask addresses and locking these addresses upon casting a vote, the submission of a second vote by any citizen is effectively prevented. This correlation, coupled with the existence of a one-time-password generated through the input of personal data known only to each citizen, renders the 'theft' of a vote impossible. Additionally, the transmission of this password via SMS to the mobile phone registered on the day of enrollment necessitates the physical presence of the citizen or continuous communication with the individual who funded the vote purchase. Due to these stringent security parameters, the alteration or coercion of a vote can only occur through two specific avenues.

1. The first scenario could only unfold if a citizen were to sell their Metamask password received during registration, along with all their personal data (ID number, mobile, etc.), an action that would likely be vehemently rejected by any vigilant citizen. Furthermore, on the day of voting, both the citizen and the potential 'attacker' would need to maintain constant communication for the timely transmission of the unique code enabling the vote. This process makes it exceedingly challenging to execute successfully.
2. The second case involves the physical presence of an individual next to the citizen called to vote. This physical presence allows the accompanying person to manipulate the voter, as there is no provision for monitoring the voter to ensure they are alone during the voting process.

Vote Anonymity Threat: Our system satisfies the principle of election integrity through the association of citizens with Metamask addresses and the encryption-based control of personal data. The use of the SHA256 cryptographic algorithm is ideal for our case, given its resistance to decryption. Thus, all personal data remains secure, allowing for verification through the matching of generated hashes. Simultaneously, the system employs a unique function storing all the encrypted votes, without the origin of each vote. Consequently, tracing the source of each vote, combined with hash decryption, becomes impossible, meeting the principle of voting confidentiality.

Even in the retrieval of receipts from the blockchain, facilitated by each transaction originating from a specific address and the encryption of personal data, identifying the sender's details for each vote remains an insurmountable challenge. The robust security measures, including address-specific transaction origins and data encryption, ensure that the privacy and anonymity of the voters are rigorously maintained throughout the entire process.

Vote Validity Threat. This principle is satisfied by the implemented system. Through multiple checks in both the user interface and our smart contract, the submission of an invalid vote is prevented. To store a vote, a unique code must be matched with the Metamask address, indicating the successful completion of the verification stage. Otherwise, vote storage is not possible. Additionally, due to the electronic nature of the voting system and the necessity to select a candidate from a predetermined list to cast a vote, storing an 'invalid' vote is impossible. Furthermore, the existence of a list of valid voters helps avoid numerous errors that could occur during the voting or vote counting process. By combining all the methods employed by the implemented system, storing an invalid vote (a vote that should not be counted) is rendered impossible.

Through electronic voting, this principle can be maintained, alleviating many problems associated with traditional voting methods. Controls for storing a vote can easily be modified by any system to align with its specific needs.

5.2   Potential Threats and Resistance to Attacks

Attacks in Blockchain Network: Like any other technology, Blockchain has its drawbacks despite its transparent and immutable digital ledger. Various types of security threats make Blockchain networks vulnerable.

51% Attack

A successful 51% attack would be catastrophic for our system, as it could alter the results of elections or impede the entire electoral process. However, such an attack is challenging and demanding on a network with a significant participation rate, accompanied by substantial costs.

Beyond the cost, a group attempting to attack the network through a 51% attack must not only control 51% of the network nodes but also introduce the modified blocks into the blockchain in a very expensive timeframe. Even if they hold 51% of the network's hashing power, they may be unable to keep up with the block creation rate or introduce their chain before valid new blocks are created by the real blockchain network.

After Ethereum's transition to proof-of-stake, a 51% attack on the Ethereum blockchain became even more expensive. To execute such an attack, a user or group would need to possess 51% of the staked ETH in the network.

Protection against this type of attack is one of the main reasons for choosing the Ethereum network to implement the voting system. Large cryptocurrencies are unlikely to suffer from 51% attacks due to the prohibitive cost of acquiring such significant hashing power and the fact that they make it impossible to introduce a modified blockchain. Therefore, the 51% attack threat primarily affects cryptocurrencies with lower participation and hashing power.

DOS Attack

Due to its digital nature, the blockchain is susceptible to attacks and exploitation. DOS and DDoS attacks on a blockchain focus on the protocol level, with the most significant threat being transaction flooding. Traditional DDoS attacks can be executed against a blockchain to slow down its operations.

In the case of a DDoS attack, some nodes may be temporarily disabled. The distributed nature of the blockchain network ensures that transactions can continue even if some nodes go offline. However, this does not imply that blockchain networks are fully resistant to DDoS attacks.

DDoS attacks are considered "weapons of mass destruction" on the Internet. It is more challenging to defend against these attacks, and currently, there are no precautions that any organization can apply to be 100% secure. The greater the computational power, the higher the chances of facing a blockchain DDoS attack. This is another reason for choosing the Ethereum network to implement the voting system, as it offers a broad range of security against such massive DDoS attacks.

Sybil Attack

In a voting system, a Sybil attack can be employed to influence the outcome of the vote. The attacker can use multiple identities to cast multiple votes, thereby affecting the voting results. Additionally, the attacker may spread false votes in the system, causing confusion and uncertainty among genuine voters.

The system we have created is entirely resistant to any form of Sybil attack. This is possible due to the multifactor authentication methodology required for the voting process. With a list of valid accounts (voters) and the necessary authentication steps for storing a vote, attempting to cast multiple votes from one account is not feasible. Moreover, the use of the Ethereum network prevents a significant increase in blockchain traffic, preventing Sybil attacks on a node.

By taking appropriate measures to create a list of valid voters and continuously monitoring the smart contract each time someone interacts with it, in combination with the use of Ethereum and corresponding protocols, the system implemented in this thesis is considered absolutely secure against Sybil attacks. Unauthorized users are not allowed to interact with the smart contract, ensuring the system's security.

Operational Attacks on the Voting Process: We will analyze the security of the system against attacks that could harm its operational processes.

MITM Attack

Information gathered during an attack could be used for various purposes, including identity theft or voter manipulation.

There are three types of attacks:

- IP Spoofing: An attacker disguises themselves as an application by changing the packet headers to an IP address. Users attempting to access a URL may be redirected to the attacker's website.
- ARP Spoofing: The attacker's MAC address is linked to a user's IP address on a local network. This causes all messages to be transmitted to the attacker.
- DNS Spoofing: An attack on a DNS server with the goal of changing the addresses of a website. Users trying to enter a website might be directed to the attacker's site.

To successfully execute a Man-in-the-Middle (MITM) attack, the attacker needs to decrypt the received data. This decryption might involve various techniques, such as SSL stripping, downgrading an HTTPS connection to HTTP, bypassing TLS identity checks sent from the application to the user.

To prevent such attacks on our system, several measures should be taken. The most crucial is the establishment of a secure connection. Besides end-to-end encryption, policies like HTTP, HSTS could be configured to enforce the use of SSL/TLS security on multiple subdomains. This enhances the website and web application's security against protocol downgrade attacks and cookie tampering attempts.

Due to the use of Metamask and the security methods it provides, even in the scenario of an attacker conducting ARP spoofing and downgrading to HTTP, the server would not function from the user's side, as SSL encryption is required for the proper operation of Metamask.

Moreover, citizens should be educated by authorities during their registration in the system to protect themselves from phishing emails that might lead them to fraudulent websites or prompt them to download malicious code to their devices.

Exploitation of Smart Contracts

In smart contract exploitation attacks, an attacker takes advantage of vulnerabilities or weaknesses in the contract code. Here are some common types of smart contract exploitation attacks, along with how they are mitigated in our system:

1. **Reentrancy Attacks**: This attack occurs when a smart contract is repeatedly called by another contract during a transaction, with the goal of extracting resources before the original transaction completes.

   In our system, sensitive personal data variables and functions are defined as private. Therefore, they cannot be called by other smart contracts. Additionally, public functions include identity checks, preventing unwanted addresses from interacting.

2. **Front-running Attacks**: Front-running attacks happen when an individual anticipates the execution of a smart contract and executes it first, before the original transaction is completed. This can lead to capital loss or malfunction of the contract.

   Our system is resistant to front-running attacks due to identity verification measures. To vote, users must be authenticated and linked to a One-Time

Password (OTP). If someone attempts to vote before the initial voting, their vote won't be confirmed without prior identity verification and OTP assignment.

3. **Timestamp Attacks**: Timestamp attacks occur when an attacker creates a transaction and changes its timestamp to achieve a desired state in the contract affected by the transaction.
   The system is protected against timestamp attacks through timestamp checks implemented in the smart contract. Authorities also collect votes at the exact moment the voting deadline expires, preventing manipulation of results through altered timestamps.

4. **Variable Overflow/Underflow Attacks**: these attacks occur when the prices of a variable in a smart contract exceed their range limits, causing a variable in a smart contract to go out of range, causing unpredictable behavior of the contract and possibly loss of capital. In order to enhance the robustness of the smart contract and minimize the risks associated with variable overflow and underflow, we opted for the integration of mappings alongside the dedicated vote storage table. This strategic choice provides a secure and automated mechanism within the Ethereum environment, effectively managing data storage and mitigating potential issues related to exceeding predefined range limits.

6   Discussion and Conclusion

The implemented system has some weaknesses, the resolution of which could make it ideal and ready for use even at the level of national elections.

The first weakness that needs to be resolved concerns the sending of the one-time password via SMS. It is not possible to send SMS, but also in general to call APIs from the smart contract. Furthermore, due to the storage of a substantial volume of votes, the necessity to retrieve them in batches can result in considerable time consumption during the vote tallying process, potentially leading to delays.

Oracles could be a solution to these problems, so we could call APIs from the smart contract, and handle SMS or API communications. Oracles are third-party services that act as intermediaries between smart contracts and external systems. They can provide smart contracts with access to external data and services, including the ability to make HTTP requests. Moreover, enhancing more suitable cryptographic algorithm to align with the specific security requirements of voting could further enhance the safety, integrity, and the speed of receiving the voting data and results.

The implemented system serves as a fully integrated and functional model, paving the way for the successful development and deployment of voting systems for a wide range of applications. By implementing an innovative user identification system that effectively fulfills the requirements of voting without endangering personal data, and coupled with robust vote encryption, the system could be deemed deployment-ready. It particularly suits applications like university elections, which require fewer resources. Additionally, its adaptable technology and generic framework make it a solid foundation for building even more secure systems in the future.

With the continuous advancements in Solidity and blockchain technologies, the prospect of an even more enhanced e-voting application is on the horizon. Nevertheless, through the encryption of API keys and the exclusive handling of messages by the smart contract, the proposed application can be considered secure and suitable for use in national elections, providing a robust foundation for future improvements in the field.

References

1. Garg, K., Saraswat, P., Bisht, S., Aggarwal, S., Krishna Kothuri, S., Gupta, S.: A comparitive analysis on e-voting system using blockchain. In: 2019 4th International Conference on Internet of Things: Smart Innovation and Usages (IoT-SIU) (2019)
2. Ehin, P., Solvak, M., Willemson, J., Vinkel, P.: Internet voting in Estonia 2005–2019: evidence from eleven elections. Gov. Inf. Q. **39**(4), 101718 (2022)
3. Baltic, T.: Estonian electronic ID - card application specification prerequisites to the smart card differentiation to previous version of EstEID card application (2013)
4. Ayed, A.B.: A conceptual secure blockchain-based electronic voting system. Int. J. Netw. Secur. Appl. **9**(3), 1–9 (2017)
5. Khoury, D., et al.: Decentralized voting platform based on ethereum blockchain. In: 2018 IEEE International Multidisciplinary Conference on Engineering Technology (IMCET). IEEE (2018)
6. Anjan, S., Sequeira, J.P.: Blockchain based E-voting system for India using UIDAI's Aadhaar. J. Comput. Sci. Eng. Softw. Test. **5**(3), 26–32 (2019)
7. Roopak, T.M., Sumathi, R.: Electronic voting based on virtual ID of Aadhar using blockchain technology. In: 2020 2nd International Conference on Innovative Mechanisms for Industry Applications (ICIMIA). IEEE (2020)
8. Abayomi-Zannu, T.P., Odun-Ayo, I.A., Barka, T.F.: A proposed mobile voting framework utilizing blockchain technology and multi-factor authentication. In: Journal of Physics: Conference Series, vol. 1378, no. 3. IOP Publishing (2019)
9. Anwar ul Hassan, C., et al.: A liquid democracy enabled blockchain-based electronic voting system. Sci. Program. **2022**, 1383007 (2022)
10. Pramulia, D., Anggorojati, B.: Implementation and evaluation of blockchain based e-voting system with Ethereum and Metamask. In: 2020 International Conference on Informatics, Multimedia, Cyber and Information System (ICIMCIS). IEEE (2020)
11. Vairam, T., Sarathambekai, S., Balaji, R.: Blockchain based voting system in local network. In: 2021 7th International Conference on Advanced Computing and Communication Systems (ICACCS), vol. 1. IEEE (2021)
12. Ochoa, X., Peláez, E.: Affordable and secure electronic voting for university elections: the SAVE case study. In: 2017 Fourth International Conference on eDemocracy & eGovernment (ICEDEG). IEEE (2017)
13. Ahn, B.: Implementation and early adoption of an ethereum-based electronic voting system for the prevention of fraudulent voting. Sustainability **14**(5), 2917 (2022)

Author Index

Printed in the United States
by Baker & Taylor Publisher Services